SEPIK RIVER SOCIETIES

SEPIK RIVER SOCIETIES

A HISTORICAL ETHNOGRAPHY OF
THE CHAMBRI AND THEIR NEIGHBORS

DEBORAH B. GEWERTZ

YALE UNIVERSITY PRESS
NEW HAVEN AND LONDON

Published with assistance from the Louis Stern Memorial Fund.

Designed by Sally Harris
and set in Electra type by Graphic Composition, Inc.
Printed in the United States of America by
Murray Printing Company, Westford, Mass.

Library of Congress Cataloging in Publication Data

Gewertz, Deborah B., 1948–
   Sepik River societies.

   Bibliography: p. 251.
   Includes index.
   1. Chambri (Papua New Guinea people) I. Title.
DU740.42.G48 1983   306'.0899912   82–48902
ISBN 0–300–02872–5

10 9 8 7 6 5 4 3 2 1

To my parents and my daughter
Max Goldsmith
Frederica Goldsmith
Alexis Gewertz

CONTENTS

LIST OF TABLES, MAPS, AND FIGURES

Maps

Figures

ACKNOWLEDGMENTS

It is with gratitude that I thank those agencies which assisted in the researching and writing of this book. The East-West Center Population Institute, the Graduate School of the City University of New York, and the National Geographic Society sponsored my first fieldwork between 1973 and 1974. The National Endowment for the Humanities and the Miner D. Crary Foundation of Amherst College supported my second research trip during the summer of 1979. And a grant from the Wenner-Gren Foundation, together with a trustee-faculty fellowship from Amherst College, allowed me to investigate archival material and write the manuscript between 1980 and 1981.

Many people contributed to the completion of this project. Among those who deserve special mention are Murray Chapman, who taught me to do fieldwork and to compile my data properly; William Heaney, Louise Morauta, Richard Scaglion, and Andrew Strathern, who were both encouraging and hospitable; L. A. Babb, Jan Dizard, Frederick Errington, Adrian Hayes, Donald Pitkin, Paula Rubel, and James Watson, who read and criticized the first draft of sections of the manuscript; and especially Mervyn Meggitt, who continues to insist that I do my best.

I am also indebted to my friends for their advice and encouragement. I particularly wish to thank Tom Moylan and Virginia Guilford for rescuing me from the "no good weed"; Craig Malone for his excellent maps and diagrams; Diane Kaplan for her word-processing wizardry; Ellen Savulis for her care in indexing; and Krystyna Starker for her continuing support and inspiration. Special thanks I send to Kenneth Gewertz, without whose editorial advice, photographic assistance, and encouragement this book would never have been written.

Of course I thank the people of the Middle Sepik, especially the Chambri people. To Matias Yambumpe, Andrew Yorondu, Patrick Yarapat, Michael Kubusa, Wapiyeri, Francis and Scolastica Wusuai, David Wapi, and Michael Kambon, I owe special thanks. And to Godfried Kolly and Joseph Kambukwat, my brothers and assistants, my debt is beyond repayment.

I also wish to thank my Wewak hosts, Brenda and Mick Cantwell and Sharon Gould and Lee Tobbits, for making resupplying trips something to look forward to.

Finally, I am grateful to Mary Catherine Bateson and Ann McLean for allowing me to examine and refer to the unpublished data of two masters of fieldwork, Margaret Mead and Reo Fortune.

INTRODUCTION:
THE CHAMBRI WITHIN THE
MIDDLE SEPIK: A STUDY IN
HISTORICAL ANTHROPOLOGY

My interest in writing a historical ethnography of the Chambri began some years ago when a student of mine came to discuss her selection of a major. She had taken a number of anthropology courses but was also interested in history and could not decide between the two disciplines. She portrayed her dilemma metaphorically, describing both subjects as intellectual journeys. History was an excursion on water skis in which she was propelled along the surface of what she could only assume were deep and complex environments, while anthropology was a trip on broken snow shoes, in which she was drawn into the depths of foreign terrains so that she could hardly get anywhere at all. If only, she bemoaned, we would articulate the two disciplines, historians substantiating their narratives with ethnographic detail, and anthropologists admitting that times change in a manner inconsistent with their notion of autonomously homeostatic societies.

I answered her questions to the best of my ability, describing alternative methodological perspectives and advising her that social research, like life in general, is a matter of constraint and compromise. Anthropologists who opt to study the complete sociocultural lives of the peoples they describe tend to shun reconstructions of the past as potentially ethnocentric misinterpretations of foreign ways of life. Historians who choose to uncover the stories of extinct or transformed peoples must find their data where they can.

It has become relatively common for anthropologists to agree with my student by labeling their colleagues as obstructionally ahistorical (see, for example, Cohn, 1980; Rosaldo, 1980). They argue that the empirical bent most of us share is not enough to save our discipline from its atemporal perspective, and by and large I agree with them. It is difficult to understand, after all, how we are to explain the present or predict the future unless we have come to terms with the past. Underlying most anthropological examinations of social systems has been the assumption that their subjects exist in static equilibrium. It is a convenient assumption when the materials for such analyses have typically been gathered during a year or two of research among a preliterate people incapable of offering what the ethnologist considers accurate records of their precontact past. Both logical argument and empirical fact demonstrate, however, that societies must change through time like other systems subject to evolutionary forces. Thus history in preliterate societies becomes like the tree that falls in the forest: can we assume that no sound (or fury) existed merely because we were not present to observe its occurrence?

My reasons for writing this book, however, are even more basic than an attempt to avoid the erroneous assumption of static equilibrium. My most immediate concern is not to justify ethnographic theory with reference to historical processes, nor to devise a theory to account for social change, but simply to locate the present among the many old and new customs and behaviors that today coexist in the Middle Sepik region of Papua New Guinea. In other words, there are some parts of the world which simply cannot be described ahistorically, because the peoples who inhabit them survive only by changing in interaction with one another through time. This is not to suggest that some societies are "hot" while others are "cold," according to their cultural dispositions to incorporate or reject the new (see Levi-Strauss, 1960), but simply to argue that change for some peoples is more of a socioeconomic necessity than it is for others. In this book I explore the necessity for change in one region of Papua New Guinea. This is primarily an ethnographic account of the Chambri people and their neighbors from a historical perspective, written on the assumption that we weaken the validity of Middle Sepik ethnography by drawing temporal boundaries between the present and the past.

When I journeyed to Papua New Guinea for the first time in 1974, my preoccupation was not with time, but with space. I came to examine the integrative potentials of dispersed networks of trade, migration, and marriage as they were related to sociopolitical integration within this emerging nation. Ethnographic evidence seemed to indicate that each New Guinea village, far from being separate and self-contained, was connected by trading relationships that facilitated the movement of people and produce throughout a network that was, perhaps, island-wide. I believed that the preservation of indigenous social structures was likely to facilitate national integration, and that it was incumbent upon social scientists to determine the capacities of existing networks to fuse their heterogeneous components. My goal was to produce a distribution network matrix, or quantified map, of the trade and migration routes within the Middle Sepik, leading to a typology of networks applicable to a region far more extensive than the one I planned to study. Committed to the notion that the boundaries my predecessors had placed around their villages and tribes were arbitrary and misleading, I determined to travel exhaustively throughout the area, measuring the movement of people and produce throughout their indigenous networks of exchange.

Finding it necessary to start somewhere, I allowed myself to be persuaded by Matias Yambumpe, then the President of an Australian-imposed political division called the Gaui Local Government Council, to stay for a time among his people, the Chambri. Since old patrol reports described the Chambri as purveyors of stone tools and mosquito bags* through extensive trading networks, and since they seemed centrally located on an island south of the Sepik River and north of the Sepik Hills, that seemed a reasonable place to start my work. My only anxiety, as a fledging ethnographer who sought to describe the unfamiliar, was that Margaret Mead and Reo Fortune had studied the Chambri (Tchambuli) some forty years before (Mead, 1963; Fortune, 1933). However, I pacified myself with the thought that I would not be staying among the Chambri for long, but would merely be incorporating them as the first "node" in my matrix.

One of my earliest projects was a migrational survey, a record of all of the individuals who journeyed to or from Chambri Island, their actual or proposed destinations, the number of days they stayed or planned to be away, and their reasons for traveling. What I discovered convinced me to abandon my original research design and live among the Chambri for a longer time than I had initially anticipated.

I found, quite simply, that I could make absolutely no sense of the data I was collecting. It was not only that I knew an insufficient amount about the Chambri and their neighbors to understand their migrational patterns but that, more immediately, I could discover no comprehensive patterns from my record of their migrations. Many Chambri journeyed to the towns of Pagwi, Maprik, or Wewak to sell fish to the laborers who lived there or to sell artifacts to European tourists. Others traveled to barter markets in the Sepik Hills, where they exchanged their fish for sago flour. Still others chose to attend barter markets located north of the Sepik River, where the neighboring Iatmul and Sawos peoples generally met to exchange their produce. Others did not travel much at all, except occasionally to visit their non-Chambri friends, or to go for treatment to one of the nursing stations or hospitals. Some stayed away from their homes for an afternoon, others for up to six months, and time did not seem to be significantly correlated with either destination or purpose. Where, among all of these movements of people and produce, was I to discover indigenous networks of exchange

---

*Chambri women produced the cylindrical, ten- to fifteen-foot-long mosquito bags of plaited sago-shoots or bast that were used throughout the Middle Sepik. Family members slept together in these bags to protect themselves from the ferocious mosquitoes which infest the area.

that would facilitate national integration? If these networks were to be found, I would have to stay put and learn what they meant to the people who were using them. In other words, I had discovered that I could not hope to draw a map of indigenous trade and migration routes until I had learned what was indigenous about them.

At the time I would have defined the word *indigenous* to mean regulated by relatively permanent social rules and generalizable over broad distances, if not pantribally. In the back of my mind were the many ethnographers of tribal societies who explain exchange relationships among the peoples with whom they work as a means of protecting land from usurpation (see, for example, Vayda, 1971; Harris, 1975; and Brown, 1978). All of these ethnographers seem to have found the same sorts of social behaviors regulating man-land relationships among the many different peoples they have studied. Consider, as an example of these social behaviors, the two types of exchange relationships that have been found to unite populations of New Guinea Highlanders into socioeconomic systems. The first, trade, is directly linked with local diversity in the production of commodities, and consists of "contingent, finite and private transactions between individuals" (Meggitt, 1974: 169). Trade "lack[s] ceremony, do[es] not involve the extension of credit and [is] not formally or structurally connected with the networks of public prestations" (ibid.) which comprise the second type of relationship.

These prestations are "elements in a system of delayed exchanges which include the notion of credit, are highly elaborated or 'ceremonialized' and usually take place with the maximum publicity between groups of people" (ibid.). As such, they establish and maintain status differentials both within and between local communities. Groups that are in an unstable alliance with one another compete to maintain their equality by striving to insure that they do not receive more than they are given. And Big Men emerge as leaders who can provide this insurance by persuading their constituents to assist them in mounting an exchange. Those who support a Big Man frequently obtain the goods they offer him from their individual trading partners, and thus trade provides a significant portion of the commodities needed for ceremonial prestations.

The relationship between individualized trading partnerships and delayed exchange relationships allows Highland societies a degree of social and cultural elaboration perhaps unsurpassed in the tribal world. Essentially, New Guinea Highlanders translate mechanical into organic solidarity by transferring the goods they acquire through their generalized trading partnerships into networks of delayed and balanced exchanges (see Durkheim, 1933). Thus, hundreds of individuals belonging to many different groups are linked together into regional socioeconomic systems.

Underlying these systems is, of course, a domestic economy based upon the cultivation of sweet potatoes and the husbandry of pigs. Families or larger kin groups own land upon which they grow crops to feed themselves and their animals. They invest their horticultural surpluses, swine, and special products in economic transactions that establish political alliances. Without these alliances the land upon which they depend would become vulnerable to intrusion by expanding groups who need additional acreage upon which to support themselves. In this sense, the socioeconomic system characteristic of Highland New Guinea both begins and ends with land. Land allows Highlanders to produce surpluses, and these surpluses allow their producers to maintain control of their primary resource.

But at the same time, the economic transactions that insure political alliances demand increased production of exchangeable items, for the more extensive are an individual's alliances, the more he must produce to maintain them. In other words, Highland exchange systems make demands upon domestic economies, and an individual's control of his land is always contingent upon his ability to support himself and his exchange partners. Thus, there is a feedback between exchange, trade, and production which links all three elements and the social and political relationships they generate. This feedback translates the past, the present, and the future into a system of spatial relationships between people and their land, a system that is expressed by anthropologists through concepts like carrying-capacity, and by natives through sociosymbolic associations between groups and their territories.

As comprehensible as the association between society and land appears to those who value the latter, we must be wary of imposing it upon those who do not depend upon land for subsistence. The Chambri and their neighbors of the Middle Sepik would find the association puzzling, for they have seen land disappear in minutes through the action of the far more powerful element, water. To them, society does not consist of areas of land whose boundaries change as sociopolitical circumstances change. Rather, it consists of relatively fixed points surrounded by the fluid and unpredictable element of water, which can change sociopolitical relationships as it inundates new areas and recedes from old ones.

The water I refer to comprises the Sepik River and its tributaries and backswamps. Beginning in the Thurnwald Range just south of Telefomin in the West Sepik Province, the river flows for over seven hundred miles to the north coast, emptying into the Bismarck Sea, some sixty miles southeast of the town of Wewak. In places along the river's middle reaches, the channel is fifty feet deep and five hundred yards wide, and it is here that the inhabitants of the Sepik appreciate the power of water.

These peoples are unfamiliar with the imposing mountains and lush valleys of the Highlands; their environment is essentially flat, punctuated by occasional hills which foreshadow the Torricelli and Hunstein ranges, visible in the distance to the north and south respectively (see map 1). But it is the Sepik River which is the majestic topographical feature here, winding through its flood plain in meanders as convoluted as those of a cranial suture.

Indeed, the metaphor is more than structurally apt, for just as a person would be helpless if his two cerebral hemispheres were not joined in mutual interdependence, so too would the societies of the Sepik be unlikely to survive without the articulation provided by the river.

This articulation allows people to exchange locally produced commodities with ease and efficiency, resulting in what Mead has called, in her study of the Mountain Arapesh, their "importing culture" (1970: 178–206). By this she not only means that Sepik peoples are preoccupied with exchanging locally produced cultural items, such as ceremonial masks, artifacts, and dance complexes, but also that their cultures depend upon importation for subsistence. Neither the Chambri nor any other people within the Middle Sepik could survive today without obtaining foodstuffs from their neighbors. They trade not only to enrich their cultures and to establish and maintain political alliances, but also to support themselves.

Their dependence upon the acquisition of foodstuffs from their neighbors makes my initial definition of the word *indigenous* irrelevant to Middle Sepik exchange relationships. My search for relatively permanent and broadly applicable social rules was doomed to failure in such a heterogeneous environment, where trading connections are far from generalized. Unlike the situation among the subsistence horticulturalists of Highland New Guinea, where traded commodities are frequently superfluities, and where ceremonial prestations can easily be shifted from one group to another, each Middle Sepik people must vigilantly maintain particular relationships with those who produce what it needs for survival.

A brief cultural geography of the Middle Sepik region will make this last point clearer to those unfamiliar with life in such a heterogeneous environment. Two points must be emphasized. First, the Sepik River not only acts as a conduit of trade items, but it also creates the need for their exchange. Second, it often poses serious survival problems for those living in its vicinity, for the Sepik is not a tranquil river. It is constantly changing its course by eroding its convex outer banks and depositing alluvium on its inside beds. Three breakthroughs have been recorded since 1940, one cutting off a seven-mile loop of the river. They are rapidly sealed by clay plugs on both ends, but, since complete silting takes a long time, the resulting oxbow lakes remain a prominent feature of the landscape.

These transformations in the physical characteristics of the Sepik and its floodplains occur as the river overflows its banks during the northwest mon-

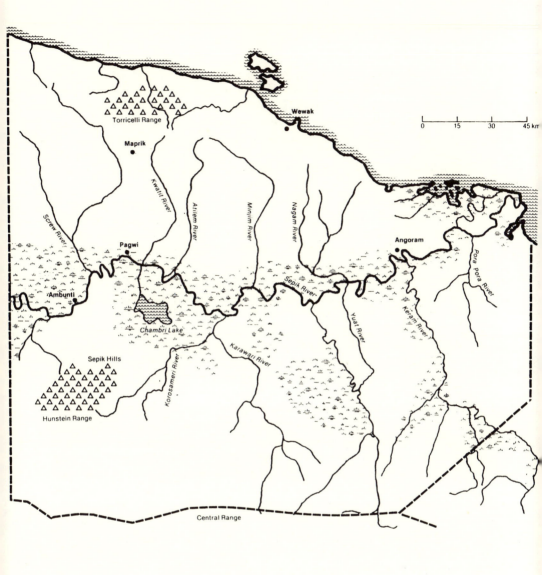

The East Sepik Province from Ambunti to Angoram

soon season from December through March, when rainfall nearly doubles in intensity from a dry season average of 5.12 inches to 9.44 inches per month, and the river rises up to twenty feet, depositing thick layers of mud and silt upon its banks which form discontinuous levees up to six miles long. The Iatmul who live along the river build their stilted houses along these levees and hope that the water will not rise above floor level. Occasionally (local tradition has it once every seven years), the stilts prove too short and the people take to their canoes, abandoning their houses, whose thatched roofs alone remain above the water like straw hats in a pool. (See map 2 for the location of the peoples mentioned in this chapter.)

Although vulnerable to the vicissitudes of their environment, the Iatmul dominate the other societies of the region much as the river does the topography. They are the headhunters described by explorers and missionaries as "fierce," "proud," and "treacherous," and by themselves as "the first people of the Sepik." Living in twenty-five large villages of between 250 and 1,500 members, they were inveterate warriors who displayed their prowess through capturing heads for display in their men's houses. They have become well known through Gregory Bateson's account of their rituals of role-reversal in *Naven* (1958). Bateson argued that the ethos of Iatmul culture emphasizes intermale competition to such a degree that Iatmul villages would self-destruct if the *naven* ceremonies did not reverse what he described as their positive feedback system of symmetrical interaction.

Although Bateson also described the complementary behavior of Iatmul women vis-à-vis their aggressive husbands and fathers, he did not emphasize their autonomous activities. These are extremely important to Iatmul society, for the women are the fishwives and marketers, capturing fish with nets and traps placed either in the Sepik or its tributaries and bartering their fish for sago palm flour at markets held in the plains. Although both men and women plant gardens, the yams, pumpkins, and sweet potatoes they grow are frequently destroyed by the rising waters of the river, and they subsist primarily upon the fish and sago provided by the women.

Flooding is also a regular event in the Middle Sepik Plains, which extend north and south of the river, covering 9,600 square miles. These plains are divided by Sepik tributaries which originate in the Torricelli Range to the north and in the Central and Hunstein ranges to the south and southwest. Flowing downward through lowland seasonal rainforest, through lowland-hill forest, through floodplain forest and through swamp grassland, they reach the Sepik, whose levee banks frequently impound them into floodout deltas or shallow lakes. The levels of these deltas and lakes fluctuate greatly, for during the rainy season they act as reservoirs for the Sepik floods.

The Sawos, who live in the lower portion of the northern flood plain, tend to build their houses near the larger tributaries which, like the Sepik,

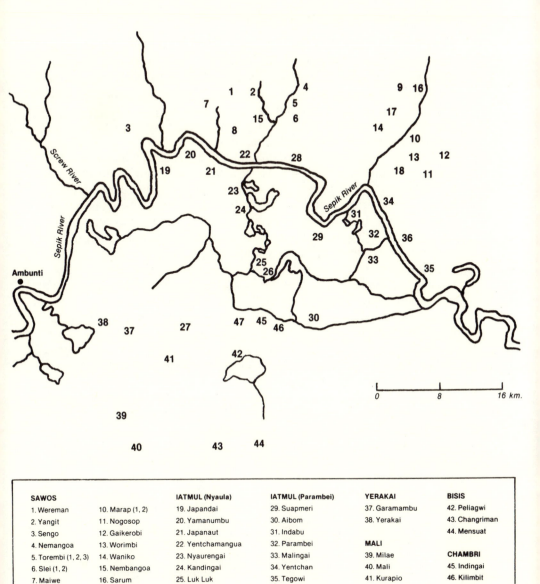

SAWOS		IATMUL (Nyaula)	IATMUL (Parambei)	YERAKAI	BISIS
1. Wereman	10. Marap (1, 2)	19. Japandai	29. Suapmeri	37. Garamambu	42. Peliagwi
2. Yangit	11. Nogosop	20. Yamanumbu	30. Aibom	38. Yerakai	43. Changriman
3. Sengo	12. Gaikerobi	21. Japanaut	31. Indabu		44. Mensuat
4. Nemangoa	13. Worimbi	22. Yentchamangua	32. Parambei	MALI	
5. Torembi (1, 2, 3)	14. Waniko	23. Nyaurengai	33. Malingai	39. Milae	CHAMBRI
6. Slei (1, 2)	15. Nembangoa	24. Kandingai	34. Yentchan	40. Mali	45. Indingai
7. Maiwe	16. Sarum	25. Luk Luk	35. Tegowi	41. Kurapio	46. Kilimbit
8. Vagiput	17. Miambe	26. Arinjone	36. Kanganaman		47. Wombun
9. Yakiap	18. Kaimbiam	27. Timbunmeri			
		28. Korogo			

Some Villages of the Middle Sepik

form levees along their banks. Although only one ethnographer has thoroughly investigated these people (Schindlbeck, 1980), they have figured in various ethnographic accounts of the region, for they supply the Iatmul with sago and ceremonial valuables (Bateson, 1933; Laycock, 1961; Mead, 1963). In 1977 their de jure population was approximately 6,200, occupying twenty-two villages. They supplement the sago they produce and the fish they acquire with yams and wild game.

The Sawos language is related to Iatmul, both being members of the Ndu language family. Indeed, Sawos may be a dialect of Iatmul, for members of both groups find their languages nearly mutually intelligible. Laycock places their common origin in the foothills at the head of two of the Sepik's southern tributaries, the Korosameri and Karawari rivers (1965: 191–97). Moving toward the Sepik River, each successive wave of Ndu migrants pushed their predecessors further north toward the Torricelli Range.[1] It is the Iatmul, however, who have achieved control of the Sepik, thrusting their Sawos cousins into the backswamps of the flood plain where, living in their small villages, they have been vulnerable to Iatmul headhunting forays.[2]

South of the river live the Chambri, whose population in 1979 was approximately 1,400. They live on a jungle-covered hill which rises out of the back swamps. This hill is a remnant of a topography drowned during the late Pleistocene, when rising sea levels caused the Sepik to back up and deposit the clays and silts which today form its floodplains. Thus, while it now appears an incongruous by-blow of the forces that created the mountain ranges to the north and south, this hill once reigned supreme over others which have since been buried beneath the mud.

The Chambri would probably not be surprised to learn that there are mountains beneath their land. They live in a world in which inundation and submergence is the norm. Indeed, they occur as regularly as the wet time of the year. Unlike the river people, whose environment remains more or less riverine, these swamp dwellers live surrounded by herbaceous vegetation during the dry season and by water during the wet season. Every year they see their hill turned into an island and their anchored grasslands transformed into floating mats of ferns, grasses, and sedge. These mats, in turn, are consumed by the rising waters, which sometimes snatch them from sight with crocodile quickness.

Margaret Mead described the Chambri (Tchambuli) as "a rather minor and special version of the great Middle Sepik Iatmul culture" (1972: 249). Their specialness has elevated them to the status of icons in the literature of women's studies because Mead believed their women to be dominant. In particular, she felt that the Chambri reversed "the expected relations between men and women . . . that are characteristic of our own [and of Iatmul] culture. For it was Tchambuli women who were brisk and hearty, who managed the business affairs of life, and who worked comfortably in large and cooperative groups" (ibid.: 251). But neither female dominance nor a "Iatmulized" culture was a special or permanent characteristic of the Chambri people. Both, as we shall see, were the temporary results of certain specific historical circumstances.

The Chambri are certainly linguistically unrelated to the Iatmul, for they speak a multiple-classifying language with full concord, with all adjectives, possessive pronouns, numbers up to three, and certain intransitive verbs changing according to noun class, of which there may be as many as thirteen. These traits distinguish the Chambri from Ndu speakers, whose languages mark only a masculine-feminine distinction in the second-and third-singular pronouns (Laycock and Z'graggen, 1975: 751–52; 754–57).

Both peoples are, however, similarly dependent upon the barter of fish for sago. Those from whom the Chambri acquire sago live in the region known as the Sepik Hills. Extending from the limits of the Sepik's southern flood plain to the Central Range, the hills range in height from 100 to 700 feet and are inhabited by over 6,600 speakers of fourteen or fifteen related languages. These peoples live in tiny hilltop villages and hamlets, subsisting on sago, supplemented with fish and wild game and, among certain groups, on cultivated yams and sweet potatoes. Apart from the Heve, who live in the most southern part of the region (Townsend, 1969), they have not been investigated by ethnographers. Members of the Summer Institute of Linguistics, however, have surveyed their languages and conclude that there are significant lexostatistical interrelationships and considerable typological agreement between the Ndu and Sepik Hills tongues, and that they should, therefore, both be placed within a single-language phylum (Dye et al., 1969).[3]

Only the Bisis and Mali speakers who live in the steep hills closest to Chambri Lake exchange their sago for Chambri fish. The Bisis live in three semipermanent hamlets between the lower Salumei River and the lake, and the Mali in three shifting hamlets between Mali Lake and the Salumei River. Between their hills are valleys completely covered with sago palm vegetation, and although the Bisis and Mali also have access to the fish that live in their rivers and lakes, they prefer to acquire this food through exchange.

The Chambri also exchange their fish with another hill people, who seem linguistically unrelated to any other group inhabiting the Sepik (Wurm, 1971: 638). These four hundred Yerakai speakers live in several hamlets on a hill called Garamambu, which is located west of Chambri Lake and north of Mali territory. They practice a way of life similar to that of other Sepik Hills peoples, producing sago from their natural reserves and supplementing this carbohydrate with fish and wild game.

This brief excursion through the cultural geography of the Middle Sepik has revealed distinct social, cultural, and political groups living in heterogeneous environments and exchanging their surpluses of fish and sago. These exchanges organize the people who maintain them into a regional socioeconomic system which contrasts with the more familiar Highlands pattern. Whereas Highlanders exchange to maintain control of their autonomous domestic economies, Middle Sepik peoples barter to support their autonomous sociopolitical groups. In the former case, exchange leads to domestic production indirectly, as it insures land ownership through the maintenance of political alliances. In the latter case, exchange is primarily responsible for social, if not biological viability. Both situations result in political economies that are truly systems, in the sense that neither production, nor exchange, nor social reproduction could occur without stimulating the other functions to activity. The contrasting emphasis upon exchange within each system, however, has produced significant differences between them.

One of the most important of these differences concerns the relationships between people in time and space. In the Highlands, as I have already suggested, the past, the present, and the future can be translated into a system of spatial relationships between men and their land; boundaries change as sociopolitical circumstances change, with intergroup interaction remaining much as it was before the changes occurred. But in the Middle Sepik, where distinct societies have had to incorporate sociocultural elements of one another within their separate social, political, and economic systems, the relationship between time and space is not so easily fused. Groups have developed together—in complementary opposition rather than in mutual interchangeability—and their developments comprise a map of their relationships through history. In both cases the regional system is greater than the sum of its parts, but in the Middle Sepik these parts have developed through the establishment of heterogeneous socioeconomic relationships, rather than through the establishment of relatively homogeneous man–land dependencies.

This difference requires that we amend the theoretical principle basic to most recent analyses of social process among subsistence horticulturalists. Known broadly as the reproductive model (see Sahlins, 1976; Tourraine, 1977; and Wiener, 1976), this principle asserts that within any given environment a people must reproduce certain crucial social relationships in order to keep itself distinct and intact. The ethnographers who use this principle begin by discovering the rules that regulate a society in order to extrapolate about the past and perhaps about the future, or to demonstrate the processes which have generated change.

Although I embrace this principle as methodologically sound, I must reiterate that social reproduction in the Middle Sepik is not accomplished within isolated groups. Villagers interact with their neighbors, acquiring food, goods, services, and complexes of cultural items, and reciprocating according to their customs and capabilities. The rules that regulate such interdependent polities are dynamic and multifaceted, as peoples contend with one another's separate but interrelated social systems. Chambri ethnography, therefore, is necessarily also the history of a regional socioeconomic system involving political relationships between interacting groups of people.

In other words, the reproductive model cannot be applied to the societies of the Middle Sepik unless it can be made to account simultaneously for their social dependencies and their cultural distinctions. In order to do this we must invoke another principle, Romer's Rule of Conservative Evolution (see Romer, 1959), which suggests that innovations are adaptive only in that they allow organisms—or societies—to maintain traditional ways of life in the face of changed circumstances. Although Romer had extraordinary changes and adaptations in mind, such as the drying up of the seas during the Devonian—when lungfish developed the legs that allowed them to *get back* to the water—I see no reason why his rule cannot be applied to smaller, sociological modifications and innovations. Indeed, its application can help us to understand how interdependent groups maintain their sociocultural distance in the face of their continuous interaction: they simply apply their old cultural ends to all new means, be these dance complexes, ritual techniques, or Australian shillings, and thereby maintain, at least temporarily, their autonomy.

The rule also helps us to understand how autonomy is lost, by forcing us to distinguish between the consequences and the causes of change. The legs of lung fish were not caused by their adaptive consequences: the fish did not desire to become amphibians any more than amphibians have remained unchanged through time. In other words, by applying this simple distinction to the analysis of social process, we avoid the logical double bind of structural-functionalism. Societies only appear to be static and bounded when we assume that they have reproduced certain sociocultural "consequences" ad infinitum, and their histories only appear to be progressive and purposeful when we assume that they have inevitably accommodated to the contradictions that they have generated in their attempt to achieve old ends with new means. To free ourselves from the choice between stasis and purpose we must recognize that interacting social groups, using the extent of their cultural capacities in an attempt to maintain the known, create contradictions with which they frequently cannot contend. New social rules result, and these affect regional systems by creating additional contradictions for those peoples who have become accustomed to regular applications of the old rules. In other words, by attempting to maintain traditional social relations and values in interaction with one another through time, the Chambri and their neighbors have created new circumstances with which they all have had to struggle to contend. The process of incorporation generating contradiction and in turn generating reformulation constitutes Middle Sepik history. It is this process, beginning when the Chambri and their neighbors entered the region and continuing until today as Chambri culture suffers rapid erosion by socioeconomic, cultural, and ecological forces, that I wish to document in this book.

The problem of documenting social history among preliterate peoples is, of course, immense (see Vansina, 1961). The major difficulty, as I see it, is to establish a minimal chronology of dates and events based upon independently verifiable historical facts—that is, upon data that have been recorded by several different people working independently of one another. Without this minimal chronology, the interpretation of changes through time becomes so highly speculative that one moves from ethnography to disembodied social theory in a manner which most anthropologists would find objectionable.

Fortunately, I have gained access to a considerable number of facts. Both Margaret Mead and Reo Fortune worked among the Chambri during the early 1930s and I have studied their unpublished genealogies and other field notes. Gregory Bateson was also an early ethnographer of the area, living primarily among the Sepik River Iatmul, but also with the people of Aibom Island within Chambri Lake. Their data, in conjunction with the reports of German and Australian Colonial Administrators and missionaries, have provided me with a time depth spanning Middle Sepik history from the turn of the century.

This is not to say that the field notebooks of anthropologists or the patrol reports of administrators and missionaries are culture-free— filled with nothing but objectively presented and unquestionably accurate historical facts—for they are not. Anthropologists, colonialists, and religious proselytizers are all members of their own cultural traditions, wearing their own epistemological blinders. The key, I believe, to developing an accurate chronology does not depend exclusively on gaining access to documents from the past, but rather on juxtaposing them. The documents can be used to filter one another, until eventually it becomes possible to separate those facts that are "true" generally from those that are the product of a particular perspective.

To fill in the gaps in these early reports, and to deduce the history of precontact times, I have depended upon the linguistic, ecological, sociological, and ethnohistorical data I collected during my two field trips (the first in 1974–75, and the second in 1979), and upon comparable material gathered in recent years by other researchers in the Middle Sepik. Linguistic data about lexicostatistical regularities between the languages spoken in different parts of the region have helped me to generalize about long-term migrations from one part of the Sepik to another; ecological and sociological information about peoples interacting within their particular microenvironments has helped me to predict the constraints upon group formation within different parts of the region; and ethnohistorical narratives have helped me to understand indigenous conceptions of the social process.

The deductions I base upon these data must be taken as approximate, to be judged exclusively by Occam's razor, as the simplest possible explanation of changing relationships through time. This is particularly true when I use ethnohistories, because people tend to relate their remembrances of things past to present-day sociopolitical contexts, making it difficult, for example, to determine whether a "mythic" war was actually fought, or whether the myth-teller is simply justifying prevailing antagonisms in terms of a fictitious historical precedent. Although it is possible to argue that native historians are operating in accordance with the same epistemological principles we use—that their histories are no more or less accurate than our own, since both are based upon cultural assumptions about the ways in which human beings behave—I find that this argument leads to a relativism that is counterproductive to the entire explanatory enterprise. Thus, I have tried to verify independently the ethnohistorical accounts I use, for no other reason than to satisfy the requirements of the cultural paradigm in which I am constrained to operate.

It is, however, true that native historians, while using their tales to justify present-day antagonisms, also reveal aspects of the social processes that motivate men and women to act (see Rosaldo, 1980). While they may not place these activities within a temporal context that would satisfy those of us who seek relationships between dates and events, they do tell us about the cultural values, structural possibilities, and social contexts that compel and regulate these activities. Taken at face value, ethnohistories seem to provide no more than static descriptions of prevailing relationships from the native point of view. But when used in conjunction with complementary historical information, and viewed through the lens of Romer's Rule, ethnohistories allow us to unwind the thread of time by asking about the traditional ends that were valued by those who applied new means to achieve them. As interpreters of history, in other words, native historians may misconstrue the facts of the past, but they provide, nonetheless, invaluable maps of human motivation.

History, as I see it, is a narration of human activity through time, and while Middle Sepik peoples are constrained by their biologies, ecologies, and interdependent societies, they have acted in accordance with the images, goals, and values that give history its meaning for them. Although I have gained some insight into the nature of their constraints, they know far more about their own motivations than I can ever hope to learn. Frequently, their value-directed actions have held dire consequences for their sociobiological viability, a fact that is apparent from the large-scale migrations, wars, exiles, extinctions, social transformations wrought by pre-European contacts with other groups, and from the significant ecological and economic erosion that has occurred since the European intrusion. That they have not been passive recipients of these changes, but have both created them and have acted to maintain themselves in the face of them, is the theme of this book.

1

IATMUL HEGEMONY AND THE EVOLUTION OF MIDDLE SEPIK BARTER MARKETS

The Middle Sepik region of Papua New Guinea has interested anthropologists for some time because it consists of many distinct ecological zones inhabited by different peoples who nevertheless embrace common cultural themes.[1] These similarities seem to occur not only because many of the cultures found in the area have a common origin,[2] but also because their representatives have been interacting within their environments through the centuries. Rivers flowing from the Hunstein Mountains to the south and from the Torricelli Range to the north integrate the area into a regional system. The flow of water links rivers, floodplains, and hills into a system of interpenetrating ecological zones, and the movement of local products translates this interpenetration into socioeconomic terms. This is to say that the ecological heterogeneity of the Middle Sepik has stimulated the trade of local products, and these exchanges link villages together into a regional socioeconomic system.

Margaret Mead, in her comprehensive description of the Mountain Arapesh, refers to this regional system when she writes that:

> In localization of industries, this part of New Guinea closely resembles the even more widespread Melanesian pattern. A great many of the communities are only partially self-supporting in the matter of food, depending upon frequent and fixed markets to provide them with fish in exchange for carbohydrates, or sago for fish. Even where communities are self-supporting in foods, other forms of dependence occur, for weapons, tools, tobacco, lime, currency, valuables, etc. Associated with the localization of industries is a regular institutionalization of trade, the institution of the trade friend, definite trade routes, paired trading relationships between adjacent communities, and the regular market in which one kind of food is exchanged for another. This trade crosses every type of boundary, linguistic, social and geographical, and forms the basis for the purposive diffusion, sale, and exchange of ceremonial paraphernalia, magical charms, methods of divining, new forms of social organization, etc. [1970: 18–19]

In this chapter I begin where Mead left off, with different peoples engaged in various forms of exchange, and attempt to explain these variations in historical terms. I am assuming that such trading patterns were not merely a matter of cultural predilection—that Mead was wrong to imply that a people could have chosen one pattern of exchange as easily as another—but that they occurred with regularity in relation to other social developments. Here I limit myself to tracing these developments among the Iatmul, relying heavily upon the published and unpublished data of others to supplement my own observations made during the four weeks I visited among the Iatmul and the Sawos. These data indicate an evolution from small-scale and individualized trading partnerships to standardized intervillage markets, a shift that took place in conjunction with the development of hegemony by Iatmul fish-suppliers over their barter partners.

Fish-for-Sago: Iatmul Barter Markets

Under the influence of the Gaui Local Government Council and the Catholic Mission, the Middle Sepik barter fish for Sawos sago at markets held twice a week, on Wednesdays and Saturdays or on Tuesdays and Fridays. Traditionally these markets were held every three days. In all of their villages women control the fishing and are also solely responsible for the marketing. On market days the fishwives carry out the highly regularized incursions into alien territory on which the sustenance of their families depends, generally traveling to the market located nearest to their villages.

They rise well before dawn to load their canoes. Dried fish, smoked whole over an open fire or split and flattened before smoking, are transported in baskets loosely woven from coconut fronds. Fresh fish, retrieved from nets on the way to the market, are strung on rattan strips and left to expire in the canoe. Turtles, their legs trussed, are stuffed into string bags. The women place their produce on large pieces of palm bark to keep it from the bilge water that sloshes about their feet.

The journey to market can take as long as three hours, depending on the destination and the season. Although many of the northern tributaries that link the Sawos market sites to the Sepik River dry up in August, during the rest of the year accessibility is no problem for the women's light, narrow canoes. Moving in single file, the canoes make silent, steady progress against the current. Women rarely travel singly; they prefer to make the journey in groups of four or five, using the largest canoes available, which they paddle in a kneeling position. A fire burns at the stern of each canoe, both to ward off mosquitoes, which swarm out from the swamp grass and forest, and to cook fish for breakfast.

On reaching the shore, the women remain in their canoes until all participants are present. Then they swing their bulging string bags onto their heads, the straps tight against their foreheads, cushioned by pads of folded leaves, and march to the market site, which is rarely more than a hundred yards from the shore. The bushwomen arrive there at the same time, having tramped along muddy paths from their villages. They carry string bags filled with sago and betel nuts. Once at the market place, the unpacking begins. The bushwomen produce large cinder-block-sized chunks of sago and cut them into nine to twelve pieces. The goods are displayed on palm bark or water-lily leaves. The women group themselves by villages and, their unpacking finished, sit brushing flies from their fish or sago while they wait for the bartering to begin.

Suddenly, the bushwomen rise. Holding the small chunks of sago shoulder high, they march in single file and obsequiously offer their wares to the fishwives. The latter, who remain seated, are haughtily indifferent to the sago-suppliers; even when they accept a piece of sago in exchange for a fish, they do so contemptuously. In one transaction I witnessed, an Iatmul woman from Korogo, having previously exchanged fish for sago with a Sawos woman from Torembi, changed her mind when she saw another woman with larger, fresher chunks. She waited until her original partner came around again, and thrust the sago at her. She demanded that her fish be returned, yelling: "You think I want this pig-feed sago. You must be crazy!" The Torembi woman took back her sago and returned the fish without a word.

The behavior of Iatmul women toward their Sawos barter partners duplicates, in many ways, the complementary relationship described by Bateson as existing between Iatmul men and women.[3]

> A relationship between two individuals (or between two groups) is said to be chiefly complementary if most of the behavior of the one individual is culturally regarded as of one sort (e.g. assertive) while most of the behavior of the other, when he replies, is culturally regarded as a sort of complementary to this (e.g. submissive). [1958: 308].

Throughout *Naven*, Bateson describes the interactional patterns of Iatmul men and women as antithetical. Men are "proud," "histrionic," "buffoonlike," "self-assertive," and "harsh" while women, when they reply, are "unostentatious," "cooperative," and "quiet." Certainly these two sets of adjectives can also be applied to the interaction between the aggressive Iatmul fishwives and their submissive Sawos barter partners.

Bateson finds that these complementary interactional patterns tend toward schizmogenesis, "a process of differentiation in the norms of individual behaviour resulting from cumulative interaction between individuals" (1958: 175).

If, for example, one of the patterns of cultural behaviour, considered appropriate in individual A, is culturally labeled as an assertive pattern, while B is expected to reply to this with what is culturally regarded as submission, it is likely that this submission will encourage a further assertion, and that this assertion will demand still further submission. We have thus a potentially progressive state of affairs, and unless other factors are present to restrain the excesses of assertive and submissive behaviour, A must necessarily become more and more assertive, while B will become more and more submissive; and this progressive change will occur whether A and B are separate individuals or members of complementary groups. [1958: 176]

Iatmul barter markets present Bateson with a problem, however, for while complementary in nature, they do not tend toward schizmogenesis.

Cases in which group A sometimes sell sago to group B and the latter sometimes sell the same commodity to A, may be regarded as reciprocal; but if group A habitually sell sago to B, we must, I think, regard the pattern as complementary. The reciprocal pattern, it may be noted, is compensated and balanced within itself and therefore does not tend towards schizmogenesis. . . . It is certain, as in the case quoted above in which group A sell sago to B while the latter sell fish to A, complementary patterns may sometime have a stabilizing effect by promoting the mutual dependence between the groups. [1972: 69]

Bateson's suggestion that the complementary interactional patterns of Iatmul and Sawos women promote mutual dependence between their groups, thus explaining the apparent stability of their barter markets, does little more than restate his problem. The problem itself, however, is worthy of consideration once it is reformulated in economic terms. If fish-for-sago exchanges can be described as complementary, then they should, according to Bateson, be subject to inflationary pressures. His problem, in other words, is to explain why the Iatmul and the Sawos have continued to barter one fish for one piece of sago through time.

The Value of Exchange

By asking why these fish-for-sago barter relationships are not inflationary, Bateson assumes that the desire of the Iatmul and Sawos to obtain that which they cannot produce represents a maximizing impulse. This assumption is based on the doctrine of capitalist economics, that all people allocate their limited resources to alternative and conflicting ends—that human socioeconomic relationships are motivated by a compulsion to acquire as much of scarce resources as possible.

Stated in this manner, it appears that the Sawos have been getting the worst of the one-for-one exchange rate, for they work harder to produce sago than the Iatmul do to catch fish. Although Markus Schindlbeck, who did fieldwork in the Sawos village of Gaikerobi, suggests an equivalence between the amount of labor invested by the Sawos and the Iatmul in the items they exchange, I think his reasoning is mistaken. He argues that:

> A fixed rate exists for the exchange of sago and fish. . . . On the average a woman gave two kg sago for one unit of fish (half of an eel, half of the fish *wandjok*, or a whole fish *makau* . . .). Considering that a woman produces 3.7 kg starch per hour, she gets about two units of fish per sago working hour. As we may deduce from the work by Hauser-Schaublin (1977: 28) an Iatmul woman may catch on the average 9 fishes a day (working time half a day). A Sawos woman works at about five hours sago for ten fishes [*sic*]. Now we see that there is a balance in the work between Iatmul and Sawos. . . . [1980: 552]

Schindlbeck recognizes a difference between the quantity and the quality of work, reminding us that "fishing and sago working are very different in relation to the energy consumed" (ibid.), but chooses to ignore his own reminder when trying to explain the fixed rate of fish-for-sago exchange. This difference cannot be overlooked, however, for although a Sawos and Iatmul woman each invests approximately five hours of labor, the former works much harder than the latter.

The process of preparing sago begins when the Sawos fell a sago palm (*Metroxylum rumphii*), peel back its bark, and pulverize its pith with blunt-headed adzes. Women then place the pith in a palm-bark trough that is set on stilts close to a shallow pool or stream. The trough is tilted and a coconut-fiber screen is lashed near the lower end. A large piece of palm bark is warped to form a shallow bowl and placed on the ground to catch the run off. The women scoop up water with ladles made of coconut-shell halves and pour it through the pith to wash away the starch. The starch-laden water flows through the trough into the shallow palm-bark bowl. The inedible sago strands are filtered out by the coconut-fiber screen. After the starch settles, the women pour off the water and place the block of starch into a basket, where it dries out.

In comparison, the Iatmul fish for a few hours every morning, each woman gathering her catch from the traps or nets she keeps submerged in clan-owned waters. Fish are plentiful and relatively easy to catch, and although an Iatmul woman may limit her catch to nine fish per day, she need not do so. Indeed, members of the Department of Agriculture, Stock, and Fisheries estimate the weight of fish of legal size that could be caught from

Sepik waters for commercial purposes to be approximately 50,000 tonnes a year (Thorpe, personal communication).

Although I have accomplished no statistical measure of the calories expended by either Sawos or Iatmul women at work, casual observation suggests that the former labor at least three times as hard to produce sago as the latter do to catch fish. This suggests that fish must be worth more than sago—enough, in fact, to counterbalance the additional effort the Sawos must expend to acquire the fish. But worth more in what sense? Certainly not intrinsically, for our only measure of sago's worth is the apparently unfair one-for-one exchange rate.

Could it be that the unfairness of this exchange rate is illusory, and that the Sawos are maximizing in this sense: that it would be harder for them to obtain fish on their own than it is for them to acquire it from the Iatmul? Although it appears reasonable when we realize that the Sawos live in a territory where fish are not plentiful, this hypothesis cannot resolve the issue of why the Sawos should want fish at all. We can assume that they need a regular supply of high-quality protein to support their sedentary populations, but then we must account for their preference for life in permanent villages. Bigger villages, where a regular access to fish may become necessary for survival, are not necessarily better villages, nor necessarily preferable villages.

The only way of approaching the question of why the Sawos prefer to live in sedentary villages—and of why they accept what is an essentially unfair exchange rate—is to realize that exchange in preindustrial societies is as much a social as it is an economic relationship, and that tribal groups exchange both to acquire goods and to keep the peace (see Sahlins, 1972). Can it be that the social relationship established between the Sawos and the Iatmul through their exchange of fish for sago is worth three times as much to the Sawos per transaction? Let us investigate this possibility through an analysis of two occasions when the peace between the Sawos and the Iatmul was disturbed. (See map 3 for the locations and linguistic affiliations of the villages mentioned throughout this chapter.)

Case 1: Suapmeri versus Yamuk

My information about the Iatmul village Suapmeri comes from the brief migrational history collected in 1973 by Assistant District Commissioner L. W. Bragge. I reproduce his account verbatim:

> Suapmeri is an ancient village site with stone monoliths similar to those found at Parambei and Chambri. The stories of origin state that Suapmeri was the first village on the Sepik and in the distant past the Suapmeri people migrated from Tipmangei. Legend has it that as the village grew trade relations were set up with

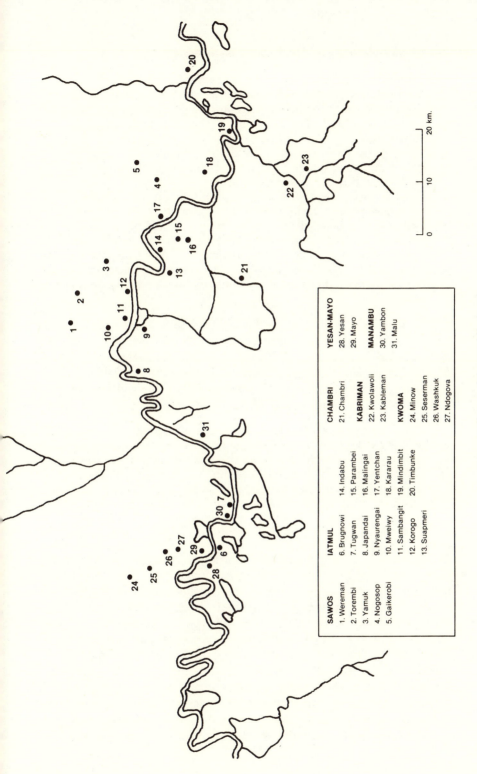

SAWOS
1. Wereman
2. Torembi
3. Yamuk
4. Nogosop
5. Gaikerobi

IATMUL
6. Brugnowi
7. Tugwan
8. Japandai
9. Nyaurengai
10. Mweiwy
11. Sambangit
12. Korogo
13. Suapmeri

14. Indabu
15. Parambei
16. Malingai
17. Yentchan
18. Kararau
19. Mindimbit
20. Timbunke

CHAMBRI
21. Chambri

KABRIMAN
22. Kwolawoli
23. Kableman

KWOMA
24. Minow
25. Seserman
26. Washkuk
27. Ndogova

YESAN-MAYO
28. Yesan
29. Mayo

MANAMBU
30. Yambon
31. Malu

20 km.

10

0

Some Villages of the Middle Sepik

Yamuk. Yamuk raided Suapmeri, however, and Suapmeri retaliated with the result that Yamuk ceased to trade sago with them. Without its staple food, Suapmeri broke up. One migration went to Nyaurengai and other migrations went all over the countryside, leaving few people at Suapmeri. The people who moved away turned upon those who stayed, and this is the justification for the wars between Suapmeri, Nyaula and Parambei.[4] Suapmeri was sandwiched between these two forces, and was hit from both sides. Finally it was abandoned and the people fled to Indabu and to Kwalingai where just prior to the German Administration, a Nyaula raid destroyed both villages, on the same day, and the Suapmeri survivors scattered. Most went to Malingai, some to Yentchan and some to Parambei. They gave two women to Malingai, and the refugees at Parambei then also came. They lived at Malingai until the 1930's when they moved back onto their own land. [page unknown]

This account is interesting for the relationship it suggests between the size of a village and its dependence upon marketing: "as the village grew trade relations were set up with Yamuk. . . . Without its staple food Suapmeri broke up." Iatmul villages are large, containing between 250 and 1,500 members. Moreover, their "social organization, kinship and religious systems are developed to an extreme of complexity" (Bateson, 1958: 4).

The community is subdivided into groups according to two independent systems with very little congruence between one system and the other. On the one hand there is a division into two totemic moieties which are further subdivided into phratries and clans; and on the other hand there is a division into two cross-cutting pairs of initiatory moieties which are subdivided into age grades. None of these groups are strictly exogamous. Membership of all the groups is determined by patrilineal descent. [1958: 4]

To support villages of this size and complexity necessitates a well-regulated supply of subsistence products. Since these are available to the Iatmul neither through cultivation nor foraging, they must be acquired through trade.

Sawos villages, in comparison, are small. While the mean population of Iatmul villages was 315 in 1959, Sawos settlements averaged only a hundred persons.[5] Moreover, casual observation suggests that the social and ritual complexity of Iatmul villages is not even approached by most of their Sawos counterparts, for the large and elaborate men's houses and well-kept dance groups so characteristic of the former are absent from many of the latter.[6]

It seems safe to assume, therefore, that far from being three times as dependent upon barter, the Sawos, living in their small settlements and organized into relatively flexible and unelaborated social groups, have less need for a regular supply of fish than the Iatmul have for sago. Schindl-beck, who studied an unusually large Sawos village, suggests as much when he describes the market behavior of Gaikerobi women. A few of these women shun the market altogether, finding that their own small lakes and rivulets contain sufficient fish to support themselves and their families. Thinking it likely that women with large families would visit barter markets more fre-quently, Schindlbeck collected data to confirm or disconfirm his hypothesis and found no correlation between the size of a woman's family and the frequency with which she attended the market (1980: 177–84).[7] Since the Gaikerobi live nearer to fish-filled lakes and streams than most Sawos vil-lagers, Schindlbeck's findings are particularly significant. They suggest ad-ditional dimensions to the social relationship between barter partners that transcend subsistence requirements and explain the Sawos willingness to invest a considerable amount of their labor in maintaining them. Perhaps the second case, which describes the processes by which marketing rela-tionships were initially established, will illuminate the issue.

Case 2: Japandai

The migrational history of the Iatmul village of Japandai as it is presented by the linguist Philip Staalsen is extraordinarily complex. I am particularly interested in two incidents, the formation of the Minow market[8] and the Japandai attempt to accustom the Yesan-Mayo bush-people to the practices of water-people. I give the significant passages from Staalsen's article:

> At this time . . . [the people of] Japanday[9] came up river and they built a house at Tugwan. Japanday gave fine women to [the people of] Malu and Yambon. . . . They also gave pay for pigs and ground. They put down a great deal of pay. Then [the man] Ngumberiygumbon wanted to kill [the man] Bensiynduma so he gave a tanget* to the men of Sesermen. Sesermen received the tanget at the market.
> In times past there was no market there. But three men Ngum-beriygumbon, Bensiynduma and Poriygumbon brought Seser-men out of the bush and inaugurated the market at Minow.
> The people of Washkuk saw the people of Sesermen eating shrimp and fish and asked them, "Where did you get that sweet food?" "We got it from Ngumberiygumbon and Bensiynduma," they re-plied. Having said this, they agreed to have a market. . . . While at the market . . . they both gave tangets to the people of Seser-men and Washkuk. Bensiynduma gave a tanget to the Washkuks so they would shoot Ngumberiygumbon, and Ngumberiygumbon gave a tanget to Sesermen so they would shoot Bensiynduma.

---

* *Tangets* are used throughout New Guinea to measure time. The leaves of the shrub *Taetsia fructicosa* are knotted, each knot representing a unit of time, usually a day.

Washkuk and Sesermen later met and said, "Why should we shoot these men? They are good men. Should we shoot one and not the other?" That's all they said. . . . They shot the two men at Ndogova on the appointed day. . . .

Yambon decided to fight again. . . . While we were discussing revenge, white men came. . . .

We said, "When the white man leaves we will attack them. For now we will go up river and stay at Brugnowi." We did not come and stay there without paying. We gave much pay to Yesan and Mayo. . . . We always say, "You people of Yesan and Mayo, you are not river people. You are from the hills. You are penis and vulva, having no breech clouts and grass skirts. . . ."

They (Yesan and Mayo) are another kind of people. We introduced them to women's cowls, grass skirts, paddles and canoes. We taught them how to live, but they wouldn't learn. We said, "Shoot fish like this. Paddle like this. Jump in the water and wash like this. Put on a grass skirt like this." But they would not go near the water. They did not know how to swim; they just sank. . . .

"It is not good," we said, "that river people and bush people should live together." They are of one kind and we are of another. Our forefathers put Yambon on the river and Yesan on the river. . . . So the boundaries of Japanday are from Nibarangi up river to Komaragu. The boundary of Mwewiy is from Sabangit up river to Nibarabgi. Mwewiy's market is at Ngungusu. Japanday's market is Wereman. . . . [1965: 186–87]

This account recapitulates the pattern we uncovered in the first case, for it suggests that the Iatmul took the initiative in establishing regularized barter markets, and we have seen that the Iatmul were once more dependent upon trading for sago than the Sawos were upon trading for fish: "Ngumberiygumbon, Bensiynduma and Poriygumbon brought the Seserman out of the bush and inaugurated the market at Minow." It does, however, furnish an additional insight, namely that barter markets grew from individualized trading partnerships: "The people of Seserman saw . . . shrimps and fish and asked. . . . 'Where did you get that sweet food?' 'We got it from [the men] Ngumberiygumbon and Benisynduma. . . .' Having said this they agreed to have a market."

To evaluate the historical validity of this ethnohistorical account, let us begin by recalling that Staalsen's Japandai informant distinguishes between these earlier trading relationships and the inauguration of intervillage marketing, attributing the latter to the genius of his people. He also suggests that necessary to the establishment of these markets was a process he describes variously as "bringing the Seserman out of the bush" and "teaching the bush people to live." By this I suspect he means two things. First, in bringing Seserman out of the bush, the Iatmul transformed the tiny and semipermanent hamlets of their hunting and gathering trading partners into larger and permanent villages of sedentary marketers. Today's Iatmul–Sawos barter markets reveal this structural transformation. While they are impersonal—without permanent trading partners—they are also patrilineally inherited— "owned" by sections of Iatmul and Sawos villages. Gaikerobi women whose husbands or fathers come from the village sections called Kraiembət and Indeləpma, for example, tend to barter at the Djametuvu market with Kanganaman women whose husbands or fathers live in the men's houses called Mindjemət and Kosimbi. And Sawos women from the villages of Marap 1 and 2 trade with Parambei women whose fathers or husbands come from the men's houses called Andimbit and Nambaləman, while the remaining Parambei women exchange with Sawos women from the villages of Nogosop and Yakiap (see Schindlbeck, 1980: 192–93). Thus, Iatmul–Sawos barter markets are conglomorates of what were once individualized trading partnerships. [10]

The second thing I suspect Staalsen's informant means is that, by teaching the bush-people how to live, the Japandai encouraged them to develop a consciousness of themselves as a group both related and opposed to all of their Iatmul barter partners, and I think their new awareness is illustrated by the question: "Should we shoot one [Iatmul] and not the other?" In other words, by transforming individualized trading partnerships into regularized, intervillage markets, the Iatmul intensified the awareness of distinctness for both groups. Today, both the Sawos and the Iatmul express this distinctness in kinship terms. They describe their relationship as being like that between mothers and children. (The mother-child relationship, however, is actually one of considerable stress.) The Sawos I spoke to, for example, would admit that they accept an unfair exchange rate, insisting that: "We must feed the Iatmul like a mother feeds her children." The Iatmul, on the other hand, while accepting the same analogy, interpret it differently, arguing that: "The Sawos, like women, are weak and inferior."

I do not mean to suggest that Ngumberiygumbon, Bensiynduma, and Poriygumbon, the Japandai men described by Staalsen's informant, devised an elaborate plan one night in their men's house to organize all of their people's individual trading partners into permanent and regularized markets. The bringing out of the bush-people was not an event which occurred at any one point in history. Rather, through the course of time, both sago-producers and fish-suppliers experienced changes in their life-styles which made regularized marketing both advantageous and necessary.

The conflicting marriage systems of the Iatmul provide hints of these changes. [11] Bateson reports three marriage preferences: marriage with the *iai* or the father's mother's brother's sons' daughter; marriage with the father's sister's daughter; and sister exchange (1933: 279–86). Neither I nor Rubel and Rosman (1978: 32–50) gained any confirmation of the second preference, and we learned of a prohibition on marriage with real first cousins, both the father's sister's daughter and mother's brother's daughter. It can therefore be assumed that Bateson misinterpreted the Iatmul statement that "the daughter goes in payment for the mother" (Bateson, 1958: 89).[12] This leaves the Iatmul with a preference for sister exchange—provided the sisters be classificatory and not their husbands' cousins—and *iai* marriage, each of which conflicts with the other.

In the case of *iai* marriage, each exogamous patriclan requires two wife-giving and two wife-taking groups, and a minimum of eight is required for the total system to work: "In the first generation, ego's group C receives a woman from B and gives a woman to D. In the second generation, group C receives from A and gives to E. The third generation recapitulates the first" (Rubel and Rosman, 1978: 37–38). Thus, wife-givers and wife-takers are always separate, and no return is ever made for a marriage. The opposite, of course, is true for sister exchange, which involves two groups in an ongoing relationship.

Whereas sister exchange allows for a flexibility conducive to shifting alliances between groups such as hamlets, *iai* marriage demands stable clans within large villages. It may be, therefore, that *iai* marriage developed when the ancestral Iatmul, speakers of the original Ndu language, moved into the area from their hamlets at the headwaters of the Korosameri and Karawari tributaries and found themselves capable of a sedentary life-style in large and stable villages (see Laycock, 1965). They may have previously exchanged sisters to link each of their semipermanent hamlets to others in a pattern of shifting alliances. This earlier marriage pattern remained a cultural possibility as permanent villages developed and expanded. Tuzin, who has studied a similar process at work among another Sepik people, the Ilahita Arapesh, suggests that village boundaries there "conceptually expanded to embrace preexisting relations *between* [hamlets] and apply them to the emergent organizational problems of a growing, consolidating population" (1977: 262).[13] He thinks that a similar process occurred among the Iatmul, and if we understand the preexisting, interhamlet relations he describes to involve affinal connections through the exchange of sisters, then he is correct in hypothesizing that the Iatmul experienced a separation of integrative mechanisms above the level of clan-pairs from their original roots in kinship and marriage (ibid.: 315). To this we must add that the intravillage, affinally related clan-pairs provided each large Iatmul village with more permanent integrative mechanisms than they had previously been able to achieve.

Thus, the Iatmul did not spring cohesive from the headwaters of the

Sepik's southern tributaries and then teach the Sawos the rules of their game. They arrived at the river to find that its fish and communicational advantages allowed the establishment of permanent villages. The integrative mechanisms which developed at this time, including *iai* marriage and its concomitant exchange of valuables for bride-price and other affinal reimbursements, made demands upon their economy and created a necessity for a more regular supply of subsistence and ceremonial goods. And it was the Sawos who could provide them with both.

I think we must assume that the increasing Iatmul demand for sago stimulated similar consolidary processes in Sawos hamlets. These bush-dwellers, after all, were gaining regularized access to "sweet-tasting shrimps and fish," which undoubtedly released them from their dependence upon a migratory hunting and gathering life-style while it allowed their hamlets to grow larger and more solidary. Schindlbeck's reconstruction of Gaikero-bi's history confirms this point. He was able to investigate six former settlements of those who became the Gaikerobi people, where he discerned the remains of dancing places and cult houses, and where he discovered pottery fragments and cultivated palm trees, data that helped him to verify his informants' ethnohistorical accounts. His descriptions of all but the last of these former settlements indicate that those who inhabited them were probably semi-nomadic hunters and gatherers, organized into small patrivirilocal groups. [14] These people adopted what might be called an "Iatmulesque" village lay-out only after they joined together at the settlement called Ng-ətəpmə, during the last half of the nineteenth century.

Certainly, Yamuk's attack upon Suapmeri could only have occurred if Staalsen's Japandai informant was correct to suggest that in bringing the Sawos out of the bush they allowed them to become consolidated, "just like us." In fact, Yamuk's attack suggests that the Sawos occasionally took being like the Iatmul far too seriously for Iatmul safety, necessitating periodic reminders on the part of the Iatmul that "they are of one kind and we are of another."

These reminders took the form of military incursions into Sawos territory for the purpose of collecting the heads with which Iatmul men decorated their men's houses. Bateson provides only one such example of "a raid on one of the neighboring bush villages" (1958: 138), when a woman and her daughter were killed, but I was told that they occurred with great frequency. [15] Indeed, the Sawos were considered by Iatmul headhunters to be easy prey, for their bush villages were smaller than the smallest water village, providing the Iatmul with a considerable military advantage.

That the Sawos recognized the military advantage of the Iatmul is best illustrated by a myth they tell about the first barter markets. It was collected by Schindlbeck in several versions from various Sawos informants of different villages (see 1980: 215–31). I include a condensed translation of the most complete version below.[16]

Ngumoekumban started the first market. All the women washed sago—it really wasn't sago, it was yono tavəno[17]—they didn't have sago yet. And Ngumoekumban brought fish, turtles, crocodile and river crabs. He landed his canoe at Lami.[18] The women took their grass skirts off, and lay in a row.[19] He went up and put his penis into them, and when he was finished, they stood up and put their grass skirts back on. They then loaded his canoe with food, and took the fish he had brought them.

A small girl wanted to go with her mother to market. Her mother refused to allow her to go, because men and children were forbidden to go to market. But the girl was too strong, and her mother was forced to take her along. When the women took their grass skirts off, they covered the girl with them so that she would not see what they did. But she made a slit in the skirts, and saw everything they did. She saw a strong man who wore mother of pearl shells and bird of paradise plumes on his head. She thought: "Ah, it is this strong man who has sexual intercourse with the women and brings them food."

After they all returned to the village, the girl decided to tell her father what she had seen. She said: "It is true, father, it is always like this. The food we eat is no good. I have seen the custom of my mother."

"What kind of custom have you observed?"

"Oh, father, the mothers do it so. They have sexual intercourse with a strong man with light skin. He's a big man with a headdress of mother of pearl shells and bird of paradise plumes. They covered me with grass skirts, but I pushed the skirts aside and secretly watched. After he had sexual intercourse with them, he gave them food."

The father thought about it, and then beat the drums. The men decided to kill Ngumoekumban. They sharpened bamboo points, dried them in the fire, and then fastened them to their spears. When the women next went to market, the men hid. When Ngumoekumban appeared and wanted to have intercourse with the women, the men threw their spears. But their spears could not penetrate his skin. They broke off and fell to the ground. His skin was made of stone.

So the men made two bullroarers, went to the market place, and dug two pits. They put the bullroarers into the pits, and tried them out on a dog. They put the dog into the center of one pit, and the bullroarers, now crocodiles,* cut the dog up. "Oh, good,"

---

*Throughout the Middle Sepik bullroarers are believed to transubstantiate as magical crocodiles.

they thought, "now the crocodiles can wait for Ngumoekumban."

When the women went again to market, Ngumoekumban wanted to go about his business. He walked toward the women, but the crocodiles rose up and cut up his leg. He went into the water, back to his home at Ngusai.[20] He thought to himself: "Because of this woman they want to kill me." He came back to the market, grabbed the woman and dove down to Ngusai. He took her with him. I don't know, perhaps she is a white woman now. [reduced and translated from Schindlbeck, 1980: 216–19]

The relationship between sexual prowess and military might is acknowledged by the men of all Middle Sepik cultures, who believe that one implies the other. I was surprised to learn that the Sawos myth about the first barter markets explicitly attributes a superabundance of these capacities to Iatmul fish-suppliers. Sepik storytellers tend to focus their narratives on their own successes or on the failures of their enemies. Instead, this story portrays the Sawos as helpless incompetents dependent upon the seducer of their women for food.[21] Incapable of defeating Ngumoekumban's powers, is it any wonder that the Sawos would barter one fish for one piece of sago at markets? Can it be, then, that here—with the military advantage of the Iatmul—we find the reason for the Sawos acceptance of an unfavorable exchange rate? Is it simply that the Sawos had no choice?

The Complementary Nature of Iatmul Hegemony

It is safe to assume that the Sawos wished to free themselves from Iatmul dominance. As we shall see, they attempted to do so by playing one Iatmul village against the other, occasionally quite successfully, as in the case of the Yamuk attack upon Suapmeri. And it is within this context of Iatmul hegemony that we can understand the value of exchange in the form that Gregory Bateson finds problematic. The Sawos, threatening to undermine Iatmul control over the river and its resources, had to be contained within the bush: "'It's no good,' we said, 'that river people and bush people should live together. They are of one kind and we are of another.'" Their "otherness" may have been assured by Iatmul military capabilities, but it was the ritualized and complementary interactional patterns at fish-for-sago barter markets that served as a continual expression and reminder of bush inferiority. Thus, it is not that complementary patterns of interaction promoted mutual dependence between groups of Sawos and Iatmul, but rather that their mutual dependence generated social contradictions which were resolved through culturally prescribed behavior patterns expressing the military and organizational superiority of the Iatmul.

That military superiority was expressed in complementary terms follows from the fact that:

> In egalitarian societies in which the ideal is of aggressive individ-
> ualism and in which virtually any man can challenge any other
> to show what he is made of . . . people who are by definition
> unequal cannot compete; their exchanges being of different things,
> cannot be subjected to any exact accounting or comparison. . . .
> [Forge, 1972: 537]

Thus, at every fish-for-sago exchange, the Iatmul defined the Sawos as unequal noncompetitors, a designation we must assume was only acceptable to the Sawos so long as they feared Iatmul military strength, as the following story—told by Bateson (1933: 282–85) about the Iatmul of the Lower Sepik and their relations with sago-suppliers living on the Korosameri River—suggests:

> A husband in a neighbouring bush village of the Kwolawoli
> tribe had quarrels with his wife, who refused to receive him sex
> ually. Apparently in desperation, he sent a bunch of five *Dra-
> caena* leaves to [a Iatmul] man in Timbunke, this being a ritual
> invitation to Timbunke to send over a party of men who should
> all of them have connection with his wife. . . . It appears that the
> Kwolawoli man was acting in accordance with tradition, except
> that he sent the leaves to Timbunke instead of Mindimbit. Each
> of the villages of the main river jealously guards its own rights in
> the bush tribes, and in this case the bush village was one in which
> Mindimbit had trading rights, etc.
>   The man in Timbunke sent on the *Dracaena* leaves to Min
> dimbit, together with a leaf tied to a ring, representing his heart—
> a symbol of his friendship for Mindimbit. (It is possible that the
> heart was a forgery made by Mindimbit.) Mindimbit determined
> to accept the invitation. In preparation, one of the leading men
> of Mindimbit secretly attached some tumeric leaves to a part of
> the spear shaft, and showed this to the other men of Mindimbit,
> explaining to them that the Kwolawoli had sent the shaft to Tim
> bunke, inviting Timbunke to beat Mindimbit. There had previ
> ously been some quarrel between Kwolawoli and Mindim
> bit. . . . The Kwolawoli alleged that the bloods of Mindimbit had
> raped . . . [a] Kwolawoli woman . . . , as is not unlikely.
>   Now it was stated that the spear shaft had been sent by the
> Kwolawoli as a token that Timbunke should beat Mindimbit in
> revenge for this incident, but the spear shaft was a Mindimbit
> forgery—I believe that nobody in Mindimbit knew of this forgery
> except two important men.
>   In due course, a party of ten or fifteen men left Mindimbit and
> went to the Kwolawoli village, taking with them the *Dracaena*

leaves, the heart, and the spear shaft. They arrived about midday and proceeded to debate in the Kwolawoli ceremonial house. . . .

It is difficult to make out what was said at this debate, but so far as I could disentangle the story, the men of Mindimbit scolded and abused the Kwolawoli on the following grounds:

(1) That the Kwolawoli had accused Mindimbit of raping the woman mentioned above and had sent the spear shaft to Timbunke. In proof of this, the spear shaft was shown. . . . Mindimbit claimed that Kwolawoli should buy the spear to make amends.

(2) That formerly, when the Kwolawoli were more powerful they had obtained a number of women from Mindimbit (I think as part of a peace-making) and that of these women one, Mambi, had never been "backed," i.e., no women had been given in exchange. . . .

(3) A spear was produced said to have been given to Kavleman village by some of the Kwolawoli as a token that the Kavleman should ambush one of the Kwolawoli men. (I do not know the history of this spear; probably it was a forgery—dragged in to get the victim on to the side of Mindimbit . . .).

On the above three counts the debate raged until nightfall, but I gather nothing was said about the *Dracaena* leaves and the woman who would not receive her husband. It is clear that the purpose of the debate was to make the Kwolawoli feel so thoroughly in the wrong that they would be ready to carry out the pledge implied by the five leaves.

Only after nightfall was the woman mentioned. Then she was called for, but neither she nor her husband could be found. Accordingly, the Mindimbit went to the dwelling-houses and took the (now old) Mambi and her daughter and brought them into the house, holding them as hostages. Finally the husband and wife were produced. Accounts differ as to what followed, but all agree that the woman was held while her husband had connection with her, and that some at least of the Mindimbit had connection with her. From my general knowledge of the people I suspect that all did.

Next morning the husband ceremonially presented valuables and betel nut to the Mindimbit for their services.

The debate was then resumed on the subject of Mambi and continued until finally the Kwolawoli agreed to hand over a woman. The woman decided on was the same one . . . mentioned at the beginning of the story. . . .

The woman was brought back to Mindimbit where she gradually settled down as wife of one of the men, though she easily could have run away back to her own people.

A few days later a payment of valuables and a pig was taken to the Kwolawoli, but this may have been done solely to enable the

Mindimbit to justify themselves in case of Government interference.

Bateson uses this story to illustrate the nature of family life and the methods of obtaining wives.[23] Although these concerns are certainly expressed in the story, I find it more interesting for its depiction of bush–water relations. Three points are particularly significant in this regard. The first involves Timbunke's betrayal of Kwolawoli's invitation: "The man in Timbunke sent on the *Dracaena* leaves to Mindimbit, together with a leaf tied to a ring, representing his heart." Clearly, the Timbunke valued Mindimbit's friendship more than he wished for an alliance with Kwolawoli. Bateson tells us that water villages jealously guarded their own rights in the bush tribes,[24] and we can therefore assume that, had the Timbunke accepted the Kwolawoli invitation, they would have alienated their Mindimbit allies in both a political and an economic sense.

Although Middle Sepik Iatmul did not guard their rights in the bush tribes as jealously as the Mindimbit and Timbunke seem to,[25] there have been occasions when bush settlements have allied with water groups through some joint interest. Such was the case between the Iatmul village of Yentchan and the Sawos villages of Nogosop and Gaikerobi. The former is said to have been formed by sentries sent from the Iatmul village of Parambei to guard against a military alliance between Gaikerobi, Nogosop, and the water villages of Suapmeri, Kararau, and Nyaurengai. Once well established, however, the Yentchañ settlers turned against their parent village by joining the alliance, only to suffer defeat when the Parambei convinced their enemies to help them destroy the upstart village (Bragge, 1973: page unknown). Thus, water villages generally accepted assistance from bush villages when they were involved in hostilities with other villages, and there was no such enmity between Timbunke and Mindimbit.

One might, of course, have predicted as much, for bush villages did not have the numbers to be themselves a threat to Iatmul hegemony. And their only means of supporting sufficient numbers was to insure themselves a regular supply of Iatmul fish. Sandwiched between expanding populations of Iatmul in the south and Abelam in the north,[26] they were in a double bind, able to achieve the potentiality of real political power only by maintaining their trading relationships, but prevented from acting together as a political force by their dependence upon these relationships.

The Iatmul were equally encumbered, for a regular supply of sago was necessary to their sociopolitical survival. Theirs was an importation culture par excellence, for without the fish-for-sago trading arrangement they would have broken up into component groups, whose members would have been forced to scour the backswamps for natural products much as the Sawos once had to do. Thus, their existence depended upon keeping their sago-suppliers trapped in the double bind between organizational capacity and political autonomy.

This brings us to the second interesting point made by Bateson's story about the Kwolawoli invitation, for it seems that this bush village once managed to transcend the double bind and gain a degree of political autonomy: "formerly, when the Kwolawoli were more powerful, they had obtained a number of women from Mindimbit." We do not learn what Bateson means by power, but we can assume that the Mindimbit would not have been interested in making peace with this bush village unless they feared its power to command their behavior through military means.

Nor do we learn how they achieved this power. What may have occurred is that Timbunke, or another Lower Sepik Iatmul village, had, in the past, accepted an invitation from the Kwolawoli similar to the one Bateson describes them as offering, and that, allied with this water village, the Kwolawoli gained temporary ascendancy over the Mindimbit. If this is the case, then their water-village allies must have rapidly withdrawn support, for Kwolawoli's power was quickly lost. Mambi, one of the only women they seem to have received from Mindimbit, was still alive when the incidents Bateson describes occurred, indicating that Kwolawoli ascendancy could not have lasted for long.

Having obviously lost their power over Mindimbit, it seems likely that the Kwolawoli were attempting to reestablish it through a new alliance with Timbunke. This would explain why the Mindimbit were so angered by Kwolawoli's invitation to Timbunke; they were not afraid of losing their rights to trade in this bush village per se, but were afraid of losing them through an alliance between Timbunke and Kwolawoli.

This interpretation of Bateson's story is also indicated by the nature of the Kwolawoli invitation, which is the last point I wish to discuss. Timbunke was invited to help a Kwolawoli man whose wife refused to receive him sexually: "this being a ritual invitation to Timbunke to send over a party of men who should all of them have connection with his wife." I can think of no greater slight to a Sepik man than the gang rape of his wife. Indeed, "the most serious insult is to call a man . . . child begotten by the assembled men" (Bateson, 1933: 271), and it seems to me that the Kwolawoli invitation was designed to communicate their submission to Timbunke will, even by this most humiliating means.

Once we realize all this, the course of events that day in Kwolawoli becomes comprehensible. First Mindimbit arrives, sabotaging the Kwolawoli hope for a new alliance with Timbunke. Then the Kwolawoli and Mindimbit debate, reviewing the history of their relationship: "You wish an alliance with Timbunke, and we know it," the Mindimbit inform them. "But you will not achieve this alliance for the Timbunke are our allies and have informed us of your designs. We will never again be in your power, and will send you no more women. Moreover, we will force you to compensate us for that time in the past when you had temporary ascendancy—we will make you reciprocate our woman with a woman of your own. You, after all, no longer have power; even your own members scheme against one another. And do not think that by receiving your woman we mean to establish the reciprocal relationship appropriate between equals. You are not our equals, and we will teach you this by accepting the offer you made to the Timbunke to gang-rape the recalcitrant wife. We know that you do not wish us to do this, but you had better pretend to be glad of our actions by compensating us for our pains." Thus, the events at Kwolawoli were designed by the Mindimbit to instruct their sago-suppliers in Iatmul hegemony—to assure this bush village that it was still trapped in its double bind.

Conclusion

It seems, then, that Bateson was right in describing the ritualized interaction between fish-suppliers and sago-producers as complementary, for it does express the socioeconomic instabilities that he would characterize as indicative of schizmogenesis. The Iatmul needed sago and created the Sawos need of fish by encouraging their sago-suppliers to expand until they could no longer support themselves. This expansion, however, threatened Iatmul hegemony over the river and therefore had to be contained through periodic military incursions into the bush territory, together with more frequent reminders of Iatmul superiority through challenges such as those which occurred in Kwolawoli.

Bateson was wrong, however, in assuming that complementarity can sometimes promote stability by encouraging mutual dependence between groups of Sawos and Iatmul. His mistake, I believe, was in looking for schizmogenesis in the nature of their interaction or in an inflation of their exchange rate. Instead, he should have sought it in the history of the social contradictions generated by the dependence he knew to exist.

FROM TRADING PARTNERSHIPS TO BARTER MARKETS: THE CASE OF CHAMBRI COMMODITY PRODUCTION

While the Iatmul were establishing their intervillage barter markets with the Sawos, they were also trading with their partners to the south, but not for sago. Until relatively recently, the Chambri supplied the Iatmul with canoes, mosquito bags, and stone tools. Reports of the trading partnerships between these peoples are our best data about this once general mode of exchange.

Unfortunately, I did not see these partnerships operate myself. The Chambri no longer produce their specialized commodities; moreover, they, like the Iatmul, have made the transition from individualized, male-dominated exchange relationships to intervillage barter markets. In this chapter I record what I know about these partnerships and establish certain of the crucial socioeconomic differences between the barter markets that I have already described in operation between the Sawos and the Iatmul and those which evolved south of the Sepik.

The Specialized Commodities

Unlike their Iatmul partners, Chambri men traded their own specialized commodities, produced from natural resources found on their island or in the lake. The largest of these were the cylindrical, ten- to fifteen-foot-long mosquito bags (*arɔnk*) of plaited sago shoot or bast that were made by Chambri women and used throughout the Middle Sepik.[1]

Before the Europeans introduced cotton and nylon mosquito netting, these bags were the people's only protection against the ferocious mosquitoes that infest the area, particularly during the transitional periods from wet to dry season and from dry to wet. The stagnant pools of water that collect along the shore are breeding areas for various species of mosquitoes, including the malaria-carrying *Anopheles faranti*. Malcolm Philpott, while administering an economic survey throughout the East Sepik District in 1971–72, described the mosquito situation as "even in the daytime—just barely endurable" (1972: 128), and I found it necessary to remain under my mosquito net for as long as two weeks at a stretch during these times of seasonal change.

Mosquito bags were no longer in use when I was in the area, but Mead, who witnessed their distribution, described the process thus:

> The people of the middle Sepik purchase these mosquito-bags, in fact they are so much in demand that purchasers take options on them long before they are finished. And the women control the proceeds in *kinas* and *talibun*.[2] It is true that they permit the men. to do the . . . trading [in] mosquito bags. The men make a gala occasion of these shopping-trips. . . . [1963: 254]

These revenues, amounting to as much as five *talimbun* and five large *kina* per bag,[3] came in quite frequently, for mosquito bags rarely lasted for more than three years. Chambri women, therefore, were producers of a commodity that brought "more *kina* and *talibun* into circulation, and it [was] by the presence of *kina* and *talibun* that the ceremonial life [was] kept moving, each dance, each ceremony necessitating the expenditure of food and valuables" (ibid.: 266).

This is not to suggest that Chambri men were completely dependent upon their wives, for they also had a source of shell valuables. They produced stone tools (*wanank*) that were used throughout the East Sepik Province. Both the production and distribution processes were male-dominated activities, with buyers journeying to their trading partners to purchase the adzes necessary for canoe building, sago processing, house construction, and sacred carving.

The Chambri operated six quarries. Each was thought to be inhabited by a particular ancestor, and each was supervised by one of that ancestor's descendants.[4] When a new supply of stone[5] was to be gathered, those concerned sacrificed a pig or some chickens to this ancestor, thereby warning him that he would be visited on the following day. They then climbed Chambri Mountain, lit a fire, and spent that night close to the quarry. At daybreak they gathered loose chunks of stone which had separated from the main boulder or "ancestor's house." If no chunks had fallen, they chipped away at the boulder until they had collected enough and then returned down the mountain to their spirit-houses to prepare the stone.

The processing involved shaping and polishing the stone with a harder variety of rock,[6] found not at the quarry but close to the streams that ran down from the mountain. Often those who had inherited access to the quarry were without a source of this harder stone, and they acquired it in exchange for the quarried variety.

The Chambri acted as a central distribution agency; their "stone-iron" network extended through primary, secondary, and tertiary contacts and encompassed the villages throughout the northern and southern drainage systems. Their stone adzes were made in four sizes.[7] The largest was designed for felling trees, the next for building canoes and houses, the third for sago processing, and the smallest for carving sacred wooden objects. Purchasers also acquired polishing stones, with which they resharpened the Chambri-made "stone-iron," reducing the frequency of replacement of tools to once every two to five years.

Although the Chambri accommodated their Sepik Hills trading partners by carrying "stone-iron" to exchange at Hills villages, they preferred to dispose of the tools within their own spirit-houses. The stone, after all, was a sacred object, which was demystified through its exchange. Sacrifices, designed to pacify the ancestral stone dwellers, followed the exchange of each tool, at which times the "uncheban" were assured that the tools had fetched a good return.[8]

Each individual man made "stone-iron" transactions on his own behalf. He met his obligations to the quarry custodian by furnishing food at the ceremonies that preceded the stone gathering and followed "stone-iron" exchanges. The presence of fifteen spirit-houses in the three Chambri villages, in contrast to the two or three in similar-sized Iatmul villages, may reflect the compartmentalization of "stone-iron" transactions. Each man desired a ceremonial location in which to carry out his own business.

Before the introduction of steel tools, Chambri men also made many of the canoes used throughout the region. This was not because the Iatmul lacked the skill to produce them, but rather because the Chambri had easier access to the large trees from which they were made. Living on the river left the Iatmul dependent on driftwood from which to carve their craft and build their houses. The Chambri, however, could acquire timber from several heavily wooded islands within the lake, and from their trading partners in the Sepik Hills.

After the Europeans destroyed the Chambri monopoly over tool production by introducing steel, the direction of this trade partially reversed. As Mead suggests, the Chambri began to "offer a market for the canoes made on the Sepik, as the Sepik natives obtained iron canoe-making tools much earlier and in larger amounts than the Tchambuli. . . . [But now] with newly obtained iron tools they . . . build their own canoes instead of purchasing them at exorbitant rates from the Sepik" (1963: 243–44).

The exorbitant rate to which Mead refers is somewhat of an exaggeration. Part of that rate inevitably reflected the price of the wood from which the canoe was made. As the Chambri were able to supply their own wood, they were not obliged to pay "exorbitant" prices. Indeed, they only traded for Iatmul canoes within the context of their trading partnerships. If an Iatmul asked too much for a canoe, his Chambri partner could simply take his "business" and his relationship elsewhere. In fact, many Chambri preferred to take the time to produce their own craft, particularly since only by carving their canoes themselves could they be assured that the correct totemic markings would appear on the sides. As one of my informants put it: "Sometimes we traded for canoes with the Sepiks, but the marks they used were always wrong. They would never learn to put our marks on the canoe."

The Reciprocal Nature of Trading Partnerships

Although the commodities produced by Chambri men and women were in great demand throughout the region, their distribution did not involve market competition. This is not to say that Chambri men did not wish to obtain a good price for their wives' mosquito bags or for their own stone adzes and canoes, but rather that supply and demand were tied to long-term social relationships between trading partners.

These relationships were inherited from father to son and were the most "reciprocal" of all interactions. When speaking Neo-Melanesian, trading partners called each other *poroman*, a word meaning a pair to any object. Thus, one shoe is *poroman* to the other. Before Neo-Melanesian was introduced, Chambri and Sepik Hills trading partners applied the Chambri term *casik* (older brother) to one another, thereby implying a relationship of mutual obligation without dependence. They say that if *yemen* (younger brother) had been the reply to *casik*, the reciprocity of equals would have been undermined by the de facto dependence of younger upon older brothers. As one of my informants put it: "It is no good if I help my younger brother too much, for he would be shamed and then we would fight and I would look at his blood and cry."

Exchanging their surplus on a delayed basis, trading partners facilitated the conversion of their perishable foodstuffs into durable wealth items. The gifts consisted of local products, such as fish, yams, sago, betel nuts, tobacco, and various meats, and specialized commodities, particularly mosquito bags, stone tools, canoes, and pottery. Shell and feather valuables were also given, the former occasionally carried up the Sepik River from the coast, but more frequently over land through the Sawos bush. Most Iatmul were completely dependent upon their trading partners to introduce new supplies of the valuable shells into their ceremonial systems, acting as middlemen between those who produced the commodities and the peoples living in the north, west, and east.

But trading partnerships implied more than the delayed exchange of surplus products and specialized commodities. Partners were also obliged to provide each other with safe conduct. Should war break out between their villages, they were to act as mediators and, if necessary, as protectors of their partners and their partners' clan co-members. Bragge feels that it was the extensiveness of Chambri trading partnerships which allowed them relative immunity from Iatmul headhunting forays (1973: page unknown), and they do not seem to have become intensively involved in intertribal warfare of any kind until their specialized products were replaced by their imported European equivalents.

Occasionally, however, intravillage obligations demanded the betrayal of intervillage trading partnerships. Such, my informants told me, was the actual case when Kanda of Chambri arranged the death of Kwaremanki of Garamambu.

> Kwaremanki worried over the Garamambu killed by Chambri.[9] He decided to retaliate by killing those Chambri who came to market with Mali and Changriman, and so he built a small grass island and he and his kinsmen hid under it. When the Chambri canoe manned by Memunwan, Kapunkame and Tsilan tried to pass over the island, it got stuck. As the Chambri were trying to free it, Kwaremanki and his men surprised and killed them all. Other Chambri saw the attack, but did not pursue Kwaremanki into the bush for they were afraid of the sago ancestors, Mai-yum and Abandimi, who would asphixiate them all if any blood spilled on their sago.[10] Now the Chambri worried over their dead, particularly those belonging to the clan, Minginor. They wanted to attack Garamambu, but Kwaremanki's trading partner, Kanda, decided instead to call his friend to Chambri. He made the magic of the "*balus*"* which caused Kwaremanki to long for his friend, and when he came to Chambri to see Kanda, Kanda told him: "Tomorrow you will die, but today I will make magic which will allow you to die like a man."
>
> All the young men of Chambri wanted to kill Kwaremanki to earn the right to wear black paint,[11] and they all tried to spear him. He stood firm and called them "little boys." Kalak speared him in the liver. Elundimi speared him in the eye. Blood covered his body but still he stood firm. Kabansebe finally killed him, but only because Kwaremanki decided to repay Kanda by allowing himself to be killed.

The implication of the story is that as his last reciprocal exchange Kwaremanki gave his life in return for Kanda's gift of magical strength. Kanda, credited with Kwaremanki's death, undeniably gained status within Chambri, but only by maintaining a reciprocal relationship with his trading partner. And, to generalize from this example, the point of the zero-sum trad-

---

* The *balus* is a bird whose sad call reminds the Chambri of friends far away.

ing partnerships is to establish obligations and credit that can be utilized in intravillage strategies where winner takes all, a point I shall return to later in this chapter and in the next.

The Acquisition of Sago: From Trading Partnership to Market

Until World War II the Chambri acquired most of their sago through the same trading partnerships that allowed them to dispose of their mosquito bags and stone tools, although they occasionally produced the carbohydrate themselves from their natural reserves on Chambri Island. The transition from these partnerships to marketing arrangements is illustrated in a myth about the discovery of sago, which I reproduce below. The myth has been adopted and transformed from an Iatmul story, and the different versions manifest the differences between Iatmul–Sawos barter markets and those the Chambri have developed with the sago-producers from the Sepik Hills.

A long time ago the people of Chambri had no sago. They ate white earth which they found beside small streams.[12] Sometimes they dried the earth in the sun before eating it, and sometimes they smoked it over a fire.

One day Sengabi, a man from Indingai, had a craving for frogs, so he decided to go and hunt for some. He followed the Warramar waterway and landed close to Mensuat, telling his two wives to remain in the canoe while he hunted.

As Sengabi was searching, Wulian of Mensuat[13] saw him. Wulian strung his bow, planning to kill Sengabi. But he was afraid, so he approached Sengabi and said, "I am Wulian and you must not kill me. Why have you come here?" Sengabi replied, "I am here only because I hunger for frogs." Sengabi called to his wives, telling them to bring fish, tobacco, and white earth so that he and Wulian could eat and smoke together. Wulian refused to eat the white earth and asked Sengabi to wait until he brought a better food from his camp. He was absent only a short while and returned with sago.

The first time Sengabi tasted sago he vomited. He tried it again and vomited again. On the third attempt he kept the food down. He then gave Wulian some tobacco. Until that time Wulian had only smoked the water plant, *pliplimank;*[14] when he inhaled the tobacco he fainted. He inhaled again and fainted again. After the third puff he felt fine.

Sengabi gave Wulian some shell money. Then he said: "From now on your wives and sisters prepare sago for five days, and on the sixth day they meet my wives and sisters at Aiwul. My family will bring fish and tobacco to exchange for your sago." Wulian and Sengabi tied six knots in two tanget leaves [*Taetsia fructicosa*] to mark the market cycle. Sengabi took his tanget back to Chambri, and Wulian took his to Mensuat. After each day they cut one knot from the leaves. When only one knot was left they knew that the next day was market day. [see Schuster, 1965 for alternate versions of this myth]

Three aspects of the Wulian/Sengabi story are of interest here, namely, that: (1) Although Sengabi journeyed to Wulian's territory, Wulian was afraid of Sengabi; (2) Wulian offered sago to Sengabi who had not come in search of it, but it was Sengabi who wished to regularize marketing; (3) Sengabi defines the market as an interfamily relationship. I would like to examine each of these aspects in turn to determine their relevance to Iatmul and Chambri marketing.

Wulian's Fear of Sengabi

The Chambri, like the Iatmul, barter in their sago-suppliers' territory. They explain this with reference to Hills' incompetence. "We would have them come to us," one informant told me, "but they were too stupid to learn to use canoes." Although it is sometimes possible during the dry season to walk from the Sepik Hills to Chambri Island, the weight of sago (one large block weighs between 20 to 30 pounds) would have made the trek across miles of muddy, weed-choked lake bottom an onerous one. And in any case, for over half the year the trip is impossible except by canoe

Because the Chambri are intruding on another group's territory, one might expect their manner to be conciliatory. Yet this is no more the case for the Chambri than it is for the Iatmul. Gardi, for example, describes a fish-for-sago transaction he witnessed in the early 1950s at a market site near the Bisis hamlet of Changriman:

> In Chambriman,[15] far from the Sepik, which is reached across Lake Chambri and through narrow channels in the marshland bordering it, we were present at a transaction of straight barter where no money changed hands. Fishwives had come with their laden canoes through the channels to a point near a village, situated not by the water but up on a hill, and about fifteen of them were squatting on the ground near their canoes with the fat, smoked fish spread out before them. Soon the women from Chambriman came down the hill with their heavy carrying nets containing lumps of sago as big as a child's head and of all colours from grey to rose-red.
>
> As in the days of head-hunting, when the people were still hostile to each other, scarcely a word was spoken. A woman from Chambriman laid a lump of sago beside a dried fish which she

fancied, and waited. The fisherwoman needed only a brief glance to weigh up the size and quality, and if she did not like the goods offered she looked away and let the other wait.

Sometimes, too, a buyer ventured to pick up the fish without waiting, only to have her hand slapped if the fishmonger did not agree with the exchange. Then the woman from the hill village took away her lump of sago and put down another and bigger one. If the fishwife was now satisfied, she wrapped the sago in a fresh water-lily leaf, but kept a good watch to see that only the fish which lay beside the sago was taken and no more.

Very silently, almost wordlessly, the barter proceeded while the stocks of fish became smaller and the piles of sago behind the fishwives grew bigger, and gradually the housewives from Chambriman went back up the hill to their village. [1960: 97–98]

But submissive as the Changriman women seemed to Gardi, they were in fact engaged in a daring experiment. The village on a hill to which he refers is not the original home of the Changriman people. It is located close to the shore of Chambri Lake, and was built by refugee Chambri after their defeat in a war with the Iatmul village of Parambei (see chapter 5). When the Chambri returned to their island, the Changriman gradually moved down from their own hamlets to occupy the abandoned village. By 1950 their descent was complete, making them the first of the Hills people to exhibit sufficient trust in the Australian government's pacification program to abandon their relatively secure hill hamlets. Other Hills people followed suit, each moving from their homes to villages nearer the shores of Chambri Lake. In the past each of the shore settlements had been temporary hunting and fishing camps, but now they are more or less permanent villages.

Traditionally, the mountain hamlets of these Hills peoples, like those of the Heve who live on the northwest edge of the Sepik Hills linguistic group,[16] were "continually changing in composition as families shift[ed] from virilocal residence to uxorilocal residence to residence with some other close kin. . . . This mobility serv[ed] to redistribute people in relation to resources, and dependants in relation to food-producers. . . . The preservation of resources to maintain a hunting-gathering economy demand[ed] a small scattered population" (Townsend, 1969: 179).

The Chambri argue that the small scattered hamlets of the Sepik Hills people were potentially vulnerable to headhunting attacks by the larger and better unified populations of Chambri and Iatmul. Clearly, by living on top of large hills, the sago-producers reduced their vulnerability to attack. A Chambri or Iatmul war party would have had to hike for hours before reaching a Hills hamlet, sufficient time for the inhabitants to become alerted to the intruders and to disappear into the jungle.

We know that the Sawos were always vulnerable to Iatmul attacks—indeed, it may be argued that they live where they do because of Iatmul military successes. But since Hills vulnerability appears to be an artifact of pacification, when the Assistant District Commissioner warned that "without law enforcement these small [Hills] groups would be in constant danger" (Bragge, 1973: page unknown), he was asserting the precise opposite of what was in fact true.

Wulian's fear of Sengabi, therefore, if translated as the Hills people's vulnerability to Chambri attack, appears to have a relatively short history. If translated as the Sawos's vulnerability to Iatmul attack, however, Wulian's fear is based on long-standing fact.

Wulian Offered Sago/Sengabi Regularized Marketing

The relationship between economic interdependence and peaceful coexistence is a complex one and varies significantly among different peoples. The Iatmul and Sawos, for example, live in sedentary villages and are incapable of supporting their populations for long without the products supplied by the other group. The Iatmul dependence upon their sago-suppliers is evident from the lengths to which they have been driven when the supply has been cut off. Their ethnohistories are filled with large-scale village migrations that were undertaken, it is asserted, when access to sago markets was curtailed during warfare with other fish-supplying villages. The Sawos, aware of this need, have allied themselves to certain Iatmul villages and against others in hope of gaining increased access to Sepik fish. They have occasionally miscalculated, however, for their Iatmul allies have not wished them to move closer to the river and have remained supportive only so long as the Sawos reciprocate with sago. Thus, if we read the Sengabi/Wulian story as a description of Iatmul/Sawos relationships, its meaning is clear. Sengabi regularized marketing because he needed Sawos sago and could insure its supply through his military strength.

It is not as easy to apply the story to the Chambri–Hills relationship. Although the Chambri need the Hills' products to support their large and sedentary population, they cannot have coerced the Hills people into marketing, for they had no military advantage prior to pacification when the Hills people descended to the shores of the lake. If Wulian is to be read as a Hills man, then a desire for peace cannot be his motive for offering sago.

Nor can it be said that he offered sago because he needed Chambri fish and tobacco. The Hills people have always had some access to the rich fish resource of the region, and could adjust the social relationships between their small and scattered mobile populations to fit their productive capacities (see Townsend, 1969: 179). They were, therefore, the more self-suffi-

Table 2.1: The Trading Partnerships between Certain Indingai and Sepik Hills
Men circa 1910

Indingai Clan	*Man*	*Affiliation of Partner*
Mangemeri	Kabansebe	Milae
	Parombank	Changriman
	Kalak	Milae
	Kanda	Milae
	Kambukwat	—
	Yuwandai	Milae
	Kandonk	Milae
Simbuksaun	Yerke	Mensuat
	Tumban	Mensuat
Yalus	Masoki	Mensuat
	Kwosai	Mensuat; Changriman
	Agutmeri	Changriman
Yambukay	Masamdu	Garamambu
	Kwolikumbwi	Garamambu; Milae
	Egundimi	Garamambu
Minginor	Wusuai	Garamambu
	Akaman	Garamambu; Mensuat; Changriman
	Uwanme	Garamambu
	Kingisu	Garamambu; Mali
Sekumbumeri	Walinakwon	Mali
	Marikumban	Garamambu
	Clemeri	Mali
	Saimeri	Mali; Garamambu
Kalumembank	Yangintimi	Changriman; Mensuat; Garamambu
	Numbuk	Changriman
	Pandin	Changriman
Walintimi	Askame	Mensuat; Changriman
Werumbank	Toremi	Changriman
	Sanguntimi	Changriman
Manjanakwon	Manjanakwon	Mensuat
Kwimembi	Sakarmandu	Mensuat
Yaraman	Wokup	Mensuat; Changriman; Mali

cient of the two groups. Indeed, the relationship between the Hills and Chambri peoples here resembles that described by Schwartz between the Usiai and the Manus of the Admiralty Islands, where the Usiai:

> might have been as self sufficient as many of the interior peoples of Melanesia and New Guinea; but with the availability of fish, they seemed as committed as the Manus to trade. They were much more heterogeneous than the Manus culturally and linguistically. Their villages were smaller, usually fewer than 100 persons, located in hilltop clearings in the rugged and heavily forested interior. [1964: 61]

Since the Hills people neither feared Chambri attack nor desired Chambri fish, their reasons for accepting Sengabi's offer to regularize marketing become somewhat mysterious.

The Market as an Interfamily Relationship

The key to solving this mystery lies in removing the Iatmul overlays from the Chambri pattern of exchange. Recall Gardi's description of the fifteen Chambri fishwives who arrived at Changriman village to barter for sago. They interact with the Hills women much as the Iatmul do with the Sawos, but their numbers are considerably smaller. Hundreds of women attend the Iatmul–Sawos barter markets, but I have never seen more than thirty Hills and Chambri women exchange their produce. Although their lower numbers are due to their smaller populations, it is unclear why they demarcate four sites at which to exchange, two in Bisis territory, one near the Mali, and one close to Garamambu Mountain. Unlike the Iatmul, Chambri fishwives cannot be said to choose the market closest to their villages. All three Chambri villages are equally close to all four market sites, and Chambri women choose the market located in the territory belonging to those with whom their families have maintained long-standing patrilineally inherited trading partnerships. Table 2.1 portrays the trading partnerships held by members of the Chambri village of Indingai with men from the Sepik Hills, and indicates that clan co-members generally exchanged within the same Hills hamlet. Indeed, it is likely that the market observed by Gardi was attended by the wives, daughters, and sisters of one Chambri clan. Their interaction with the bushwomen, however, had already become less personal, or more "Iatmulized." Compare the account of marketing given to me by Patrick Yarapat, a leading Chambri, whose father figures in the story.

> The night before the market Wabiyangal built a fire on top of the mountain and my father, Kanda, saw it. The fire talked: to-

morrow we shall meet and exchange. Kanda then answered Wabiyangal's fire with one of his own. After they both made their
fires die, Kanda hit his split gong and called all his family to his
house. He told them: "Wabiyangal made a fire and I answered it.
Tomorrow we will meet and exchange." Now the market place is
called Wangma. It is a patch of kunai grass [*Imperata sp.*] with a
grove of sago nearby. Kanda and his family readied five canoes
and paddled to Wangma. Wabiyangal and his family came down
from their mountain and walked to Wangma. The two families
met and exchanged. Sometimes they exchanged fish for sago,
Chambri fish for Milae sago,[17] and sometimes sago was bought
with shell money. Wabiyangal brought the eggs of wild-fowl and
cassowaries, and also sago grubs and pig meat. Kanda brought
crocodile meat, eels, and tobacco. When the market was finished,
Kanda or Wabiyangal gave presents. Kanda gave tobacco or banana leaves or shell money. He gave to Wabiyangal, his good friend.
And sometimes Wabiyangal gave him presents back at once. But
sometimes he waited for the next market. They were good friends
and Big Men and they gave each other many presents. Then the
two friends tied the *tanget* with six knots, one for each day. Kanda
would cut one knot off on each day and when five were gone he
would look for Wabiyangal's fire. The fire would tell him that the
sixth day was the market day. If another family went to exchange
with Wabiyangal, Kanda would get very angry. They should go to
their own markets. If another man exchanged with Wabiyangal at
Milae, this man would die. Kanda would kill him.

Yarapat's description of marketing emphasizes the exchange of foodstuffs
between trading partners who engage in "a formal reciprocative, paired relationship . . . in which both sides benefited from steady exchange of their
complementary products" (Schwartz, 1964: 79). The exchange of complementary products between trading partners is formal, regular, and apoliti-
cal.

The value of a particular trade partnership depended on the level
of exchange to which it was set, and *did not depend closely on the
actual balance of the account between the two.* Most large cross-
ecological transactions took place through trade partnerships, as
well as a good deal of routine exchange of foodstuffs paralleling
the market exchange. *Delay allowed also for the co-ordination of
different ecological and ceremonial calendars of the two partners.*
[Schwartz, 1964: 79, my emphasis]

As among the Manus islanders described by Schwartz, Chambri trading
partners were not in competition for power. Rather, they introduced the
goods acquired through their trading relationships into their separate social

systems. When a Chambri male returned from the Sepik Hills with six bird-of-paradise plumes, his success was measured not in terms of the Hills man's failure, but in terms of comparable successes or failures of co-Chambri. The political significance of such success or failure is distinct from the interaction of trading partners and is judged solely in respect to the comparable but separate interactions of other Chambri. Like the *Kula* trading system of the Trobriand Islands, Chambri trading partnerships have "two prongs: one bridges the 'essential hostility between two strange tribesmen,' whilst the other suspends the political identity between two *fellow* tribesmen . . . it parcels them out . . . duly . . . prepared to compete amongst themselves . . . " (Uberoi, 1971: 147).

Herein lies the difference between Iatmul barter relationships with the Sawos and those observed by Gardi between Chambri and Hills women: While the former involve intensive competition among Iatmul settlements to maintain access to sago markets and between bartering villages to insure regularized exchanges, the latter were basically individualistic connections between potentially jealous but relatively secure trading partners; that is to say, Iatmul barter arrangements are group interactions while Chambri exchange relationships were then, primarily, family affairs. Although they were in the process of fusing into impersonal markets, they had not yet become fully consolidated.

Conclusion: From Trading Partnership to Marketing Arrangement Reconsidered

By the early 1950s, Chambri marketing arrangements, although not fully crystallized, had nevertheless been considerably transformed from more traditional trading partnerships. Consider, for example, the exchange items mentioned by Gardi and Yarapat in their accounts of the transactions they witnessed. Yarapat described eleven different items exchanged between the trading partners from Chambri and Milae: Kanda brought fish, shell money, crocodile meat, eels, tobacco, and bananas, while Wabiyangal reciprocated with sago, wild-fowl eggs, cassowary eggs, sago grubs, and pig meat. Gardi, on the other hand, refers only to the fish and sago exchanged between Chambri and Changriman women.

This difference does not, of course, mean that the Chambri lost their taste for sago grubs, or that the Milae no longer desired tobacco in exchange for their cassowary eggs, but rather that they began to acquire these items separately from their fish-for-sago market exchanges. In other words, Chambri and Hills men continued to maintain their trading partnerships, while their women began to exchange fish and sago at barter markets. The same is also true of the Iatmul, who continued to acquire shell valuables, stone tools, mosquito bags, and canoes from their Sawos and Chambri trading partners while their wives bartered fish-for-sago.

Thus, the transition to marketing arrangements from trading partnerships involved a separation between the functions of each. The former became subsistence oriented, while the latter remained concerned with specialized and ceremonial goods and services. This separation, in turn, not only allowed an increase in the number of people attending and supported by the subsistence markets, but also involved a shift in the sex of those controlling them.

The following Chambri myth, about the formation of a trading partnership between a Garamambu from Kamsur and a Chambri, describes the earlier condition:

> Wusi and Abio were brothers. One day Abio and his family scrubbed sago for Wusi, expecting to be given some of the sago flour in return for their labors. But Wusi decided to keep it all for himself.
>
> That night, Abio heard his children crying tor hunger. He became angry with his brother and decided to leave Chambri Island. He boiled a pig and a chicken in coconut milk and, after a night's sleep, journeyed with his family to the island of Marikuman.
>
> Upon landing their canoe at the shore, Abio and his family went in search of sago palms. But they found Wukio, a man of Kamsur.
>
> Now Wukio had no asshole, and because of this he ate nothing but pig bones, in hopes that their sharpness would bore through his rectum. Abio felt sorry for him and decided to help him. First he offered to share his chicken and pig with Wukio. Then the two men left the women and children and climbed into the mountains.
>
> Once there, Abio built three platforms. It took him a month to complete the job. Wukio sat on the first platform and Abio speared him from underneath. Only water came out. So Wukio sat on the second platform and Abio speared him from underneath. But only bones came out. So Wukio sat on the third platform and Abio speared him from underneath. This time, Wukio lost consciousness.
>
> Abio bound his friend's rectum with tanget leaves over which he had recited his totemic names. Wukio slept for three days so bound. On the fourth day he awoke and passed many feces.
>
> Returning to Abio's family, Wukio and his friend were very happy. Wukio thanked Abio by giving him many bricks of sago flour. Abio reciprocated by offering his second wife to Wukio. Wukio accepted and gave Abio the use of the bush near Kamsur to scrub sago. They remained friends, and visited each other periodically to exchange presents.

They would meet and exchange fish, sago, tobacco, sago grubs, kina, pig meat, cassowary feathers, bird of paradise plumes, and crocodile meat. They gave each other everything sweet, and that's how they stayed good friends.

The myth illustrates three of the points I have already discussed in some detail. (1) It describes the reciprocity inherent in trading partnerships by contrasting the successful Wukio/Abio relationship to the failed Wusi/Abio partnership. (2) It depicts the diversity of items exchanged between partners. And (3) it portrays trading relationships as male interactions. The last point is doubly emphasized by both the situation surrounding the establishment of the partnership and by the items initially exchanged. Although wary of overpsychologizing mythology, I could argue that Abio impregnated Wukio with his spear and then provided his partner with a woman through whom to have their child.

Be this as it may, I am interested in the myth because it associates the acquisition of fish, sago, shell valuables, edible delicacies, and women. All seem to have been potentially available from trading partners. This fact corroborates the suggestion I made in chapter 1 that the exchange of women once bound small groups of Ndu hunters and gatherers into flexible and shifting alliances, and that the transition from trading partnership to marketing arrangement occurred when kinship-oriented integrative mechanisms became limited to intravillage relations. In other words, the myth supports my argument by placing trading partnerships and intervillage, even interethnic, marriages within the same time-frame.

But the myth is told by the Chambri, not by the Iatmul. Although Chambri villages seem to have become increasingly complex through time—maintaining a 91 percent rate of intravillage marriage in 1974—there is every indication that these changes occurred prior to the establishment of barter markets with the Hills people. Moreover, while it is easy to argue for a transition from restricted to generalized marriage systems among the Iatmul—from the exogamy inherent in sister exchange to the endogamy of *iai* marriage—the Chambri may have always preferred marriage with the classificatory mother's brother's daughter for as long as they have been living on their island.

The myth, then, while adding some support to my argument, also detracts from it, leaving me with several problems. The first is to account for the transition from trading partnerships to marketing arrangements among the Chambri, who, unlike the Iatmul, have not grown larger and more complex in relation to an increasing dependence upon sago. And the second is to explain the Hills people, who never were intimidated by Chambri hegemony and yet appear to have shifted from the reciprocal exchange relationships described in the myth to one in which women exchange fish and sago at an essentially unfair, fixed rate.

Thus we are left with an enigma. History appears to have repeated itself for unknown reasons. It would be fruitless to argue that similar human materials were transformed by identical determinants, for the Chambri possessed neither the numbers nor the military might to command the behavior of their Hills trading partners. Nor would it be satisfactory to suggest that the diffusion of cultural traits convinced Chambri and Hills women that they should voluntarily adopt an unequal exchange rate, for this would demand the revision of all that we know about socioeconomic behavior.

In other words, we do not yet have enough data to understand the evolution of Chambri barter markets, a situation I begin to rectify in the next chapter. My focus will be upon women, for it is their markets that we are trying to explain.

3

WOMEN IN PRODUCTION
AND EXCHANGE

Since it is women who are the primary producers in both Chambri and Iatmul societies, this chapter focuses on them. My concern is to describe both their autonomous subsistence activities and the social mechanisms used by men to insure themselves of the products of female production and reproduction.

Women and Production

Among both the Chambri and the Iatmul, subsistence requires the deployment of considerably less labor than it does among horticulturalists. Indeed, Chambri and Iatmul women generally accomplish all of their tasks during a few hours each morning.

A woman's day begins when she rises before dawn to check the fishnets and traps she has left in the water overnight. Generally, she returns with enough fish for the day's consumption as well as a considerable number to smoke and put by or to exchange with her sago-suppliers.[1] These fish are of various species, including trevally, catfish, and sawshark, but *Tilapia mosambica* are by far the most common. The *Tilapia*, or *makau* in Melanesian Pidgin, are recent arrivals in Sepik waters. They escaped from experimental ponds at Maprik into the Screw River and from there spread rapidly into the Sepik River. By 1965 *Tilapia* were abundant throughout the region. Although *Tilapia* have been extremely successful, they appear to have replaced indigenous species rather than filled an empty niche, and there is every reason to believe that Chambri and Iatmul women always returned with their baskets filled with fish.[2]

Although most women check their baskets every day, each has generally put by enough smoked fish to feed her family for up to three months. This is especially true during the dry season, when surpluses rise extraordinarily, for fishing becomes a matter of scooping fish into canoes from the shrunken rivulets where they have risen to the surface to seek oxygen. When Chambri Lake dries up, for example, its two constitutive tributaries are lined for thirty feet with dead and dying fish. During this time, Chambri and Iatmul women keep their smoking fires burning all night long to prepare as many fish as possible for storage.

Although sago can be stored for a considerable time, it tends to ferment and become unpalatable to Chambri and Iatmul tastes. Women, therefore, rarely bring home more than a week's worth of flour from barter markets and prepare fresh sago pancakes every morning, usually four for each family member. Using small clay griddles, they bake the pancakes over open fires built in large pottery hearths that are located inside their houses. Resembling omelets, the finished pancakes are dry and flakey on the outside and dense and gummy within; they have little food value other than the calories they provide. The Chambri and Iatmul think them delicious, however, and will say that nothing satisfies hunger more than a sago pancake.

Only on ceremonial occasions when special foods are prepared do Chambri and Iatmul women serve food to their families. Normally, they place the fish and sago pancakes they have cooked for the day into baskets hanging from hooks attached to the ceilings of their houses. When a family member is hungry, he simply takes some food out of one of the baskets. Some women designate one basket for each family member, but more frequently they store the day's food communally.

They may even share food when several families comprise a household. Among both Iatmul and Chambri, the dwelling houses tend to shelter several families of patrilineally related men. Thus, a typical house will contain a man, his sons, their wives, and children, and perhaps a few matrilateral relatives as well. (See table 3.1 for the composition of households in the Chambri village of Indingai during 1974.)

Occasionally a man will build separate houses for his several wives, particularly when the women come from different clans or villages. Yandi, for example, will have nothing to do with Ambunowi's second wife. Continually pregnant and nursing, she prefers to have her seven children go hungry rather than accept help from the childless Sapui. Ambunowi has built separate houses for his wives, Yandi's two hundred feet up Chambri Mountain and Sapui's along the shore. Both women assiduously avoid one another, each doing her best to discourage Ambunowi from visiting the other.

Only when relationships between co-wives and sisters-in-law are amicable do they live together in one large house. Each occupies a particular area of the house, where she places her pottery hearth, her household possessions, her clothes, those of her children, and the mosquito bag she shares with her immediate family. This is not to suggest that there is rigid territoriality within a large Sepik household, because it is common for the women living together to share their possessions. The fact that any one of them

Table 3.1: The Composition of Indingai Households during 1974

House No.	M (age)	F (age)	Relationship*
1	23		head
		20	wi
	12		bo
	3		so
2	59		head
		55	wi
		17	da
		19	da
	8		so
	25		so
		23	da-in-law
		4 mos.	grda
3	23		head
		20	wi
		39	class. z
	7		class. z so
		9	class. z da
	14		class. z so
4	44		head
		41	wi
	18		so
	16		so
		13	da
		5	da
	3		so
	11		so
	9		so
		6 mos.	da
5	54		head
		54	wi
		41	wi
	20		so
	19		so
		14	da
		11	da
	9		so
	14		so
		9	da
		7	da
	3		so
6	44		head
		42	wi
		17	da
		14	da

House No.	M (age)	F (age)	Relationship*
	20		so
		13	da
		9	da
		16	da
	29		wi bo
		23	wi bo wi
	56		wi class. bo
7		49	head
	26		so
	22		so
		13	da
	9		so
8	45		head
		43	wi
	16		so
		14	da
		11	da
		9	da
	6		so
		3	da
9	52		head
		51	wi
	24		wi so
	21		wi so
		19	wi da
		12	da
		9	da
	7		so
10	35		head
		33	wi
	7		so
		9	da
		70	no relation
11	40		head
		38	wi
	15		so
	17		so
	11		so
	7		so
	4		so
	10 mos.		so
12	48		head
		42	wi
		18	da

House No.	M (age)	F (age)	Relationship*
		16	da
		14	da
		11	da
	7		so
		4	da
	1		so
13	48	(also heads house 12)	head
		48	wi
	16		wi so
	11		wi so
	8		wi so
		30	no relation
	10		friend's so
	8		friend's so
	6		friend's so
		3	friend's da
14	39		head
		34	wi
		12	da
		10	da
	7		so
		5	da
		2	da
15	68		head
		59	wi
		1	grda
	26		so
		23	da-in-law
	4		grso
	2		grso
	1		grso
		22	da
16	59		head
		54	wi
	7		grso
	16		so
	13		so
		6	grda
		26	da
	12		grso
		8	grda
17	40		head
		40	wi
		23	da

House No.	M (age)	F (age)	Relationship*
	17		so
	13		so
		8	da
	5		so
		4	da
18	57		head
		55	wi
	27		so
		24	da-in-law
	6		grso
	19		da-in-law's bo
		3 mos.	grda
		11	adop. da
		31	class. da-in-law
	14		class. grso
	6		class. grso
		16	adop. grda
		16	z da
19	24		head
		24	wi
20	30		head
		26	wi
	8		so
		5	da
		1	da
		40	class. z
		13	class. da
		8	class. da
	33		bo
		30	bo wi
	13		bo so
	9		bo so
		54	class. bo wi
21	38		head
		37	wi
	19		so
	13		so
		11	da
		9	da
		5	da
22		54	head
	16		so
	12		so
		34	class. z

House No.	M (age)	F (age)	Relationship*
	27		class. bo
	12		class. z so
23	35		head
		33	wi
		16	da
		12	da
		11	da
	7		so
		4	da
		2	da
		10 mos.	da
		52	class. mo
24		40	head
		26	da
25	60		head
		74	wi
		54	wi
	22		wi so
	15		wi so
		60	class. mo
	20		class. so
		15	class. da
		14	class. da
	14		class. so
26	40		head
		38	wi
	10		so
		5	da
27		40	head
	9		so
	2		so
28	36		head
		32	wi
	10		so
	8		so
	5		so
	3		so
	4 mos.		so
		6	adop. da
29	38		head
		34	wi
	40		bo

House No.	M (age)	F (age)	Relationship*
	24		bo
	10		so
		17	da
30	30		head
		31	wi
		37	wi
	8		so
	4		so
	2		so
		6 mos.	da
		4 mos.	da
		32	z
		3	z da
	2		z so
	9		z so
31	59		head
	19		so
		19	da
	2 mos.		grso
	3		grso
	13		so
		17	adop. da
	11		so
	5		so
32	40		head
		33	wi
		17	adop. da
		11	da
		7	da
		36	wi
	25		class. so
33	50		head
		35	wi
	4 mos.		so
34	26		head
		24	wi
35	66		head
		56	wi
		59	wi
		59	wi
	24		so
		22	da-in-law
	3		grso
	19		so
	44		bo

Table 3.1: Continued

House No.	M (age)	F (age)	Relationship*
		44	bo wi
	20		bo so
	11		bo adop. so
	5		bo so
		16	class. da
	13		class. so
		9	bo wi da
36		37	head
	10		so
		9	da
		3	da
	7 mos.		so
37	33		head
		33	wi
		10	da
	3		so
		11	da
38	37		head
		35	wi
	7		so
		4	da
	5		so
39	30		head
		26	wi
	5		so
	1		so
	26		class. bo
	20		class. bo

*Abbreviations: adop. = adopted; bo = brother; class. = classificatory; da = daughter; gr = grand; mo = mother; so = son; wi = wife; z = sister.

may provide all of their children with food on a particular day, expecting that another will reciprocate in the future, lends "an air of solidarity, of firm co-operation and group purpose" (Mead, 1963: 239) to the household.

The household of Wapiyeri, an elderly Chambri Big Man, is a fine example of this solidarity, cooperation, and group purpose. His three wives, Popai, Yambusin, and Kundi, all live together in his one large house. After Kundi developed a benign tumor on her forehead, she was frequently incapacitated with dizzy spells. Popai and Yambusin assumed responsibilities for the fishing and marketing, while Kundi stayed at home to cook sago pancakes. During the afternoon, the three women would weave baskets together, or repair fish traps, or just gossip about their relatives and neighbors, while sitting on the floor near one or another of their designated "areas" of the house.

Mead thought that Chambri households exemplify female solidarity and cooperation to an unusual degree. In *Sex and Temperament* she wrote:

> Solid, preoccupied, powerful, with shaven unadorned heads . . . [Chambri] women sit in groups and laugh together, or occasionally stage a night dance at which, without a man present, each woman dances vigorously all by herself the dance-step that she has found to be most exciting. Here again the solidarity of women, the inessentialness of men, is demonstrated. Of this relationship the Tchambuli dwelling-house is the symbol. It presents the curious picture of the entire centre firmly occupied by well-entrenched women, while the men sit about the edges, near the door, one foot on the house-ladder almost, unwanted, on sufferance, ready to flee away to their men's houses. . . . [1963: 257–58]

Wapiyeri's household verifies Mead's description, but Ambunowi's wives appear far from solidary and cooperative, and I mention these examples of household interaction to emphasize that female unity varies as much within Chambri households as it does between those of the Chambri and the Iatmul. I will return to a comparison between Iatmul and Chambri women in the next chapter. Here I must say, however, that the significant differences between these women did not involve the organization of their households. Both Iatmul and Chambri households are identically organized, and both Iatmul and Chambri men live in men's houses where they take part in the activity they consider to be more important than fishing, marketing, and cooking—namely, the ongoing drama of political manipulation and debate that surrounds the negotiation of marriages.

Affinal Relations

Although Chambri and Iatmul women work hard for their families, their husbands must purchase rights to them. During initiation ceremonies and other rites of passage, groups linked through marriage engage in ceremonial transactions. Regardless of how the marriage occurs—with the *iai*, through sister exchange, by abduction, or with the mother's brother's daughter as the Chambri prefer—it inevitably involves the transfer of valuables. These continue to pass, in exchange for food and ceremonial services, from wife-takers to wife-givers, at least into the next generation. Thus, marriage involves asymmetrical exchange, with wife-givers losing productive women but gaining valuable objects.

This asymmetrical exchange verifies a relationship of inequality, for wife-givers are considered "superior" to their affines, and their superiority rests on several social facts. First of all, throughout egalitarian New Guinea, an individual or group to whom another is indebted is always considered to be at least temporarily superior. Thus, in the Highlands of New Guinea, status differentials are established and maintained through competitive equal exchange. One individual gives a quantity of goods to his trading partner who reciprocates with more goods, forcing the first donor to give even more goods. Certain individuals and groups will be indebted to other individuals and groups at any one point in time, and "the only way they can maintain their alliance is by continuing positive, ceremonial exchanges of valuables. . . . [The system is one] in which reciprocative transactions prevail and the relationship between partners is relatively egalitarian" (Strathern, 1971: 214–15).

Although Chambri and Iatmul men do not engage in competitive equal exchanges, they do contract comparable inequality-producing debts, but to their affines. In a sense, Iatmul and Chambri wife-takers owe their lives to those who have provided their mothers, and bridewealth, which the Iatmul speak of as "wainga, the same word being equally applicable to the purchase of a canoe or any other object" (Bateson, 1952: 281), is the means used to repay their obligations, to purchase themselves and their children from their matrilateral kinsmen. Thus, jural membership in both Iatmul and Chambri patriclans is contingent upon the fulfillment of debts incurred to affines.

But there is another important social fact to be considered, for despite reiterated payments, affinal debts can *never* be fully settled, primarily because the exchanges between wife-takers and wife-givers cannot be subjected to any direct comparison or accounting, being of essentially different things (see Forge, 1972: 537). Valuables move in one direction and women move in the other, and the men who are linked through these exchanges are trapped in a relationship of inequality, a relationship established between men by means of women.

Let me establish the nature of affinal inequality by reproducing a myth Bateson uses to illustrate the "double emphasis" of the ethos of Iatmul women (1958: 145–47). The myth interests him because it seems to celebrate the unusual courageousness of two Iatmul women, but I think it more interesting for what it tells us about affinal relations.

> Kararau were killing us.[3] They speared women who went out to get tips of wild sugar-cane, and women who went to get water-weed (for pig's food), and women who went to their fish traps. And they shot a man, Au-vitkai-mali. . . . His wife was Tshanggi-mbo and (his sister was) Au-vitkai-mangka. They shot him and beat the gongs (in triumph). Au-vitkai-mangka was away; she was on the lake (fishing). . . . [The] sound of . . . [the] gongs came

(over the lake). She asked, "Whom have they speared?" and (the people) said, "They have speared your husband."[4]

Then she filled up a bag with shell valuables and she (went to the ceremonial house and) said, "Men of this village, I have brought (valuables) for you." But they said, "No. We do not want them," and they were ashamed (because they had not dared to accept the valuables which she had offered as payment for assistance).

Then she went down into her canoe; she loaded the valuables into the canoe; she took off her skirt and put it in the canoe. Au-vitkai-mangka was in the stern and Tshanggi-mbo in the bow. The bag of valuables was in the middle of the canoe. She went up the river to Palimbai,[5] because she had heard his gongs. . . .

They sat leaning against the ceremonial mound (a place of refuge) in Palimbai,[6] and they put the bag of valuables on the ground close to the mound. At dawn (the people of Palimbai) got up and saw (them). They were sitting stripped of their skirts, with their skirts on their shoulders.[7]

The men of Palimbai said, "They are women of Kararau"; and they were for spearing them.[8] The women said, "Why will you spear us?" Kaulievi (of Palimbai) saw them and said, "Don't spear them"; and he said "Come." Then he beat the gong to summon all the men of Palimbai, Kankanamun, Malingai, and Jents-chan. . . . The men said, "What women are you?"; and the women said, "We are the women of Ienmali." (Ienmali is the name of the old site of Mindimbit.) . . .

Au-vitkai-mangka then (calling the names of the totems of the four villages) appealed to Kankanamun: "You! Crocodile! Wani-mali!"; and to Malingai: "You! Crocodile! Kavok!" and to Palim-bai: "You! Pig! Palimbai-awan!"; and to Jentschan: "You! Pig! Djimbut-nggowi!" And she said, "I shall take away my bag of valuables."

She set out the valuables in a line; and the four villages accepted them. That night they debated, "Already tomorrow we shall raid them." Each of the four villages (brought) a fleet of canoes. They formed into one fleet on the Sepik River.

They (the men) gave a spear to Au-vitkai-mangka and the men of Palimbai gave another spear to Tshanggi-mbo. . . .

When they drifted down to the Kararau (reaches of the) Sepik, (the canoes took up formation).[9] The two women hid in the centre. Then the men shot an eel. It said "War." (A favorable omen; and here my informant reproduced the grunting of the eel.)

. . . The Palimbai people killed the people of Kararau and they caught two men (alive) in their hands. Au-vitkai-mangka speared one of them. Tshanggi-mbo speared the other. They speared them all, every one of them. . . .

The key to understanding this myth rests in the shame felt by the men of Mindimbit when approached by Au-vitkai-mangka to avenge her husband. She undoubtedly made her request of his patrilineal relatives, for "their first duty was the taking of *nggambwa* (vengeance)" (Bateson, 1958: 139).

> The rings of cane worn in mourning for the killed individual may not be put aside until vengeance has been achieved; and a pointed reference to an unavenged relative is one of the most dangerous insults that one Iatmul can use in ranting against another. . . .
> Indeed, so serious is the condition of those who are unable to secure revenge, that it . . . may lead to the sickness and death of . . . [group] members. [ibid.: 139–40]

But her husband's relatives refused to avenge their kinsman, thereby revealing themselves as fearful and weak—unequal to other men within Mindimbit, and certainly to those Parambei who eventually accepted the task. Their shame must have been doubly great because it was Au-vitkai-mangka who made it public. She, after all, by marrying into their clan, had already affected a relationship of inequality between her own family and theirs, and was now transforming this affinal inequality into a patron–client relationship between unrelated groups of men.

By taking the valuables to Parambei, Au-vitkai-mangka was asking Kaulievi and his supporters to assume her in-laws' responsibilities. The message she brought was this: "My in-laws are rubbish-men. They have neither the will nor the strength to avenge my husband's death. You must do so, and thereby become his relatives and my affines." By sitting at the ceremonial mound stripped of her skirt, she was declaring herself already married into Kaulievi's clan, for this is the posture assumed by mothers during *naven* ceremonies (Bateson, 1958: 6–22 and my footnote 8).

Her message would have been immediately comprehensible to any Iatmul or Chambri. Among both peoples, individuals and groups that are not linked through marriage are considered equal, "differentiated from other identical individuals and groups only by sets of cultural signs, typically names, that are intrinsically mutable, not by reference to any sort of current external or past distinction in nature, or ancestry" (Forge, 1972: 533). Every Chambri and Iatmul, and each of their patrilineages, patriclans, patrimoieties, and villages owns an equivalent number of totemic names, such as those mentioned in the myth.[10] Differences in status are established and maintained between these groups of equal men when those that are "more than equal" assist their "less than equal" neighbors to meet their affinal debts. When an Iatmul, or a Chambri, and his clan co-members cannot amass sufficient valuables to compensate their wife-givers, they will seek assistance from an unrelated clan. The unrelated clan, by giving assistance, gains power over its clients. This is what the Iatmul mean when they say that an unrelated individual "bosses" the resources, names, and powers of his clients. "Tchuikumban," they would tell me, "is not the father of this crocodile; he bosses it, that's all." Thus, competition between equal clans is played out within the context of unequal affinal exchange. One's own affinal relationship is a source of inequality, but the affinal relationships of others provide unrelated men with the opportunity of proving themselves equal competitors. And this is the opportunity Au-vitkai-mangka provided the Parambei. She asked them to assume her husband's relatives' responsibilities, to become their patrons.

In this sense, the myth is not only about the origin of the traditional feud between the Iatmul village of Kararau and those of Parambei and Mindimbit, but it is also about the development of patron–client relationships between Parambei and Mindimbit. A man from Kararau killed a man from Mindimbit; the slain man's relatives did not have the strength to avenge his death; Parambei assumed responsibility, initiating the feud and gaining status and power over the shamed village.

We see, then, that the Mindimbit myth is more an admonition than a panegyric. It was told not merely to glorify the courageousness of two unusual Iatmul women, but rather to warn against the danger inherent in the relationship established through women. This danger is twofold: wife-givers maintain superiority over their wife-takers, and unrelated groups may transform this affinal inequality into that between patrons and clients.

Women and Reproduction

Forge, writing about Middle Sepik male sensibilities in general, feels that underlying the fear of the unequal relationships established between men through their marriage to women is a more fundamental ambiguity, specifically, that "women are treated as inferior by men, who nevertheless believe them to be superior" (1971: 142). And certainly many Iatmul and Chambri have told me that women are in need of careful watching, for they once owned the men's houses, sacred flutes, and other accoutrements of culture, and threaten to regain their lost possessions someday. Indeed, on top of every Iatmul and Chambri men's house is the carved figure of culture's progenitress, who reminds the occupants that women once sat where they now do.

Without wishing to analyze the psychological components of this fear, I think it fair to say that Iatmul and Chambri men feel ambiguous about their dependence upon the reproductive capacities of women, not only because reproduction entails claims by matrilateral kinsmen, but also because it is through the power of inferior women that "equal" men are produced.

Essentially, Iatmul and Chambri men are committed to the notion that like should generate like, although they are aware that it can never do so. Their initiation of young men into patriclan membership, for example, involves scarification and bloodletting, both designed to free the initiates from the deleterious effects of the mother's blood that they are bound to internalize prior to birth. These ceremonies are the culmination of years of affinal exchanges and express the basis of the prestations, as men attempt to earn their social freedom from their male in-laws and their psychophysiological freedom from their mothers. What we see is a recapitulation of the same structural ambiguity on two levels. Inferior and inequality-producing women reproduce equal men. More than equal wife-givers provide the women. And a man, within his patriclan, must establish his autonomy from both.

The following Chambri myth illustrates both the degree to which men blame the existence of affinal inequality upon the women who link them together as unequals and the lengths to which they will go to live without the relationships established through women.

Tsambali Kanusaraman, who lived by himself on an island in Chambri Lake, decided to create two large wooden carvings [chambən][11] in the image of women. He named the carvings Wobunprendu and Kabunprendu, and upon doing so he enlivened them. He called them daughters and instructed them in sago preparation and other domestic chores. The three lived happily together for many years, the only people on their island.

One day as the two sisters were preparing sago, two hawks fell from the sky and landed next to their sago baskets. The girls hid the birds underneath their baskets, after placing a feather from each of the birds through the holes in their ear lobes. They returned to their work, but were interrupted when two brothers, Wundan and Pumbun, arrived in search of the hawks. The two men knew by the feathers in the girls' ears that they had come to the right place, but the girls denied having seen the birds. When Wundan found them underneath the sagʋ baskets, he demanded that he and his brother be taken to the girls' father.

Tsambali Kanusaraman welcomed his visitors and instructed his daughters to prepare the hawks for a feast. While the birds were being prepared, the two brothers asked Kanusaraman for his daughters in marriage, and suggested that he accept the hawks as bride-price. Kanusaraman agreed to the marriages and to the bride-price. He told the brothers that he was accepting such a small bride-price only because his daughters were nothing more than carvings; they had no blood and had been carved without sexual organs. The brothers were not disappointed by this news, and assured Kanusaraman that they were only interested in the girls as house-keepers and cooks.

Upon arriving home, Wundan and Pumbun were met by their

mother's brother, Owibuni. Seeing the girls they had brought, he warned his nephews that no good would come of stealing other people's women. Wundan and Pumbun assured him that they had paid for the girls, and asked him to help them open up their wives' vulvae. After building a fence to prevent onlookers, Owibuni put the women to sleep with a magic spell and then carved vaginas for each of them with a sharp piece of bamboo. Blood gushed from their wounds, but Owibuni stopped the bleeding by bandaging them with leaves. The girls rested for six weeks, and then were able to assume normal female sexual duties. Both immediately conceived children.

They lived happily until Wundan and Pumbun decided to hold a ceremonial sacrifice to their ancestors. In the past, they had used a chicken or a pig as the sacrificial victim, but this time, however, they decided to sacrifice a man. The brothers convinced Owibuni to help them collect water lilies from Chambri Lake, and while he was in the water, they stabbed him with a fishing spear and then severed his head with a bush knife.

All would have been well if Tsangirapan, the mother of Wundan and Pumbun and the elder sister of Owibuni, had not been pulling in her fish basket at the time the murder took place. In her basket she found pieces of her brother's flesh, and when she saw her sons place his head on top of their ceremonial house, she knew what had happened. She prepared a soup from the excrement of dogs and chickens, and presented it to her sons and their wives. They drank of it, as she did herself, and the five of them immediately turned into boulders which can still be seen today on the top of Mount Karundui. [See fig. 3.1 for the cast of characters.]

Let me enumerate the myth's major themes. First, it tells of a man who creates his own daughters but who cannot guarantee himself grandchildren because his daughters are bloodless and infertile. Their infertility and bloodlessness are predictable, given the Chambri belief that a child's bones are the product of its father's semen, whereas its blood comes from its mother.[12] Wobunprendu and Kabunprendu have no mother, and hence have no blood.

Second, the myth describes the girls' exogamous marriages to two brothers who pay bride-price with foodstuffs. Such marriages would have been quite unsatisfactory to the Chambri, who in 1974 practiced intraisland endogamy 91 percent of the time, and intraphratry endogamy 78 percent of the time. (See table 3.2 for a comparison with comparable data collected by Margaret Mead in 1933.) Moreover, the Chambri insist that ceremonial valuables and not foodstuffs be the items of bride-price. Although the bride-prices for Wobunprendu and Kabunprendu would have been reduced given

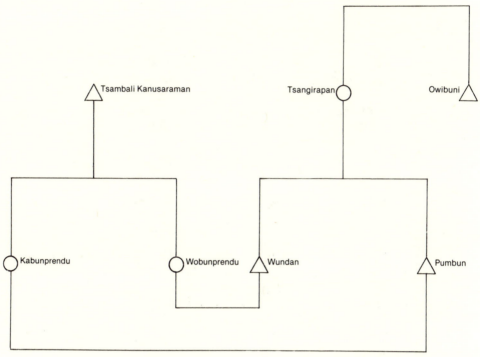

Figure 3.1.   The Cast of Characters in the Chambən Myth

their infertility, they certainly would never have consisted exclusively of eatables, and a Chambri father would sooner eat crow than accept hawk as bride-price.

Third, we learn that the brothers do care about procreation, and that they ask their mother's brother to complete their wives by creating sexual organs. Again, the appearance of a mother's brother is predictable considering the Chambri preference for mother's brother's daughter's marriage. The girls become functioning women—they are blooded, so to speak—at the hands of their husbands' mother's brother. He, I would argue, by performing the operation, assumes his rightful role as father to his nephews' wives.

Fourth, the two brothers kill their mother's brother and thus sever the affinal connection they acquired after their wives' operation. And finally, in the style of grand tragedy, the remaining protagonists are killed by the mother, who also kills herself.

The myth deals, in effect, with three different attempts to avoid the affinal bond: first, by creating one's own children; second, by practicing what might be called "terminal exogamy"—marrying women from such distant

Table 3.2: The Frequency of Endogamous Marriage at Chambri during 1933 and 1974

1933[a]

Chambri Phratry	Yambukayingai	Saungai	Walintimiingai	Totals	Sub Non-Chambri	% of Endogamy	
						Phratry	All Chambri
Yambukayingai	23	4	1	28	2	82	93
Saungai	7	18	1	26	0	69	100
Walintimiingai	4	0	12	16	0	75	100
Totals	34	22	14	70	2	75.3	97.7

1974[b]

Chambri Phratry	Yambukayingai	Saungai	Walintimiingai	Totals	Sub Non-Chambri	% of Endogamy	
						Phratry	All Chambri
Yambukayingai	64	11	6	81	7	73	92
Saungai	13	94	2	109	11	78	92
Walintimiingai	6	1	86	93	11	83	90
Totals	83	106	94	283	29	78	91

[a]Figures were derived from Margaret Mead's unpublished censuses. They are incomplete, reflecting her partial completion of the work. The percentage of extratribal marriages was actually higher in 1933, because the Chambri had intermarried with members of the Sepik Hills during their exile among them from about 1905 to 1927. See chapter 5 for a full discussion of this exile.
[b]Figures were collected by the author. They were calculated from the male perspective to avoid double-counting, and include the marriages of migrant laborers.

villages that the affinal relationship is nearly irrelevant; and third, by murdering one's mother's brother, who is, in Chambri culture, one's most important wife-giver. The myth also tells us, or rather the five boulders atop Mount Karundui tell us, that the attempts were to no avail, that relationships of inequality are inherent in the birth of equal men from inferior women.

Bateson provides several ethnographic details which illuminate this contradiction from the Iatmul perspective. The first involves a contrast between the mortuary ceremonies celebrated for men and women.

> When a great man dies a figure is set up by the members of his initiatory moiety to represent him and is decorated with symbols of all his achievements. Spears are set up to the number of his kills and baskets are suspended form the shoulder of the figure to the number of his wives. But no symbols are added to show how many children he has begotten. For a woman, when she dies, a post (*nggambut*) is set up and is decorated with the ornaments which were given to her sons by the senior age grade at initiation. Her greatness is vicarious and lies in the achievements of her sons. [1958: 48]

He also reports that: "[N]*aven* are celebrated for a boy when he takes a wife, but not when his first son is born. For a girl *naven* are celebrated when she gives birth to a child, but *not* for her marriage" (ibid.). And he explains these details with reference to three cultural premises.

> The three premises which I have mentioned deal with the relationships of the child to its father, mother and maternal clan. These may be summed up . . . by saying that the child is closely identified with its father but competes with him. . . . [T]he child is not a competitor but, rather, an achievement of the mother; and the child's achievements are her achievements, the triumph of *her* clan. [ibid.]

Although his formulation of these premises is astute, Bateson does not speculate about the relationships that underlie them: as a competitor, a son is equal to and independent of his father, but he is unequal to and dependent upon his matrilateral kinsmen. Furthermore, this affinal inequality is primary because it is caused by a son's indebtedness to his mother's clan. In other words, necessary to an equality between cognate individuals and groups is an inequality between them and those responsible for their existence. The ambiguity they feel can be expressed thus: If I am here and equal to others like me, then those responsible for my existence must be either inferior to me or better than I.

A comparable ambiguity exists in the West, where it has been resolved through the notion of a great chain of being, linking the creator with his creations in a series of hierarchically ordered steps. In Western societies, the emphasis is upon the inequality of condition, as each creature, together with those like it, remains in its proper place, suffering its inevitable deprivations and reaping its predestined rewards. Among the Chambri and Iatmul, however, the problem of ontological inequality can only be resolved through sociological mechanisms, for their societies are without state authority, and they cannot conceive of an agency empowered to regulate and explain life's condition. Thus, each Iatmul and Chambri man deprecates his women and recompenses his affines, in the hope of overcoming the inequality implied by his very existence.

Restricted versus Generalized Systems: Sister Exchange, Iai, and Mother's Brother's Daughter's Marriage

If inequality is the inevitable result of the relationships between groups of men established through their marriages to women, and if these unequal affinal relationships are as intolerable as the Chambri myth makes out, then what better way to reduce this inequality than by exchanging sisters? If men exchange their sisters, then their women, bride-prices, ceremonial services, and affinal payments move in two directions, for each group of men is simultaneously wife-giver and wife-taker to the other. Following from this, we might ask why the Iatmul and Chambri both prescribe marriages, the former with the *iai* and the latter with the mother's brother's daughter? In the case of the Iatmul the question is real, for Bateson reports sister exchange as an alternative marriage rule. For the Chambri, however, the question is hypothetical, for there is no indication that they ever prescribed anything but cross-cousin marriage.

Bateson's Iatmul data can be extended to provide an answer to the question in both its real and hypothetical senses. The first important point is this: although sister exchange reduces affinal inequality, it does not eliminate it completely. Consider, for example, a description of a "typical case of completing a brother-sister exchange" (Bateson, 1932: 280).

> The girl had first lived for some time in the house of the husband, and I was told that she had gone there without fuss or ceremony. Later, the husband made a big ceremonial present of shells and other valuables to the girl's parents and this was the occasion for a considerable ritual performance, including the ritual of walking the girl in procession from her parents' house to the house of the bridegroom. For this she was very heavily ornamented from head to foot with valuables, while her companions carried large numbers of decorated useful objects—pots, fish traps, etc.—these being

a reciprocal present to that which the husband had made to the girl's parents. . . . [My] informant . . . said that a husband would always have to consult his wife in his expenditure of valuables, he having been ruined by the bride wealth. However, my material is inadequate for a discussion of the economics of marriage and the debts incurred in raising bride wealth. [ibid.: 280–81]

Even in this most symmetrical of marriage arrangements, then, the ritual union of intermarrying groups was structured to separate the status of wife-givers from that of wife-takers. In other words, the prestations were asymmetrically organized.

Undoubtedly this was so because the exchange of sisters had been somewhat delayed, and one group was acting as wife-giver vis-à-vis the other group at the particular time the marriage was celebrated. But I suspect that the exchange of sisters was delayed for a more fundamental reason—namely, that even balanced marriages cannot overcome the inequality inherent in the birth of men from inferior and inequality-producing women.

Sister exchange can, of course, reduce the ramifications of this fundamental ambiguity. We are told, for example, that the bride's parents made "a reciprocal present to that which the husband had made to the girl's parents." And, it is logically possible for the groom to have paid his bridewealth with the very valuables his relatives initially received in exchange for their sister. My guess, therefore, would be that if Bateson had collected information about the economics of marriage, his data would indicate that fewer valuables—and more of the same valuables—change hands during sister exchange, and that the debts incurred in raising bridewealth are far less extensive than in any other form of marriage.

Thus, although the fundamental contradiction inherent in the birth of equal men through unequal women cannot be resolved through sister exchange, this form of marriage can reduce its sociological implications. We are left, then, with the same question. Why do the Chambri and Iatmul prescribe cross-cousin marriages? Perhaps we can better answer this question by concentrating on the disadvantages of sister exchange.

Of course, the most obvious disadvantage is the fact that it generates a closed system in which one gives what one gets. In other words, one cannot engage in sister exchange without having a sister to exchange. Undoubtedly the Iatmul used many of the same strategic alternatives found among the southern Arapesh, another Sepik people preferring to exchange sisters in marriage. Tuzin reports:

When no uterine sister is available, there are conventional fall-back strategies. A FBD is the one most commonly "borrowed" by Ego . . . provided she . . . does not have a uterine brother. . . . More distant agnatic kinswomen may be applied for, but the chances increase with genealogical distance that she will be committed to more closely related brothers. Anticipating the exchange needs of one's son(s) may be a factor in deciding to adopt a girl infant, or in trading opposite-sexed children with one's brother. Finally . . . the woman's group may allow the debt to be deferred until the next generation, when a child of the union is returned. . . . [1977: 100–01]

Tuzin argues that "with the various options at hand, especially that permitting generational deferral, the rule of exchange easily accommodates natural demographic imbalances" (ibid.: 101). Although accommodation may occur, I wonder whether "easily" is the right adverb. After all, the percentage of sister-exchange marriages found in 1979—between 31 percent and 50 percent of all marriages—is not particularly high. Tuzin believes that this percentage reflects a breakdown in the system, specifically, an increased capacity to default on generational exchange. Young girls, it seems, are no longer forced to move in with their prospective in-laws prior to menarche and tend to find men more to their liking than those they are supposed to marry.

Although the system may indeed be changing from its more traditional mode of operation, my guess would be that the percentage of sister-exchange marriages has remained relatively constant through time. The system's only flexibility is generational deferral, and this option will be unacceptable to all but a few Arapesh men—probably only to those wealthy men from large clans who can accommodate all of their sons through sister exchange and invest in the future by accepting a deferred payment or two.

Extending this argument to the Iatmul, who probably also practiced adoptions and generational deferrals, we can assume that somewhere between one-third and one-half of the population was able to acquire wives through sister exchange. When I asked an Iatmul informant if this were true, he replied: "It's all right to exchange women, but it's hard to know if you'll be able to. If you have a sister, good, you'll be able to get a wife. But wives sometimes ruin everything by holding back their daughters to punish your sons." He was referring, of course, to the difficulty of negotiating imbalances in the genders of children, but was doing so in a typically Iatmul manner. Essentially, he was alluding to women's power, and was bemoaning the fact that sister exchange is under the control of the unpredictable reproductive capacities of women. As another informant put it: "When you get a wife with valuables, it's better. You can work for valuables and get women. But if you want to get a woman with a woman, then it's something which women can ruin."

We are now in the position to understand an important aspect of the Iatmul and Chambri preference for cross-cousin marriages. While the inequality established between intermarrying groups of men can be diminished through sister exchange, this diminution requires their absolute dependence upon the reproductive capacities of women. Iatmul and Chambri men, therefore, are trapped between Scylla and Charybdis. Marriage, any way they accomplish it, is a no-win game, but at least generalized marriage systems provide some possibility of control.

Conclusion

The major advantage of prescriptive marriages is that they transform closed into open systems by allowing valuables to be used in exchange for women. Both *iai* and mother's brother's daughter's marriage allow Iatmul and Chambri men to control the valuables with which they pay for the women who will bear their sons. And these valuables can be acquired in a variety of ways: through the sale of specialized commodities, in exchange for produce needed by others to hold feasts, in affinal payments, through inheritance, through robbery or raids, and, most importantly, by borrowing from kinsmen or from unrelated individuals. Each of these arrangements results in connections between individuals and groups that cross-cut those based upon kinship, while they add to the complexity of the society.

Margaret Mead reports in her field notes, for example, that one shell *kina*—observed over the four months she spent among the Chambri—changed hands four times, thereby establishing or maintaining relationships between thirty-five men and women belonging to five different clans and four different men's houses. She describes how Tchuikumban received it from his classificatory sister during a ceremony held to open the Yangarman men's house, in return for his contribution of sago and coconuts; how he gave it to members of his prospective father-in-law's clan in order to help them fulfill their debt to his fiancé's dead husband's father; how he took it back when he feared that his wedding was off; and how he contributed it to pay for a pig that was given by members of his clan to their affines in order to end a major mourning ceremony.[13]

Mead's data agree with those I collected at fifteen different affinal exchange ceremonies, all of which involved the establishment or maintenance of extensive personal and corporate relationships. The least extensive of these ceremonies, a bride-price transaction, involved thirty-six individuals, thirty-two of whom were acting on behalf of eight different patriclans, while four represented their own personal interests; and the most extensive, an initiation payment, included seventy-seven individuals, seventy-three of whom represented fifteen different patriclans, while six came on their own behalf.[14] The complexity of the interconnections exhibited at these affinal transactions is a direct product of the numerous dyadic relationships that result when offers of assistance are made and accepted. Men must acquire women and recompense affines. When they can borrow valuables in order to do so, they indebt themselves to unrelated individuals, who effectively become their patrons. Very occasionally these relationships shift, through time, from patron–client to client–patron as individuals assist one another to meet their affinal debts. More frequently, however, the direction of assistance is maintained from transaction to transaction, from generation to generation, until the clients are either incorporated within their patron's clan, or until they terminate the relationship by reachieving their autonomy through discharging their obligation. But reachieving autonomy usually necessitates activating another dyadic relationship, thereby shifting dependence from one patron to another.

Thus, Chambri and Iatmul men gain power over others as they borrow and lend valuables to assist unrelated individuals to gain control of women and to win autonomy from their matrilateral kinsmen. Their patron–client relationships weave through their agnatic and affinal connections, adding organic solidarity to their otherwise mechanically organized societies. No Chambri or Iatmul is in any sociologically significant way different from any other, apart from his degree and kind of indebtedness. And it is in the differences established between individuals and groups through patronage that village strength resides, as they become committed to the irreplaceability of others in their lives.

This solidarity, then, is the product of marriage practices in which men consider valuables to be an adequate payment for women. And, at least among the Iatmul, these marriage practices developed along with and because of an increasing dependence upon regularized marketing; Iatmul villages grew, restricted marriages became less common, intravillage political connections ramified, hegemony developed, and barter markets were regularized.

The Chambri, however, are less easily understood. Their political consolidation does not seem to have demanded the regularized marketing between specialized producers of subsistence products. Mother's brother's daughter's marriage seems to have been their preferred form of marriage for at least as long as they have been living on their island. And they did not develop barter markets until after the European intrusion. In the next chapter I continue to discuss these differences by concentrating on the broader implications of interethnic trade and on the dual economy of the Chambri.

THE GROWTH AND INTEGRATION
OF CHAMBRI VILLAGES:
THE IATMUL DIRECTIVE

Chambri and Iatmul men could only gain freedom from the inequality-producing women who bore their sons by recompensing their matrilateral kinsmen with shell valuables. In this sense both peoples were alike. However, they acquired these valuables through different exchange relationships, and in this sense their positions within the regional socioeconomic system bore little resemblance to one another. While the river people acquired their sago and their valuables from the Sawos, the Chambri obtained each of these articles from a different source. Shell valuables entered the Middle Sepik from the north, passing from the Sawos through the Iatmul to the Chambri, until they left the region through the Sepik Hills. Sago, on the other hand, entered from both the north and the south—from the Sawos to the Iatmul and from the Hills people to the Chambri.

The situation had additional complexities centering on the production and use of specialized commodities. The Chambri produced the stone adzes and mosquito bags that they introduced into their trading partnerships with Hills men, obtaining specialized foodstuffs, feathers, tree sap, and timber in return. But the Iatmul used shell valuables to purchase Chambri products and then sold their acquisitions to the Sawos for additional valuables. Thus, the Iatmul were the middlemen of the region, using Chambri products to acquire the valuables with which they obtained further products. It is with this relationship—between producer and entrepreneur—that we must begin to unravel the history of Chambri development.

Chambri Origins

The Chambri tell the following story about their origins: Emosuie Apankay, the pig-man, emerged from a hole on top of Chambri Mountain to found the tribe. His one biological son, Yambukay, accomplished the peopling of Chambri Island by inviting various outsiders to become his brothers and children, guaranteeing them land on which to live. Only two of these people,

Walintimi and Saun, were adopted as brothers. Both came from the Chambri Lake island of Peliagwi and lived with Yambukay at Indingai until Walintimi left to found Wombun and Saun to establish Kilimbit.[1] Fifteen men were adopted as sons, three from the island of Garamambu, one from the island of Peliagwi, three from smaller islands within the lake, two from a now defunct hamlet on the Korosameri River, one each from the Hills villages of Mensuat and Milae, one from the now abandoned Yerakai-speaking hamlet of Ame, and one each from the Iatmul villages of Nyaurengai, Suapmeri, and Parambei. These men, together with ten of the sons they sired after arriving on the island, are considered by the Chambri to be the founders of their twenty-eight original patriclans (see table 4.1). And thus they consider over two-thirds of their ancestors to be of foreign origin.[2]

Just where the Chambri did originate is lost in prehistory. Linguistically related to villages located east of them—to speakers of Murik, Angoram, Tabriak, and Yimas—the Chambri seem to have been cut off from these other members of the Nor Pondo language family[3] by the Ndu intrusion into the area from the headwaters of the Korosameri and Karawari tributaries (Dye et al., 1969: 154). Their language is not, therefore, a conglomerate of Sepik Hills, Yerakai, and Iatmul, as their myth implies.[4] But their origin story is true in this sense: the Chambri would not have survived the Iatmul rise to prominence within the region without intertribal alliances. The story is, thus, an explanation of these alliances in genealogical terms and, as such, an argument for their continuation.

The use of kinship terms to underwrite alliances is a very common rhetorical device throughout New Guinea, and the Chambri employ it frequently. The coda of the Abio-Wukio myth that I related in chapter 3, for example, has the marriage of the now freely excreting Wukio to his trading partner's second wife blessed with eleven sons, all of whom eventually migrate to their mother's territory where they are adopted into various Chambri patriclans. The Chambri tell this story to explain their friendship with certain men from Garamambu. But the rhetorical expression of intertribal political alliances in kinship terms is in sharp contradistinction to the real nature of Chambri alliances, which are rarely based on marriage. As I have shown in the last chapter, the Chambri are a highly endogamous people— marrying one another nearly 91 percent of the time. One would, of course, expect as much of them, since they have maintained their own language over the hundreds of years they have been surrounded by and interacting with Ndu, Yerakai, and Sepik Hills speakers.

Not kinship based, Chambri political alliances were largely composed of individual trading partnerships maintained by the dependence of others upon Chambri products. As Assistant District Commissioner L. W. Bragge put it, "Chambris held a notable position in traditional trade patterns, being the

Table 4.1: The Patriclan Founders

Village	Men's House	Clan Founder	Place of Origin
Indingai	Mumbukumbit	Sekumbumeri	Nyaurengai Garamambu
		Wobanowi	Indingai (Wobanowi's son)
		Kwolimbebank	
	Yangarambit	Yambukay	Indingai (Emosuie's son)
		Bukian	Small island
	Mangembit	Sakware	Small island
		Mangemeri	Milae
		Nogusamay	Small island
		Simbenakwan	Kabentume on the Korosameri River
	Wansikimbit	Minginor	Garamambu
		Pangantimi	Ame
	Wiarmankeko	Simbuksaun	Parambei
		Kwiamemp	Peliagwi
		Yalus	Timbunmeri
Wombun	Wombunkeko	Walintimi	Peliagwi
	Nambaraman	Andikubak	Indingai (Wobanowi's son)
		Waranupan	Garamambu
	Mindimbit	Simbinakwan	Kabantume on the Korosameri River
		Kasayeli	Mensuat
		Kwolisupan	Indingai (Kwiamemp's son)
	Simboraman	Waingwunsat	Indingai (Kapwesaun's son)
Kilimbit	Suapmeriagwi	Saun	Peliagwi
	Kilimbit	Palambo	Suapmeri
		Wiarambank	Indingai (Pangantimi's son)
	Olimbit	Pangantimi	Indingai (Pangantimi's son)
	Kwaramopwi	Woliwobwe	Indingai (Yambukay's son)
		Masombank	Indingai (Yambukay's son)
	Aparowkwi	Bukian	Indingai (Bukian's son)

stone axe blade producers for the Middle Sepik, and they have therefore lived in considerable peace" (1973: page unknown).

My suspicion is that Chambri society evolved in the following manner: until they began integrating themselves within the economy established by the Iatmul, the Chambri lived a semimigratory, hunting and gathering existence. They resembled the Hills people more than the Iatmul, until the latter became increasingly interested in acquiring the valuable shells they needed to engage in affinal exchange. At this point, the Iatmul began to encourage the Chambri to supply them with the specialized commodities they needed for trade with the Sawos. In return for supplying the stone tools and mosquito bags which the Iatmul traded for these valuables, the Chambri were allowed to remain unmolested.

The data upon which I base this evolutionary reconstruction consist of three sets of facts. First, my informants consistently spoke of the "time before," when their ancestors were "bush pigs." Indeed, I was shown the remains of settlements on top of Chambri Mountain that were, they said, their original hunting and gathering camps. Moreover, the Chambri date certain totemic names from this "time before"—before they adopted elements of Iatmul culture. These elements include most of the Chambri's proper nouns, which have no lexical meaning in their own language. Thus, although they will admit that the names of the founders of the three Chambri villages are Iatmul in origin, they speak of "bush spirits" who have Chambri names, and who possess the real strength and substance of the Chambri people. Emosuie Apankay is one of these bush spirits and, together with Mepurkumban and Yerenowi, his compatriots from Wombun and Kilimbit, respectively, is considered the "root of Chambri power."

The second set of facts does not even concern the Chambri but, rather, another Middle Sepik people whom I have not yet introduced, the Aibom. These people also live on an island within Chambri Lake, and are the producers of the pottery used throughout the region (see Schuster, 1969). Their island is rich in clay, from which the women shape the hearths, sago-storage jars, and griddles used by every Iatmul, Chambri, Sawos, and Hills housewife. Thus, like the Chambri, they produce a commodity that is extremely important to the domestic economy of every tribal group within the region. And, like the Chambri, their history seems to have been neither peaceful nor settled until they began to do so. I reproduce a composite of six versions of Aibom history as it was reported by informants from Iatmul, Chambri, Sepik Hills, and Aibom villages, before discussing its relevance to Chambri origins.

> The Aibom originated on Peliagwi Island. They were nomadic hunters and gatherers who used the island of Aibom as a temporary fishing site, living in caves while there. Eventually, a few of these people left Peliagwi to settle at Aibom permanently. But they still felt attached to their original home, for "it was part of our meat we left back there, our spirits and ancestors were still there."
>
> These original Aibom may have spoken a language unrelated to any other spoken in the region, although some informants argue that it was similar to that now spoken in the Hills hamlet of Mensuat, and others say it was identical to Chambri.
>
> These early Aibom lived in fear of the Parambei Iatmul, who

eventually attacked and killed most of them. Faced with death, one of the settlers, Walintimi, fled to the Chambri village of Indingai where he was adopted by Yambukay. [This is the man who eventually founded the Chambri village of Wombun, which is why the Wombun and Aibom are close friends.] Walintimi's brother, Mepran, remained at Aibom, a defeated man with no friends or family.

Yambiyur, an Iatmul from Malingai whose mother came from Peliagwi, took pity on Mepran, and brought his family to live at Aibom. His descendants have lived there ever since, which is why the Aibom now speak Iatmul. They have lived in peace because all surrounding groups have been concerned to protect their source of pottery.

What I find particularly interesting about Aibom's history is its correspondence to that which I have suggested for the Chambri. I cannot determine whether the Aibom spoke Chambri, or when they arrived in their present location, but I think it logical that the initial Iatmul attack upon them occurred before they had begun to supply the region with ceramics, for afterward "all surrounding groups [became] concerned to protect their source of pottery." It seems, in fact, that the only way the Iatmul would tolerate sedentary neighbors was as sago-suppliers or commodity producers.

Whereas the first two sets of facts upon which my evolutionary reconstruction is based concern indigenous recollections of things past, the third set has a more objective status. Since my argument is that the Chambri lived unmolested because they supplied the Iatmul with specialized commodities, I can predict that they would suffer Iatmul attacks if they ever stopped doing so. And this seems to have been the case, for the European introduction of money, mosquito netting, and steel tools put an end to their usefulness—and to their peace. Since the turn of the century, the Chambri have been periodically attacked by Iatmul headhunting parties, and were exiled from their island by Parambei Iatmul for nearly twenty years, returning shortly before Margaret Mead and Reo Fortune worked with them in 1933. (See chapter 5 for a fuller discussion of this exile.)

I will discuss these Chambri–Iatmul wars in the next chapter. Here I wish to suggest that Chambri society—like that of the Sawos—evolved as the result of Iatmul hegemony. This is not to argue that the processes of change were identical, for the Chambri and the Sawos were not only very different peoples to begin with, but they also interacted with the Iatmul in different ways.

He Who Sits Down and He Who Walks About: A Historical Overview

There is a Chambri myth about Yambukay's loss of power suggesting a scenario close to the one that must have occurred once the Chambri settled on their island and began to trade with the Iatmul. The myth was told to me to explain differences between the wealth and power of certain Chambri patriclans. I think it is informative about social change in general.

> During the time of our fathers and ancestors, there were three important men living at Indingai, Yambukay—who was the headman of the bush, Walintimi—who was responsible for resolving the people's grievances, and Samanday—who was not as important as the other two.
>
> Now Yambukay was very strong, but Samanday was very attractive. He was best known for his beautiful jewelry, particularly for the shell valuables he wore around his neck. Yambukay's wife, Palawanpur, could not resist him, and they began to have sex together whenever they could.
>
> Walintimi told Yambukay about Palawanpur's unfaithfulness, but Yambukay did not believe him. Finally he agreed to test her. He sent her to ask Samanday to obtain sago from his Mensuat trading partner, using tobacco she would provide. Yambukay watched the two of them speak together, and saw Samanday squeeze Palawanpur's breasts. He knew then that Walintimi had been speaking the truth.
>
> Yambukay climbed Chambri Mountain. He gathered firewood and torches at Mingunsan, at Wenkopake, at Wanjinkowi, at Yanjarianpank, at Wandikan, at Injanaplan, at Changurin, and at Wobowe. He stopped at the places he knew well, eight places altogether. Finally, he arrived at Yenimp,[5] where many Chambri still lived. There, Yambukay made a spear from the roots of a bamboo plant, and called the spear Klimbangal. The people of Yenimp were afraid of Yambukay, because they knew that such a Big Man does not come for nothing.
>
> Returning to Chambri, Yambukay placed all of his pigs, roosters, and dogs in his house, promising them to Walintimi provided that he arrange to have Samanday brought to him. Walintimi agreed, and decided to invite Samanday to accompany him to Kilimbit the next day.
>
> Walintimi met Samanday near the Mubukumbit men's house at Indingai. As they walked toward Kilimbit, Walintimi began to complain of tiredness. As they approached the last of Indingai's women's houses, Walintimi told Samanday that he wished to rest inside, but that he had to catch his breath before climbing the house ladder. Samanday's son said that he would climb first. Now this young man wore jewelry just like his father's. When Yambukay, who was hiding underneath the house with his bamboo spear, heard the sound of the young man's necklaces clanging against one another, he thrust his spear between the rungs of the ladder, stabbing the boy in the foot. Samanday's son cried: "Father, I've been bitten by a snake!"

Samanday climbed the ladder next. Once again Yambukay thrust his spear between the rungs of the ladder. He stabbed Samanday through the testicles, and the spear emerged through Samanday's neck. Yambukay had killed him.

After announcing his deed on his split gong drum, Yambukay fled to Yenimp. All of the Chambri people who lived on the shore feasted on his dogs, pigs, and roosters. After the feast, they climbed Chambri Mountain and killed all of the people living there. They killed all of the Yenimp and all of the other mountain people. But Yambukay escaped.

Walintimi gave all of Yambukay's land to Samanday's descendants. That's how he resolved their grievances, and that is why they are very rich today. Today they all live in big houses and pay large bride-prices, while Yambukay's descendants are rubbish men.

The myth tells the story of a change in the political organization of Chambri villages, of the erosion of Yambukay's power-base by Samanday and his descendants. Yambukay begins as the more powerful—he is the leader of the bush. Samanday is a subordinate—he is not as powerful as either Walintimi or Yambukay, literally "underneath" them both.[6] But by the end of the story it is Samanday's descendants who inherit Yambukay's property. They become the payers of large bride-prices, while Yambukay's descendants become rubbish men.

The myth establishes five important differences between the two antagonists: Yambukay is a leader, while Samanday is his subordinate; Yambukay owns dogs, pigs, and roosters, while Samanday owns valuables; Yambukay knows the bush and can perform the magic of spear-naming, while Samanday is irresistibly attractive to women; Yambukay migrates from place to place, while Samanday maintains trading partnerships; and Yambukay's descendants decline in power, while Samanday's descendants rise in wealth. Let me discuss each of these differences in turn to determine their relevance to Chambri history.

The Leader and the Subordinate

Given what we know about the politics of affinal exchange in the Middle Sepik, one wonders whether the relationship between Yambukay and Samanday was that of patron to client, or whether it was predicated upon a different form of dominance. In the last chapter I described Chambri and Iatmul leaders as those who assist unrelated individuals to pay their affinal debts, but is this the kind of leader Yambukay seems to have been?

Walintimi is a more likely candidate for the position of patron. He is described as the man responsible for resolving problems, but he does so more in the fashion of Iago than Solomon. His resolution of the discord produced by Palawanpur's infidelity, for example, appears to be rather self-serving. With Yambukay vanquished and Samanday dead, it is Walintimi who allocates the remaining property. Indeed, the feast he decides to hold with Yambukay's dogs, pigs, and roosters may well have helped him maintain and extend his network of clients. Moreover, since it is Walintimi who gives Yambukay's property to Samanday's descendants, we can assume that he is in no great need of it himself; his largesse implies his even greater wealth.

Yambukay, as a man of action, is more like Othello. His solution to his wife's unfaithfulness is straightforward, and his leadership seems based more upon personal prowess than upon the manipulation of networks of clients.

Dogs, Pigs, Roosters, and Valuables

It could be that Yambukay was unable to establish these networks because he was without the necessary valuables. But more likely his rise to power occurred at a time when marriage did not involve the same kind of affinal debts that it does today.

If I am right in assuming that the Chambri were once semimigratory hunters and gatherers, then their marriage system may well have resembled that described by Townsend for the Heve of the Sepik Hills:

> The Heve clans are not exogamous in theory or in practice. . . . At least twenty percent of all marriages are between persons who are second cousins or closer. . . . All categories of cousin marriage occur: patrilateral and matrilateral, parallel and cross. . . . Marriage requires payment of bridewealth. . . . Bride prices are small . . . [and] form a nearly closed system; most of the shells given at a wedding were received in an earlier wedding and have not been used in the meantime. [1969: 142–46]

This marriage system is maximally flexible, a fact that should not surprise us, for, as Townsend suggests, hunter-gatherers seem to value mechanisms that allow them to adjust their populations to their resources (ibid.: 179).

What is most relevant about her description of the Heve marriage system, however, is the fact that it is "nearly closed." By this she means simply that the Heve have access to very few valuables. Living far from the source of shells, they save what few they acquire for investment and reinvestment in wives (ibid.: 145–47). Thus, the Heve marriage system is not closed because of structural considerations, but rather because of circumstances. If they had the opportunity of acquiring additional shells, they would certainly add them to their bride-prices. As it is, they can marry nearly anyone with whom they wish to establish a sociopolitical alliance and need pay only a small amount to do so.

The Chambri, like the Heve, also must have had little access to shell valuables until they began to supply the Iatmul with specialized commodities. I think it likely, therefore, that the growth of networks of control based on affinal relations is the direct result of trade with Iatmul. Indeed, the fact that most Chambri ceremonials—including their marriage, initiation, and birth rituals—are Iatmul in language and design, suggests that they developed after regular trading relationships had been established, a point I shall return to later in this chapter.

Yambukay, therefore, is an old-fashioned leader. Unlike Samanday, he owns only dogs, pigs, and roosters. He cannot establish networks of control, indeed he would not consider doing so, because in the world he lives in such networks do not and cannot exist.

The Spear and the Woman

Yambukay's power resides in his knowledge of his territory and in his adeptness at magic. He knows where he is going and what to do when he gets there, as do all successful leaders of hunting and gathering groups.

The people of Yenimp particularly fear his magical powers, for they know that Big Men do "not come for nothing." What Yambukay does come for is the bamboo from which to make a spear to kill Samanday, a spear he names "Klimbangal."

The naming of objects in order to imbue them with power is a very common Chambri and Iatmul custom. When an object is named, it internalizes the power of the ancestor for whom it is named. Each Chambri and Iatmul clan owns many of these totemic objects, about which they tell stories concerning their use through time. Some are considered to be more powerful than others, and these the Chambri attribute to the apical ancestors who brought them to Yambukay in payment for his initial gift of land. Thus, the ancestor Wobinowi is alleged to have come from Garamambu with a magic spear named Wandanakwi, and with a magic knife named Dumar. These he gave to Yambukay in return for land near the Mubukumbit men's house at Indingai. The ancestors Bukian and Sakware are said to have come from a small island within the lake, bringing Yambukay the two sacred flutes now named after their donors in return for land near the Indingai men's houses of Yangarambit and Mangembit, respectively.

The Chambri call all of these powerful objects by Iatmul names, indicating that the elaborate totemic system, of which the objects are crucial parts, did not exist among them prior to their incorporation within Iatmul trading networks. Certainly, if the Chambri had become sedentary prior to their establishment of trading relationships with the Iatmul, we would expect to find more than a few remnants of an indigenous social and ceremonial system.

Recalling that the immigration of foreigners to Chambri Island is a metaphor for the establishment of trading relationships between tribal groups, we can now see how Yambukay brought about his own downfall. By encouraging strangers to immigrate, he simultaneously admitted the valuables with which Samanday would distract Palawanpur and elevate his descendants to power; by supplying the Iatmul with specialized commodities, the Chambri became committed to playing the politics of affinal exchange, in which the man with the most valuables wins the women. If Yambukay had not named his spear for an Iatmul ancestor—if he had not adopted the Iatmul social and ceremonial organization—he might have kept his woman.

The Migrant and the Trader

As I played my recording of the Samanday-Yambukay myth for the informant who told it to me, he interrupted the tape to correct himself. He insisted that Palawanpur had not asked Samanday to acquire sago from his Mensuat trading partner, but had given him tobacco to obtain mussels. "Samanday," he now assured me, "would never ask his trading partner for sago; he was only interested in strong food."

This mistake bothered him so much that he wished to retape the entire story. He told me that the Chambri consider mussels and sago to be so different that they would laugh at him if they heard of his error. After I promised that I would play the tape for no other Chambri, he explained that mussels are considered a delicacy, while sago is just everyday fare. But, more significantly, the Chambri think of mussels as a masculine food, and of sago as a feminine one. The masculine identity of mussels is connected with the fact that the Chambri bake the mussel shells to produce lime for use as body powder in male-oriented rituals and as a condiment chewed with betel nut. In its latter capacity, the lime expresses certain exclusively male prerogatives. Women, for example, are not supposed to be seen using lime in public. But more importantly, men carry the lime in large cylindrical gourds, whose identity as phallic symbols is undeniable. To extract the powder they use bone spatulas, grooved to make a loud grating noise when withdrawn from the gourds; the louder the noise, the better the gourd, and the more it advertises the prowess of its owner. A man will further enhance his gourd by attaching feathers to the spatula, each representing a death he claims to have arranged in warfare or through sorcery. Mussels, from whose shells the lime held by the gourd is made, connote masculine potency in sex, in warfare, and in politics. It was Samanday's capacity to acquire this food that my informant was concerned to make clear.

The myth portrays Yambukay, on the other hand, as a hunter and gatherer, migrating through his territory—moving to "eight places altogether" (i.e., throughout Chambri Island) in search of firewood before arriving at Yenimp, where he makes the spear. He is not described as having trading partnerships with anyone, and his activities appear far more domestic and intrinsically focused than do Samanday's. Whereas Yambukay is interested in avenging his wife's infidelity, Samanday is preoccupied with extrinsic and extradomestic exchanges that bring him the goods necessary to win women and power.

The Decline of Yambukay and the Fall of Samanday

Interestingly, although those Chambri informants with whom I discussed the story found Yambukay the more sympathetic of the two antagonists, they perceived Samanday as the more successful. They would tell me that: "Yambukay is a good man, but Samanday is smart—a winner." And when I asked them about Samanday's death, they would say: "He should have known better than to have fooled around with another man's wife. He was stupid for himself, but smart for his children."

Although my informants may have meant no more by their words than we do by the adage Nice Guys Finish Last, the story and their discussion of it have wider implications. Yambukay, after all, did finish last. And my informants are all Samanday's descendants in the sense that they live very much like the Iatmul—in large and sedentary villages with complex social and ceremonial organizations. They do so only because the "Samandays" of their past incorporated increasing amounts of valuable shells into their marriage system. Once this was done, the Chambri became irreversibly committed to supplying specialized commodities to the Iatmul in return for the valuables they needed to pay their affinal debts.

Intratribal Transformations

I do not mean to give the impression that the Chambri were created by the Iatmul to act as commodity producers. Nor do I wish to underemphasize the importance of Iatmul hegemony to Chambri evolution. The fact of the matter is that Chambri social organization developed as the result of two interrelated processes, one external and the other internal. First, their permanent settlement on Chambri Island was encouraged by the Iatmul who needed their specialized products. Second, the Chambri themselves became increasingly interested in acquiring shell valuables from the Iatmul in order to play at the politics of affinal exchange, a game made even more problematic by the fact that not every Chambri had equal access to the means of production. Having discussed the first process at some length, I turn here to a discussion of the internal factors contributing to the development of Chambri social organization.

In regard to ownership of the means of production, perhaps the most important cultural belief was this: The six Chambri quarries were thought to be inhabited by particular ancestors, and each was supervised by one of that ancestor's descendants. A quarry's custodian would allow unrelated individuals access to the stone resource only if they organized the ceremonies necessary to pacify the *uncheban* who dwelled within the stone. The ceremonies were costly. The prospective quarry-user not only had to provide enough food to satisfy the owners and other guests, but he also had to recompense the custodian for use of the resource. Fortunately, the feast-givers could invite their wife-takers, who would be forced, as at all ceremonies, to reciprocate with shell valuables for the food provided by their wives' brothers. And a deft manipulator would use these affinal payments to recompense the quarry custodian.

But not all men could be so adroit. Some would already have pledged all affinal payments to their own wife-givers. Others would have sisters' husbands who refused to attend the ceremony. And still others would be incapable of even initiating the process for want of sufficient feast foods. Thus, although all men could theoretically gain access to the valuable stone resource, only some men could in fact do so. And these men tended to be either the owners of the quarries or those who could afford to pay for usufruct without depending on affinal contributions.

As might be expected, the latter category was generally filled by wife-givers to the quarry-owners, who were the recipients of generous affinal payments. And there were quite a few of these. Quarry-owners not only married more women than nonowners, but also tended to diversify their marriage partners or, as the Chambri describe it, "marry all around the place."

It is impossible to substantiate this point with much statistical data. My genealogies are most accurate for individuals who married after the introduction of steel tools, while Mead and Fortune only had time to complete a preliminary household survey of approximately half of the Chambri population. Mead's field notes, however, are complete about the polygamous marriages of nineteen men from eight of the fifteen different Chambri men's houses. Although these particular men's houses were inhabited by members of only three of the quarry-owning clans, other coresidents had given women to men of the additional groups of quarry-owners. Table 4.2, which summarizes this data, indicates that eight of the polygamists were themselves quarry-owners, while another five were wife-givers to quarry-owners. Moreover, while only two of the remaining six polygamists married women from outside their villages, seven of the quarry-owners and their affines practiced village exogamy. It seems, therefore, that the Chambri perception is correct—quarry-owners and their wife-givers did "marry all around," at least in comparison to their non-quarry-owning neighbors.

Although the quarry-owners undoubtedly diversified their marriages in order to display their abilities to manage many large affinal debts, their marriage proclivities had the effect of easing access to the stone resource.

Table 4.2: The Marriages of Nineteen Men as Recorded by Margaret Mead in 1933[a]

Man	Village	Men's House	Clan	Quarry-Owner or Wife-Giver[b]	Wife	Village	Men's House	Clan
1	Indingai	Yangaraman	Mongemali	Q-O	1	Indingai	Boroboraman[c]	?
					2	Kilimbit	Kilimbit	?
					3	Kilimbit	Olimbit	?
					4	Kilimbit	Olimbit	?
2	Indingai	Mongeimbit	Mongemali	Q-O	1	Indingai	Yangaraman	Mongemali
					2	Wombun	Wombun	?
3	Indingai	Mongeimbit	Mongemali	Q-O	1	Indingai	Boroboraman	Yamboke
					2	Mensuat	—	
					3	Changriman	—	
4	Indingai	Mongeimbit	Asanapwon	—	1	Kilimbit	Olimbit	Yabanunk
					2	Indingai	Yangaraman	Mongemali
5	Indingai	Wandjikinbit	Noungkwe	W-G	1	Indingai	Mongeimbit	Mongemali
					2	Indingai	Mambokinbit	?
					3	Indingai	Mambokinbit	?
					4	Indingai	Mambokinbit	?
6	Indingai	Wandjikinbit	Noungkwe	W-G	1	Indingai	Yangaraman	Yabanunk
					2	Indingai	Yangaraman	Yabanunk
7	Indingai	Boroboraman	Yalush	—	1	Indingai	Boroboraman	Mongemali
					2	Indingai	Wandjikinbit	Yamboke
8	Kilimbit	Soinmaliyapkwi	Nambut	W-G	1	Indingai	Mongeimbit	?
					2	Kilimbit		?
9	Kilimbit	Soinmaliyapkwi	Nambut	W-G	1	Indingai	Wandjikinbit	?
					2	Wombun	Wombun	?

Man	Village	Men's House	Clan	Quarry-Owner or Wife-Giver[b]	Wife	Village	Men's House	Clan
10	Kilimbit	Soinmaliyapkwi	Nambut	W-G	1	Kilimbit	Kilimbit	?
					2	Kilimbit	Kilimbit	?
11	Kilimbit	Soinmaliyapkwi	Yakum	Q-O	1	Kilimbit	Olimbit	?
					2	Indingai	Mambokinbit	?
					3	Indingai	Mambokinbit	?
12	Kilimbit	Soinmaliyapkwi	Yamboke	Q-O	1	Kilimbit	Soinmaliyapkwi	?
					2	Kilimbit	Soinmaliyapkwi	?
13	Kilimbit	Soinmaliyapkwi	Yundunamp	—	1	Kilimbit	Olimbit	?
					2	Kilimbit	Kilimbit	?
					3	Kilimbit	Kilimbit	?
14	Kilimbit	Kwalamokwi	Yakum	Q-O	1	Kilimbit	Kilimbit	?
					2	Kilimbit	Kilimbit	?
15	Kilimbit	Olimbit	Yamboke	Q-O	1	Kilimbit	Kwalamokwi	?
					2	Kilimbit	Kwalamokwi	?
					3	Indingai	Mongeimbit	?
					4	Indingai	Mongeimbit	?
16	Wombun	Agitman	Manuwi	—	1	Wombun	Wombun	?
					2	Wombun	Nambukaraman	?
17	Wombun	Wombun	Numbugke	Q-O	1	Indingai	Boroboraman	?
					2	Indingai	Boroboraman	?
18	Wombun	Wombun	Weinkwendjap	—	1	Wombun	Nambukaraman	?
					2	Wombun	Agitman	?
19	Wombun	Wombun	Weinkwendjap	—	1	Wombun	Wombun	?
					2	Indingai	Mambokinbit	?

[a]Data taken from Mead; unpublished census information. I have used her spellings throughout.
[b]Information pertaining to quarry ownership is my own.
[c]The men's house called Boroboraman by Mead is today named Wiarmankeko.

But rather than equalizing the economic differences between themselves and nonowners, the numerous wives taken by the quarry-owners tended to increase them. Wives were, after all, the producers of the other major Chambri commodity—the woven mosquito bags—and the men who married many women also acquired many primary producers.

This last point needs some qualification, for not every Chambri woman produced the bags. The work was tedious and time-consuming, involving the endless interlacing of dried sago shoots and bast to produce a mesh fine enough to prevent mosquitoes from penetrating its weave. Taking weeks to finish, the task was simply unsuited to the temperaments of some Chambri women. Thus, the women who were good at weaving the bags were highly valued and, generally, fetched high bride-prices. These the quarry-owners could easily pay, resulting in their marriages to the finest mosquito bag producers. Indeed, of the nine Indingai women remembered by seven informants (three men and four women) as excellent and hard-working weavers, five were married to members of quarry-owning clans.

It seems, therefore, that the rich got richer through their marriages to productive women. But the situation was not quite as simple as this, for Chambri men—including quarry-owners—did not directly control the valuables their wives earned. Instead, women could allocate their valuables as they cared to, provided they did not offend those upon whom they depended for protection. In other words, a woman really only had the choice of allocating her valuables to two individuals, her brother or her husband.[7] Thus, marriages to proficient mosquito-bag producers did allow the rich to become richer, but the category of rich men included both the husbands and the brothers of these productive women—both quarry-owners and their wife-givers.

Margaret Mead makes too much of a woman's freedom to allocate her valuables when she describes the relationship between men and their wives' revenues in the following way:

> when a man has the final negotiations for one of his wives' mosquito-bags in hand, he goes off . . . to spend a delightful few days over the transaction. He will hesitate and equivocate. . . . But only with his wife's approval can he spend the *talibun* and *kina* and the strings of *conus* rings that he brings back from his holiday. He has wheedled a good price from the purchaser; he has still to wheedle the items of the price from his wife. [1963: 254]

Two of Mead's suggestions need qualification. First of all, she fails to make clear the degree to which the valuables a man brought back from his trading expeditions differ from money. They could not, for example, be easily used to acquire sago or other subsistence products. Indeed, their primary use was in the payment of bride-prices and other affinal debts; secondarily, they were traded to the Hills people for valued feathers, tree sap, and hard woods. Women had neither interest in nor use for these specialized objects, and although we might expect them to try to control the course of affinal relationships, they do not seem to have done so.

Today, women rarely invest the revenues they control in affinal exchanges, a fact I will verify in chapter 8. Indeed, they are far more concerned to acquire subsistence products with the money they earn than they are to invest in marriage transactions. Men, on the other hand, tend to horde what they earn until they can mount a large ceremony at which they recompense their matrilateral kinsmen. If this contrast prevails at a time when the same valuables—e.g., money—can be used for both affinal exchanges and subsistence transactions, I feel safe in predicting that Chambri women were never much involved in manipulating affinal debts. In fact, older Chambri women will say that they never had much use for shell valuables, and that they only wove mosquito bags when their families and friends needed them, or when pressured by their husbands or brothers to do so.

It was not, then, from his wife that a man had to wheedle valuables. Rather, he had to induce his wife to wheedle them away from her brothers. As members of two different corporate groups, each of which had use for the valuable shells, and both of which claimed rights in the same women, these men surreptitiously fought for control of mosquito-bag revenues. Each tried to influence his sister or wife to disenfranchise the other. I frequently heard arguments between brothers and sisters like the following:

> *Kosemp:* "Apendoi tells me that you sold two baskets[8] when the tourists came and I was with the Father. Is this true? And why have I not received a present of two dollars from you? Am I not the child of your mother's blood?"
> *Kosempandoi:* "I did not sell two baskets, just one small one, and I gave the money to Wampi for Godfried's chicken."
> *Kosemp:* "Why did you do this? Am I not your brother, and don't you owe me allegiance?"
> *Kosempandoi:* "This is rubbish-talk. You only call me sister after I've sold a basket to the tourists."

Nearly identical conversations I have heard between husbands and wives indicate that brothers and husbands both pressure their women to ignore the other.

This leads to the second of Mead's suggestions that requires qualification. By confusing work and power, she is led to assume erroneously that the activities of Chambri men were secondary and frivolous. Consider, for example, her description of the importance of Chambri women to their economic system.

For food, the people depend upon the fishing of the women. Men never fish unless a sudden school of fish appears in the lake, when they may leap in canoes in a frolicsome spirit, and spear a few fish. . . . But the real business of fishing is controlled entirely by women. For traded fish they obtain sago, taro and areca-nut. And the most important manufacture, the mosquito-bags . . . are made entirely by women. . . . Real property, which one actually owns, one receives from women. . . . Once one has obtained it, it becomes a counter in the games that men play; it is no longer concerned with the underlying economics of life, but rather with showing one's appreciation of one's brother-in-law, soothing someone's wounded feelings, behaving very handsomely when a sister's son falls down in one's presence. The minor war and peace that goes on all the time among the men, the feelings that are hurt and must be assuaged, are supported by the labour and contributions of the women. [Mead, 1963: 253–54]

But it is the games men play—affinal transactions and the patron–client relationships that develop from them—which define the rationale of Chambri socioeconomic life. These games, and the patrilineal organization within which they take place, determine the ownership of land and water rights, the assignment of women to their productive roles, and the distribution of the products of labor. To consider them secondary is comparable to calling capital formation the by-product of assembly-line activities.

Although it is true, then, that both men and women are pressed by kinsmen to meet affinal debts, the pressure constraining women is quite different from that facing men. A woman's identity—her self-image and position within Chambri society—is not affected by her success or failure in affinal exchange. She has, in effect, established her husband's debt by figuring as the primary item of exchange. Her husband, her father, and her brothers may ask her to assist them, but their insistence is particularistic, as it is based upon dyadic relationships between the woman and each of these men. Men, on the contrary, succeed or fail as members of corporate groups.

Fortune, who analyzed the mother's brother's daughter's marriage system of the Chambri, felt that women there did belong to de facto corporate groups, insofar as female clan co-members tended to marry into the same patriclan. He wrote:

The most interesting social consequence of this system is that it is impossible for a man to marry a woman without his creating a lien in perpetuity upon the male line she comes from in favour of his male descendants. The women who are sisters of a male line are in entail, so to speak, to a vis-à-vis male line. . . . [Since] the social drama is conceived as a play between patrilineal lines, women become the object of liens in perpetuity, and this type of entail is

> validated by payments made against it by those whom it bene-
> fits. . . . It will be clearly evident that with mother's brother's
> daughter marriage, where the marriage is socially arranged be-
> tween a male line and a vis-à-vis female line, the practice of women
> in lien and in entail between kinship lines is likely to be lost, for
> the women are grouped in a social formation which stands in its
> own right. [1933: 3 and 8–9]

Given a marriage system in which patrilocality means moving a few hundred yards from where you were born, and frequently in the company of your sisters, and given the possibility of earning shell valuables for investment in affinal transactions through mosquito-bag production, one wonders why there is no indication that Chambri women ever behaved as a corporate group with political clout. Even Mead, who argues for the dominance of Chambri women, concentrates more on their behavioral style than she does on their ability to command the actions of others (see Mead, 1963, and Gewertz, 1981).

Of course, to ask why Chambri women never entered the public domain is to assume that they should have—and would have—if they could have done so, and this may be merely an ethnocentric assumption of twentieth century social scientists. The fact of the matter is simply that Chambri women were not particularly interested in manipulating affinal transactions in order to gain public recognition and power, but preferred to leave what they may indeed have considered foolishness up to their men. In fact, the more I asked Chambri women about their political activities, the more I became convinced that my questions were irrelevant to them.

Moreover, those women who were grouped together as social formation through mother's brother's daughter's marriage would be those least likely to have any real political power, primarily because their husbands, fathers, and brothers had no real power themselves. Quarry-owners never practiced mother's brother's daughter's marriage, and it was preferred only by what we might call "middle-class clans," those whose sufficient but not excessive resources were equally committed in both the wife-giving and wife-taking directions. In other words, mother's brother's daughter's marriage was a ref-uge from the politics of affinal exchange, not an invitation for women to practice it.

As Fortune has told us, within a mother's brother's daughter's marriage system it "is impossible for a man to marry a woman without his creating a lien in perpetuity upon the male line she comes from in favor of his male descendants" (1933: 3). This perpetual lien, however, was only a theoretical construct among the Chambri. Wife-givers frequently preferred to marry their daughters to successful clansmen who would pay large bride-prices and maintain a high level of affinal exchange. Wife-takers, on the other hand, depending on how wealthy and powerful they were, would either try to acquire inexpensive women or display their success by marrying high-priced women. Nearly 30 percent of Chambri patriclans, however, married members of their mother's brother's clans, and still seem to do so. As I have said earlier, these were the clans whose sufficient resources were equally committed in both the wife-giving and wife-taking directions. In order to operate properly, a mother's brother's daughter's marriage system had to involve a minimum of three clans. Women moved from clan A to B, from B to C, and from C to A, while valuables moved, in repayment for these women and their future children, in the opposite direction, from A to C, from C to B, and from B to A. Thus the relationships between A, B, and C were equitable, with all three clans both giving and receiving women and affinal recompense. Wife-givers acquired necessary valuables from wife-takers, and the marriage system was, at least temporarily, self-contained and self-sufficient.

The system worked very well until one of the clans was forced to increase its outlay of ceremonial valuables. This occurred most frequently when its wife-givers' daughters achieved maturity and became marriageable. Each time wife-takers who practiced mother's brother's daughter's marriage had to give bride-prices to acquire wives for their sons, they had difficulty amassing the necessary valuables. Those valuables they periodically received from the clans of their own daughters' husbands were used to pay for their present wives and children. There was little—if anything—to spare, certainly not enough to acquire new brides.

They could not remedy this situation by increasing their production and sale of stone tools. They did not have direct access to the stone resource and could not increase production without an initial outlay of valuables to the quarries' custodians.

The only way for clans practicing mother's brother's daughter's marriage to contribute more to their wife-givers, was to receive more from their wife-takers. And each mother's brother had the power to do this, by arranging for the initiation of his sister's son. He thereby acquired the valuables he needed to amass bride-price, while increasing the number of potentially productive males among his wife-takers. His wife-takers may have later been able to pay him a larger amount of valuables because there was a greater number of producers of stone tools among them. And, as importantly, initiated men would marry and thereby acquire wives who would, perhaps, produce mosquito bags. Moreover, these men married their uncles' classificatory daughters, thereby obligating themselves to maintain affinal exchange relationships, and so triggering another round of initiations.

In other words, when maternal uncles initiated their nephews in order to acquire valuables, the nephews had to obtain women who made it possible for them to meet their affinal obligations. To acquire these women they had to pay bride-price, and to do so they, in turn, initiated their own sisters' sons. Thus, initiations, marriages, and affinal exchanges maintained the mother's brother's daughter's marriage system, which impeded, at least for a time, the designs of large clans practicing the politics of affinal exchange (see Gewertz, 1982).

The equitability of the system depended upon its participants' coordinating their marriages, birth payments, initiations, and funerals so as simultaneously to accommodate their wife-givers and be accommodated by their wife-takers. This balancing of input to outlay was nearly impossible to accomplish and the mother's brother's daughter's marriage system was therefore inherently unstable. The "middle class clans" that practiced it inevitably failed to accommodate their affines and were taken on as clients of their larger neighbors, who were frequently quarry-owners.

The Factors Impelling Change in Social Groups

It seems, then, that Chambri society was once three-tiered, the uppermost tier consisting of the quarry-owners, who controlled access to the most important natural resource; the second of the wife-givers to the owners, who had unimpeded access to the quarries; and the third comprising the remaining clans, who practiced mother's brother's daughter's marriage until they were incorporated as clients within a clan from tier one or two. The question thus becomes, why didn't hierarchical control replace egalitarian competition as the organizing principle of Chambri society? Or, to put it simply, why didn't the quarry-custodians become chiefs?

Hierarchical societies or chiefdoms are predicated upon specialized production of commodities that are redistributed by powerful chiefs through extensive descent or local groups, and "most chiefdoms seem to have risen where important regional exchange and a consequent increase in local specialization came about because ecological differentiation was combined with considerable sedentariness" (Service, 1962: 146). The descent groups are dependent upon one another and upon the chief because no one of them has access to all the necessary resource zones. But, if all the descent groups had access to the same resource zones, then the ties between descent groups would probably not be maintained. Chambri clans all had access to the same resources, except for stone. This difference between them was simply not enough to institute hierarchic control, not because stone was insignificant to the operation of the Chambri socioeconomic system, but because its ownership resulted in certain insoluble structural dilemmas.

One of these was that the disproportionate growth of some clans eventually triggered their decline. In fact, the limits of growth were built into the relationships that integrated the system. An ordinary man who married a woman from a large clan found it difficult to meet his affinal obligations. He was forced to seek assistance from an unrelated group and thereby condemned himself to client status or to being incorporated within the patron clan. Thus, men from unusually populous and wealthy clans found it difficult to find husbands for their sisters, because their status demanded that they set high bride-prices on them. The greatest incidence of intraclan marriage occurred within the wealthiest clans. Once they had split and intermarried, the two new clans interacted as complementary affines, with separate relationships to all other "equal" clans within the village.

Such was the case of the Yambukay clan, which split to form Mangemeri in around 1860. This event is particularly interesting because the Yenimp quarry is said to have closed down while its ownership was being debated after the two clans separated. Mangemeri eventually prevailed, primarily because it had become wife-giver to Yambukay. During the unsettled time, no one gained access to the quarry, causing many political realignments throughout the three Chambri villages. And after the ownership was resolved, Mangemeri found itself in much the same position as Yambukay had occupied before—in control of a scarce resource, but incapable of displaying its wealth by charging high bride prices for fear of finding no buyers. Indeed, the only two cases of intraclan marriage recorded by Margaret Mead in her field notes occurred between members of Yambukay and between members of Mangemeri—the latter then being, in terms of clan size and number of wives per adult male, the wealthiest clan in the village of Indingai (see table 4.3).

Hence, disproportionately "more" or "less equal" clans could no longer

Table 4.3: The Wealth of Certain Indingai Clans

Clan	No. of Adult Males	No. of Married Men Recorded	No. of Chambri Wives Recorded
Kwalemémbank	6	1	1
Tchukúmbimali	2	1	1
Mongémali	6	5	11
Ashpanapwan	2	1	2
Noúngkwe	2	2	6
Kwinaṁbi	2	2	2
Yálush	1	1	1
Andikábak	2	2	2
Yamboké	4	2	2
Wopwonápwi	1	?	?
Mongéinaul	1	?	?
Yabanunk	2	?	?
Yelapalon	1	?	?
Weinkwendjap	1	?	?
Kandein	1	?	?

Source: Data taken from Margaret Mead's unpublished field notes.

adequately play for prestige but were designated as nonegalitarian and hence defined as out of the game that went on among the "equals." To put it simply, "less equal" clans lacked the valuables necessary to enter the competition, while "more equal" clans lacked willing partners. If the former could have acquired the necessary valuables without accepting patronage, they could have continued longer in the game. By the same token, the "more equal" clans would undoubtedly have found contenders if valuables had been more easily available.

It may be objected that a truly powerful clan, capable of indebting many of its neighbors, would redefine the rules of the game in such a way as to preclude its own exclusion. But we must not forget that the rules were not, ultimately, Chambri-imposed, for the ownership of quarries did not automatically provide valuables. Valuables, rather, had to be acquired from the Iatmul, and in a manner satisfactory to the Iatmul.

5

THE KAMANBO EXILE AND THE IMPORTATION OF CULTURE TO THE HILLS

When I discussed the evolution of barter markets among the Iatmul and Sawos, I suggested that the relationships between these groups were characterized by two very different dependencies. Each people relied upon the other for both food and specialized goods, the Iatmul trading surplus fish for sago and Chambri- produced specialized commodities for the shell valuables acquired by the Sawos from the Abelam. The Iatmul needed the sago to support their expanding villages, and the shells to maintain political integration within them. But, while they were able to exert control over the supply of sago through periodic military incursions into Sawos territory, they were incapable of directly affecting the provision of shell valuables. They could not, after all, coerce their Sawos partners into supplying them with valuables that these men did not have and could not produce. Thus, as the Iatmul need for sago continued to grow, they were increasingly faced with the problem of how to insure a steady flow without alienating their suppliers of shell valuables.

This alienation was not simply the result of an Iatmul propensity to take Sawos heads occasionally. As I suggested in chapter 2, trading partners were obliged to provide each other with safe conduct. Should war break out between their villages, they were to act as mediators and, if necessary, as protectors of their partners and their partners' clan co-members. If they fulfilled these obligations, warfare between their villages would not cause them to break off relations. Kwaremanki, it will be remembered, continued to act as Kanda's trading partner long after the Garamambu and the Chambri were at war. Indeed, it was he who had instigated the war (see chapter 2, pp. 41–42).

What Sawos trading partners would not have been able to tolerate, however, was the unequal exchange rate characteristic of fish-for-sago barter. Exchanges between trading partners were invariably set to the productive capacities of each individual, both partners striving to maintain equality between the items exchanged.

Thus, the necessity of insuring a regularized supply of sago through the maintenance of a one-for-one exchange rate threatened the developing integration of Iatmul villages by alienating those who supplied the valuables necessary to maintain this integration. It is my contention that by separating the domestic from the public domains—by allowing women to control subsistence transactions—the Iatmul overcame this threat. So long as their Sawos trading partners could associate the barter of sago with "inferior" and inherently "unequal" women, they would continue to supply Iatmul men with shell valuables on a reciprocal basis. In other words, the Iatmul affected the separation of the domestic and public domains in response to a conflict of interests experienced by Sawos men—as a means of allowing the Sawos to overlook the conflict's relevance to their personal trading relationships.

In this chapter I support my contention through a comparison with the Chambri data, which are far more complete than their Iatmul equivalents, the events they describe having occurred relatively recently. I shall demonstrate that Chambri women gained control of subsistence marketing when it became convenient for their men to separate the domestic from the political domains, and that this convenience was, primarily, Iatmul-induced. In other words, the Chambri were as unconscious of their dependency upon Iatmul goodwill as the Sawos were of the Iatmul propensity to generalize the category of "inferior bartering women" to include all of Sawos society. Both peoples suffered from false consciousness by denying the pervasiveness of Iatmul hegemony.

We must keep in mind, however, that although both the Chambri and the Sawos were transformed under Iatmul hegemony, each people experienced a unique process of change. While the Chambri became dependent upon the valuables provided by the Iatmul in exchange for the commodities they produced, the Sawos needed both commodities and fish in exchange for sago. While the Sawos's dependence upon the Iatmul was subsistence oriented, the Chambri needed exchange items for ceremonial and political purposes, a difference that will help us understand the contrasting histories of their barter markets.

Ritual Regulation

If my Chambri informants' fathers were told about Iatmul hegemony, I am sure that they would deny its relevance to them. Every indication suggests that, until 1900, the Chambri thought of the Iatmul— particularly of the Nyaula-speaking Iatmul—as their best friends, their staunchest allies, their classificatory brothers.[1] Consider, for example, the following Chambri story, which is still told today as an explanation of why Chambri Island is stationary.

When the land was new, Chambri Island was not fastened, but floated all throughout the Sepik—close to Timbunmeri, close to Suapmeri, and close to Kandingai.

One day, as it drifted near Kandingai, Kwolimbank happened by. He pulled his canoe up to the island, thinking it just a clump of floating grass.[2]

All of a sudden, Kwolimbank heard a pig sing out: "Who's there?"

Kwolimbank answered the pig: "Don't kill me. I'm Kwolimbank. I'm not a man; I'm half dog and half bat."

Emosuie Apankay came out from his rock and said: "Don't you kill me. I'm not a man. I'm half pig."

Kwolimbank boarded the floating island to give Emosuie a *tanget*. He said: "In six days you and I will meet here to exchange betel nuts and food." Emosuie took the *tanget* and reentered his stone home.

When the six days were up, Kwolimbank arrived to meet his friend, but Emosuie never showed up. Chambri Island had floated away, and the pig couldn't navigate it back to Kandingai. Kwolimbank, therefore, returned to his home, loaded a large canoe full of food, and set off in search of the pig-man.

Finding the island near Sunmali,[3] Kwolimbank called out: "Emosuie, where are you sleeping? I came to trade with you after six days, but you never arrived. It's no good that I must search for you throughout the water."

Emosuie brought many different wild fruits with him from inside his stone, and the two friends ate together. After they finished, Emosuie spoke: "Let's work our strongest powers to anchor this island."

They made a soup from their excrement and from insects and dirt. After they drank it, Kwolimbank worked his power over a piece of palm bark, while Emosuie worked his over a small boulder. Each recited totemic names over his object, and when finished, they threw them into the water hole close to the Yangarambit men's house. The boulder and the bark sank to the bottom of the hole, and Chambri Island was anchored fast.[4]

The Chambri consider Kwolimbank and Emosuie—the apical ancestors of the Kandingai Iatmul and the Chambri, respectively—to be jointly responsible for securing Chambri Island. Indeed, until relatively recently, when relations between Kandingai and Chambri soured as a result of Nyaula incursions into Chambri territory, the Chambri called Kandingai "the fourth Chambri village," because its inhabitants descended from "our ancestor's comrade, Kwolimbank."[5] Moreover, although I do not wish to make too much of this aspect of the myth for want of additional indicators, it seems that the Chambri recognize, on some level, the importance of stone to their permanent settlement. Emosuie Apankay, after all, uses a stone boulder to anchor his island, and he does so in order to regularize trade with the Iatmul.

What is most interesting about the story, however, is the nature of the relationship it portrays between Emosuie and Kwolimbank. Theirs seems to be a relationship of absolute equality. Both are afraid of each other. Both bring foodstuffs to trade. Both anchor the island. And both desire to do so.

I do not know what the Iatmul thought of the Chambri during the years they were supplied by them with stone tools. Those of their sons who discussed this matter with me suggested that while their fathers held the Chambri in contempt as a small and weak group of people who had adopted a 'malformed' version of the Iatmul social and ceremonial system, they nevertheless exhibited respect and allowed the Chambri their autonomy.[6] They flattered the Chambri into thinking of themselves as Iatmul equals, for "men do not trade unless they think of themselves as strong." In other words, the perception of equality was an important aspect of inter-male trading partnerships.

The Neo-Melanesian verb which, I think, best expresses this Iatmul flattery is the word "*grisim.*" The word literally means "to grease," as with pig fat, in order to make tasty and sweet. It is used in the sense of to mollify, to win over, or to sugar coat. Today, the word is frequently used to describe transactions between Papua New Guineans and Europeans. During my last field trip, for example, my Chambri friends took special pleasure in "greasing" the tourists who were interested in learning about the artifacts they were buying. Sitting together in a men's house that had been especially built to impress these visitors, the Chambri would charge them an additional *toea* to learn the story behind the carved masks they were buying. These fantastic stories were fabricated from whole cloth and generally extremely lewd. The Europeans seemed most impressed with them, however, generally writing them down in notebooks so as not to forget the secret lore with which they had been entrusted.

Although the word was not in use prior to the European intrusion, the concept seems to have been. Bateson, for example, reports the case of a bush woman captured by the Iatmul from Kanganaman, to which I have already referred in chapter 1 (see p. 29). After her capture, the woman pleaded for her life: "You are not my enemies; you should pity me; later I will marry in this village" (1958: 138). The woman must have thought her argument successful for, as Bateson continues the story:

> One of the young men, Avuran-mali, son of her captor, cut into this discussion, and in a friendly way invited her to come down to the gardens to get some sugar-cane. Accordingly he and the girl went down to the gardens together with one or two of the

younger boys, among them my informant, Tshava, who was then
a small boy. On arriving there, Avuran-mali speared her." [ibid.]

Avuran-mali, who could have easily killed the woman in front of her assembled captors, chose to "grease" her into thinking herself saved. Both the
Chambri and the Iatmul consider courage and rhetorical proficiency to be
prerequisites for leadership, and Avuran-mali must have gained considerable status among his comrades, who would praise him for possessing both
traits when he returned from the garden with the woman's head.

To be successfully greased means to be suffering from false consciousness—to be deluded into thinking that you are behaving in your own interest when, indeed, you are behaving in the interest of your deceiver. The
Chambri, I believe, suffered from false consciousness when they supplied
the Iatmul with stone tools and mosquito bags. They thought they were
viewed as equals to the Iatmul, when they were, in fact, viewed as foolish
and inferior.

This is not to suggest that the Chambri were cheated out of their stone
tools and mosquito bags by the wily and conniving Iatmul. Quite to the
contrary, the Chambri were more than willing to trade their commodities
for shell valuables. What I mean is that the hegemony sustained by the
Iatmul over the Chambri depended upon the more powerful people keeping the weaker under the impression that they were equals. In other words,
whereas the Iatmul maintained control of their sago-suppliers through periodic military incursions into Sawos territory, they preserved control of
their commodity providers by perpetuating the Chambri belief that Emosuie Apankay and Kwolimbank were equal comrades—nearly brothers. Indeed, the Iatmul tell a version of this myth as frequently as do the Chambri.

Although Emosuie and Kwolimbank gave one another foodstuffs in the
myth, the Chambri and Iatmul rarely exchanged subsistence products, for
they both had access to the same resource zones.[7] The objects they exchanged were specialized commodities and shell valuables, the former produced by the Chambri and obtained by the Iatmul for use but, more importantly, for further trade with the northerners who supplied the shells.

The Chambri needed the valuables they received from the Iatmul for
introduction into their system of affinal exchange. This system, as I have
shown, was predicated upon competition between men who were ostensibly equal to one another. If the Chambri did not define one another as
equals—if, for example, hierarchical control replaced egalitarian competition as the organizing principle of the tribe—then a regular supply of the
valuable shells would no longer have been needed. It was, therefore, in the
interests of the Iatmul to maintain Chambri competition, because as long
as the Chambri remained eager for shell valuables, the Iatmul would have
a supply of specialized commodities.

One method Iatmul traders might have used to help maintain Chambri equality would be to shift partnerships from those Chambri clans that had become too powerful to those with less extensive networks of clients. The Iatmul would have pursued such a strategy not because they understood the dangers inherent in any one Chambri clan becoming too large and successful, but rather because they would have been incapable of satisfying the demands made by powerful Chambri leaders. Trading relationships, it will be remembered, were dyadic in nature—set at a level comfortable to both partners. While the ownership of stone quarries allowed certain Chambri to establish themselves as significantly "more than the equals" of their compatriots, no Iatmul had a similar capacity. Each had access to precisely the same resources as did all of the others, and although Iatmul leaders emerged through adept manipulation of the sociopolitical system, they did not own any special means of production. Thus, no Iatmul would remain the trading partner of any Chambri leader for very long, but would withdraw from the relationship before becoming incapable of matching the Chambri leader's gifts. This is what the Chambri mean when they describe their "really Big Men" as being "alone—without any real friends."[8]

We must not forget, in this regard, that although the Iatmul controlled access to the valuable shells, they did not themselves produce them. The shells traveled from the coast, through trading arrangements between Arapesh, Abelam, and Sawos men, until they finally arrived in Iatmul territory. Each transaction was limited by those that preceded it. No Sawos, for example, could push his Abelam trading partner into providing shells that were unavailable, or otherwise invested. And no Iatmul could supply Chambri leaders with shells they had been unable to obtain from the Sawos. In this sense, the genius of the Iatmul, as articulators of Chambri commodities with Sawos valuables, was to maintain supply and demand at a relatively constant rate—and one favorable to themselves. And they did this, in the case of the Chambri, by keeping them engaged in the politics of affinal exchange—by "greasing" them into thinking themselves the equals of the princes of the Sepik.

From Trading Partnerships to Barter Markets

Relationships between the Iatmul and the Chambri began to deteriorate as a consequence of the undermining of Chambri specialized commodity production by Europeans. It was no longer necessary for the Iatmul to "grease" the Chambri, for they had begun to acquire even more effective specialized goods through their newly established relationships with European missionaries, entrepreneurs, and colonial administrators. The revelation of Chambri inequality vis-à-vis the Iatmul—the dissolution of equal exchange between them—ramified throughout the regional socioeconomic system in a curious manner, resulting in the development of barter markets between the Chambri and the Hills people. The story of these developments can best be told by dividing them into three series of events, each of which is well documented both in verbal accounts by those who participated in them, and in reports of colonial administrators (see, for example, Bragge, 1973 and 1974).

Series 1: Simbuksaun and the Parambei Wars

Around 1860, a man named Simbuksaun emigrated from the Iatmul village of Parambei to the Chambri village of Indingai. His emigration seems to have been motivated by an argument in his original village, but whether that argument was over a woman, a banana tree, or a plot of garden land has by this time become unclear. In any case, shortly after settling among the Chambri, Simbuksaun, apparently in order to distinguish himself among his adopted people as well as to prove his loyalty to them, killed Yebiyelis, a man from his former village, and took the head back with him to Indingai.

Simbuksaun's act stimulated a series of "paybacks" between Indingai and Parambei, and these escalated into a full-scale war which, by about 1905, involved all three Chambri villages. Parambei won, having acquired a shotgun from German colonial administrators, and the residents of the three Chambri villages took refuge on land owned by their trading partners, Indingai and Kilimbit moving first to the uninhabited island of Timbunmeri and then to the Sepik Hills near Changriman, and Wombun fleeing to Kabriman village on the Korosameri River.[9] In the mid 1920's, members of the Australian colonial government assured the Chambri that the Parambei would cause them no further trouble. Chambri, convinced of Australian good will, returned to their island by 1927.

These events are particularly significant because they are the first occasions on which the Iatmul and Chambri acted as antagonists. In all of their previous military undertakings, the Chambri directed their hostilities against their southern neighbors, and were generally assisted by members of one or another Iatmul village. Consider, for example, the incidents that provoked Simbuksaun to take the head of Yabiyelis. I was told that he was returning to Indingai from a protracted visit to Parambei when he heard victory drums (*garamuts*) sound from Chambri in celebration of the defeat of the Manabi. These people had been living on two islands within Chambri Lake, Timbunmeri and Peliagwi, until the Chambri, together with Iatmul allies from Kandingai and with Hills supporters from Mensuat, Garamambu, Changriman, and Yambi Yambi, totally wiped them out.[10] Simbuksaun feared that members of his clan would not have distinguished themselves in this fight, for he had not been there to help them. He therefore killed his former neighbor to insure that his men's house would also be adorned with a head taken in battle, thus initiating the Parambei wars.

The story of the defeat of the Manabi by a joint contingent of Iatmul, Chambri, and Hills men is typical of Chambri ethnohistorical accounts of warfare before the turn of the century. The Parambei wars changed all of this, beginning an enmity between the Chambri and these Iatmul that lasted until after World War II. What is most striking about this protracted conflict is that it did not escalate until after the European intrusion, and that, in its most active phase, it resulted in the exile of the Chambri from their three villages. Why were friendly relations between Chambri and Iatmul never reestablished? Was it simply because of one man's anxious pursuit of status, or were there deeper reasons?

Examining the Iatmul–Chambri wars in context, it becomes clear that the alliance between the two villages broke down completely only after the Iatmul no longer relied upon the Chambri as a source of the specialized commodities they needed in order to acquire shell valuables from the Sawos. The Iatmul received European goods well before the Chambri (see Mead, 1963: 243), and as German and later Australian administrators, missionaries, and explorers were providing them with valuable shells, steel tools, and cotton mosquito nets, they no longer had to humor the Chambri into believing themselves equals in order to secure less efficient indigenous products. The Chambri became expendable, and were dispatched—with the assistance of another European commodity, the shotgun—to a nearly twenty year exile among their exchange partners.

Series 2: The Exile

The following account of the events which led to the Chambri exile was told by Taplambun Gelepan, a seventy-five year old Indingai man who had been a child when they occurred. He did not tell the story directly to me, but in answer to a young man from Kilimbit who had asked him why the Chambri had "run in fear" from the Parambei.

> My father, Kingisu, and Yankiman's father, Tambunowi, had taken me to the bush that day to look for breadfruit and *toans* [the fruit of the tree, *Pometia pinnata*]. Many other people had gone to meet their trading partners from Garamambu at Kurapio.[11] It was the time of high water, and all of the rivulets were filled with floating grass islands. The people who had gone to Kurapio had a difficult time pulling their canoes through the grass.
> All of a sudden, many Kaminimbit, Mindimbit, and Parambei war canoes shored at Kilimbit. Everyone was amazed that they had done so without being seen. How could they pass through the

grass so easily? They must have had very strong magic. But the shotgun owned by Andemeri, one of the Parambei, was even stronger. He had obtained it from a German, and used it that day to shoot an old man from Kilimbit.

When the Chambri people saw the shotgun, they all ran away into the bush. They would have fought the Parambei, except for the shotgun. They had nothing to beat this power. And the Parambei knew this, because they did not chase the Chambri into the bush, but simply burned all of their men's houses, all that is except for Wiarman. Wiarman was Simbuksaun's men's house [inviolable sacred ground], and several people hid in it throughout the day.

Those at Kurapio saw that Chambri was burning, and they guessed what had happened. They decided to stay where they were for the time being.

When the Parambei left, all those Chambri who had fled to the bush returned to their homes. Nothing was left of their men's houses, and so they decided to leave their island.

First they killed all of their pigs and chickens, for they didn't want the Parambei to return to find food waiting for them. Then they loaded canoes with all of their possessions, including the large war canoes, Maliyambi and Walintimi. The people decorated themselves, and cried "sorry" to their homes.

Kapiwan's father, Yukandimi, didn't want to leave. He wanted to stay and fight. He decided not to, however, because he was hungry. He was starving for sago. Parambei had blockaded most of the rivulets that led to the Hills, and for months the Chambri had only been able to acquire sago occasionally. That is why they left. It was over hunger for sago. Wombun had left long before for Kabriman over hunger for sago, and now it was the turn of Indingai and Kilimbit.

According to Taplambun, then, the Chambri fled their island for fear of a shotgun and for want of sago, and I do not doubt the accuracy of his account. All of my Chambri and Iatmul informants mentioned Andemeri's ownership of a German shotgun. And although some denied the relevance of sago, pointing to the sago palms growing on one section of Chambri Island and arguing that "we could always have washed it ourselves," I do not believe this assurance to be founded in fact. During 1979 I became aware of how quickly these sago groves were depleted when access to markets was curtailed. This time the blockade was not established by the Parambei, but by the accidental introduction of a South American water fern, *Salvinia molesta*, which grew so thickly throughout the lake that no Chambri canoe could penetrate the barrier it had formed. I will discuss the details of this floral blockade in chapter 10. Here I wish only to emphasize that the Chambri cannot supply themselves with sago for more than six months, and the Parambei blockade had been going on for years, with greater or lesser intensity.

The island of Timbunmeri is rich in sago palms, and some Chambri say that they stayed there for many years. Others, however, insist that they camped out on Timbunmeri for only one night, while waiting for stragglers to arrive from the burning Chambri villages. As far as I can tell by comparing the stories of different informants, including some from the river and the Hills, the Indingai and Kilimbit exiles remained on Timbunmeri for several months, and then, fearing another attack by the Parambei, moved further south, finally settling near the hamlet of Changriman. There they did not live with their trading partners, but rather built the hamlet of Kamanbo along the lake's shore, an area that had frequently been used by the Chambri and the Changriman as a trading site. Since the Chambri's departure, the Changriman have abandoned their defensible but inconvenient hilltop hamlets and now occupy Kamanbo as a permanent home. The majority of Chambri with whom I discussed these matters were extremely anxious to have it understood that after fleeing from their Parambei antagonists, they did not live with their trading partners, but retained their distinctness by building a separate hamlet at the foot of the mountain they call Brobwi. They did not assume the identity of Hills people, but only wished the bush behind them, to allow an easy retreat should the Parambei attack once more, and to insure a regular supply of sago. As one of my older informants put it: "We did not become like Hills men. They are of the bush and we are of the water. They are cassowaries and we are crocodiles. We went there for fear of Parambei, not to become bushmen."

This statement and the data it supports suggest that by the time of the Parambei wars, the Chambri had become thoroughly "Iatmulized." They had become accustomed to a sedentary life, and to filling their carbohydrate requirements through exchange. Although still a small population— only about 375 Chambri were exiled at Kamanbo[12]—they did not disperse into the various hamlets of their separate trading partners, but stayed together with a consciousness of themselves as "of the water." Meanwhile, the Chambri continued to exchange with their trading partners as they had in the past. Both Mensuat and Changriman had relatively easy access to Kamanbo, and would walk there to acquire fish in exchange for sago and other bush products. It may seem something of a mystery why a people should bother to trade for fish acquired from a place to which they have as unrestricted access as the fisherfolk. Why not catch them oneself? The answer (at least in part) is that until relatively recently, only the Garamambu, of all the Hills people, had mastered the art of making and using canoes. And it is therefore understandable that the Hills people continued to be interested in trading their bush products for the fish, eels, and turtles that Chambri women could acquire off the shore of their new hamlet. Chambri men, while accustomed to using these water foods to verify their relationships with their trading partners, had always considered them to be secondary— superfluities they used to "decorate" the real exchange items, namely, stone tools, mosquito bags, shell valuables, tobacco, and betel nuts. However, it was just these real exchange items that they now found themselves unable to obtain. Those few foresighted Chambri who had taken their valuables with them to Kamanbo were not willing to trade them to their Hills trading partners for, as one man put it: "We were without the strength of our ancestral ground. Were we to lose the strength of our valuables as well?"

The fact of the matter is that most Chambri men had nothing but subsistence products with which to engage in exchange with their trading partners, while those who had brought specialized goods with them thought it best to withhold them. Their situation must have drastically altered the relationships between themselves and their friends from the bush, because the Chambri could no longer arrive at an exchange site "resplendent in feathers and shell ornaments" (Mead, 1963: 254), nor offer stone stools and shell valuables for trading.

Humiliated by the Parambei success and without valuables to exchange, Chambri men maintained their status by instructing the Hills people in cultural practices they themselves had learned from the Iatmul. Mead makes note of these lessons when she describes the mechanics of diffusion betwen the Chambri and the Hills peoples in her unpublished fieldnotes. She refers to two Iatmul-named sacred flutes, Yasahangwi and Babendimali, about which the Chambri had tried to teach the Mensuat. They did not, however, tell them all they knew about the flutes' secrets, ostensibly because they had found the Mensuat incapable of appreciating such esoteric information. The Hills peoples had managed, nonetheless, to learn a considerable amount from the Chambri during the exile, because it was at this time that the Changriman and Mensuat began to build Sepik- style houses, including *haus tambaran*. Moreover, one informant told me that it was Chambri scarifiers who affected the first initiation of Hills boys (including Changriman and certain Mensuat) into the responsibilities and prerogatives of masculinity in a men's house at Kamanbo. Thus, while the Chambri no longer had specialized commodities and shell valuables to offer in exchange, they did have information and ritual techniques, both of which were highly valued by the Hills men who had never before had the opportunity to identify themselves with this high culture of the water peoples.

Chambri and Hills women, on the other hand, continued to exchange fish for sago, for both groups needed the foodstuffs acquired by the other. It is understandable that the mode of exchange they adopted resembled Iatmul and Sawos barter markets, particularly in view of the Chambri men's larger strategy of maintaining status by serving as the "Iatmulizers" of the Hills people. Chambri women were undoubtedly aware of the manner in which their Iatmul counterparts conducted barter markets as well as the exchange rate they demanded, and if it did not now occur to them to look to these women as models, it must certainly have occurred to the Chambri women's husbands and fathers, who were concerned to appear before their Hills hosts as the enlightened bringers of Iatmul culture. Thus, Chambri–Hills barter markets were born, with one fish being bartered for one small brick of sago, in imitation of exchanges between Iatmul and Sawos women.

Series 3: The Return to Labor Migration

World War I intervened between the Parambei wars and the return of the Chambri to their island, and since no fighting took place in the region, its only effects were the substitution of Australian for German colonial administrators and entrepreneurs. Papua New Guinea had become a Trust Territory of the League of Nations under Australian supervision and, on September 11, 1924, the Sepik District was created, with its headquarters at Ambunti. Prior to this time, the Australians had sent several expeditions up the river from a patrol post at Marienberg for the purpose of ending intertribal fighting. They do not seem to have been very successful, however, for as the Sepik District Officer, G. W. L. (Kassa) Townsend, reported in the Annual Report to the League of Nations, issued by the Commonwealth of Australia during 1924:[13]

> Between 1914 and 1921...no systematic attempt had...been made to bring the natives of this District under control, and the whole of the District, with the exception of the portion in the vicinity of Marienberg, may, therefore, be regarded as a "new area" ....
> The patrols made during the year have been mainly up and down the river by means of a power launch, but, where opportunity has offered, the swamps reaching back from the river have been penetrated and relations of a friendly nature established with the natives. [1924–1925: 43–44]

Although Townsend's more detailed patrol reports were lost during the Second World War, we can be sure that one of his expeditions into the back swamps involved convincing the Chambri people to return from their years of exile to their original homes.

I do not know the argument Townsend used. The Chambri probably did not need much convincing, being anxious to return to their ancestral land. Indeed, Townsend, who is remembered as "a good man, who spoke good words," may only have had to assure them that he would prevent the Parambei from ever attacking them again.

I suspect, however, that the key to the Chambri return can be found in another of the statements found in the 1924–1925 Annual Report. Townsend writes:

> There are no native plantations in the known portions of the District. Each village has a few coco-nut palms but the natives do not appear to be agriculturalists.
>
> It is considered that the Sepik River is at present the best field for recruiting in the whole of the Territory. Recruiters have been active along the river, and the Expropriation Board has established a camp at Angoram, near Marienberg, for the concentration of its recruits.
>
> Whilst the actual possibilities of the District from a recruiting stand-point are not known, it seems certain that the labour requirements of the Territory can, to a large extent, be met from this source for a number of years to come. [ibid.: 44]

Table 5.1, which depicts the number of laborers legally taken to work on plantations from the Sepik District between 1924 and 1938, indicates the extent to which Townsend's prediction proved correct. During these years, the percentage of the Territory's total number of laborers indentured from the Sepik rose nine and a half times, from .016 to .152. Moreover, since many more men were recruited illegally by "black- birders," we should read the figures in the table as low estimates of the number actually at work and away from their villages.

I am unable to say how high a percentage of the newly-returned Chambri left their villages to work on plantations or in mines, but I do know that 98 percent of Indingai's adult males who were above the age of 35 in 1974 have worked at processing copra or at similar jobs for at least two years. Few had much choice. The Territory's demand for labor made recruiting a profitable business. Professional recruiters earned between £5 and £25 per man, making a profit of up to £22 after deducting the costs of delivering the recruit to his job. Such high profits encouraged many recruiters to use fraud, intimidation, and misrepresentation (see Curtain, 1978: 11–17). But there was a more subtle form of coercion applied by the Australian Government itself. Patrol Officers were impowered to collect a Head Tax of 10 shillings a year from every able bodied man living in every pacified village. Certain categories of men were, however, exempt from the tax, and among these categories were men serving under indenture. The Head Tax, therefore, induced many men to sell their labor who may not have otherwise done so (see Reed, 1943: 179).

When Chambri men describe their experiences as laborers, they do not as a rule speak of coercion and intimidation, but rather of travel and access to European commodities. I do not mention this to absolve European en-

Table 5.1: The Number of Migrant Laborers Absent from the Sepik between 1924 and 1938

Year	No. of Migrant Laborers from the Sepik	Total Migrants all Districts	Percentage of Total
1924–25	152	9,477	.016
1925–26	233	10,448	.022
1926–27	250	12,062	.020
1927–28	185	13,310	.014
1928–29	967	15,089	.064
1929–30	584	12,940	.045
1930–31	298	12,650	.024
1931–32	303	12,968	.023
1932–33	355	14,448	.025
1933–34	2,073	15,125	.137
1934–35	1,536	15,398	.098
1935–36	2,295	17,674	.130
1936–37	2,547	18,483	.138
1937–38	2,763	18,124	.152

Source: Data were taken from the 1924–38 Reports to the League of Nations on the administration of the Territory of New Guinea.

trepreneurs and administrators for the inhumane tactics and policies they employed to insure themselves a source of cheap labor, but rather to suggest that the history of the Chambri can be understood only partially if we assume them to have been mere pawns manipulated by the capitalist intruders. They participated actively in the events that occurred after the Europeans colonized their island, and frequently thought themselves to be in control of these events. Certainly they desired to incorporate aspects of capitalism's array of goods and services into their traditional socioeconomic system. And although their incorporation of these items held unexpected and often unpleasant consequences, we should not confuse these with the causes of change. Consider, for example, the following interviews I recorded with men who had sold their labor prior to World War II, each of which indicates how the Chambri perceived labor migration.

HISTORY 1 TAPLAMBUN GELEPAN   Right after Chambri returned from Kamanbo, I left for Rabaul. I worked on cargo, copra, and petrol ships there, traveling to all of the islands off the coast. The work was hard, but the food was good, and this is why many Chambri wanted to do this kind of work. Most of the men were from Kilimbit. Only Suqwe from Indingai worked with me on the ships. After I finished with Rabaul, I worked at Madang for three years, loading cargo for B.P.[14] After I was finished there, I returned to

Indingai and sat down here for good, but I have traveled to Ambunti many times. I also helped build the Pagwi road, when it was nothing but bush. This all was many years ago, after the big fight with Parambei, and after Master Townsend convinced Malmansi and Yangandimi[15] that it was safe to return home from Kamanbo. We all went to work then because of money and all of the things that white men brought, the steel tomahawks, knives, scissors, and razors.

HISTORY 2 MARUMBANK   I was born at Timbunmeri during the time of the fight with Parambei. My mother was from [the men's house] Mangembit, and my father was a Garamambu. His name was Kwaremanki, and he was a Big Man with fourteen wives. I don't remember him, because he was killed at Indingai. His body is buried near [the] Yangarambit [men's house]. After he was killed, my mother went to live with Askame near where Elami has built his house. Soon she married Clemeri, and I became his number one son. After I was initiated, I went with Yambunapan to Buka,[16] where we worked unloading ships. Then I heard that my mother had died, so I returned home. I left Indingai for Madang in 1938, and stayed there until I heard that my sister had drowned. This was in 1941. I stayed at Chambri for six months, but returned to Madang during the Christmas of 1942. Then the war came up, and I fought with the Australians until I was dismissed. I fought at Lae, at Port Moresby, and at Madang. But my friend, a Nyaula from Yamanambu, told an officer that the war was for white men, not for black men, and they let us go. After I left the army, I walked from Madang to the mouth of the Sepik. There I met a mission boat that took me to Marienberg. I stayed at the mission for a little while, and then stole a war canoe belonging to a man from Tambunum. I needed the canoe to get home. Four days after I arrived at Indingai, I married Sapui. I had money saved, and plenty of cargo, and that was why I decided to marry her then. We were married for a long time, and I can't understand why she left me for that little man she's married to now. In 1948 I went to Rabaul with Joseph Mindim. We cut copra for one year, and then returned home. I became *tultul** of Indingai. My daughter, Scola, was born in 1950; Willy came up in 1953; Valentine was born in 1957; one child died; and I had others, too. In 1964, the Village Committee and Council were formed, and I worked for eight years on the Committee, traveling to Ambunti many times to see the A.D.C. [Assistant District Commissioner]. In 1971, I left Chambri to boss the high school students living at Wewak, making sure that they eat well. I don't think I'll live at Indingai again. I'll probably die here.

*A *tultul* was assistant to the *luluai,* both government chiefs. See chapter 7, p. 295.

HISTORY 3 ELAMINAKWAN   I was born at Timbunmeri, before the Chambri went to Changriman after the big fight with Parambei. When the government sang out for us to return to our ground, I came back with everyone. Then I went to Rabaul, where I worked at Buka on a plantation for three years. I came back to Indingai, got married, and then went to Madang where I worked loading and unloading a copra ship. I did this work for one year, then I became lazy. I had gotten enough tomahawks for everyone back home, and so I returned to Indingai, and remained there throughout the war. Then I went back to Rabaul, stayed a year, and came home again. In 1953, I went back to Rabaul with my wife and child. Alamanbi was born at Rabaul. I stayed for a year after her birth and then returned home, where I have been ever since. No, that's not true, for in 1957 I took my wife to the hospital at Ambunti where Marcus was born, and I have been to Maprik three times in order to sell carvings to the tourists. I've been around quite a bit, as much as any Big Man.

HISTORY 4 LAKINDIMI   I was born at Indingai, and never went to school. As a young man, I went to Seramow, near Madang, where I worked at cutting grass and cooking food for three and a half years. I worked there for knives and laplaps. Then I returned to Indingai, where I got married. I stopped at home for a time, and then went to Manus, where I became a cook once again. I cooked for all of the boys there for two years, and then came back to my place. The war had come by then, and I stayed at home. By the time it was over, I had decided not to work anymore. I just travel around now. I've been to Wewak twice, once for four months, and I stayed with Yambumpe at Pagwi for three months. And I forgot to say that the time they had that big trouble at Ambunti, when the policemen made trouble for the government, I helped the Australians kill the trouble-makers.[17]

Every migrational history of Chambri men during the exile at Kamanbo suggests the same pattern: The men left their homes to work on plantations, or in some other capacity for Europeans; they returned to Chambri; they married—generally using the money and the goods they accumulated during their sojourns to pay their bride prices;[18] they frequently returned to work for one of several contract periods; and they settled permanently in their villages at about the same time that their younger brothers or elder sons were assuming their places as migrant laborers—and assuming their obligations to pay taxes and bride prices.

I have no statistics to prove that the Chambri engaged in labor migration more frequently than their Iatmul neighbors, but my guess would be that this was so, not only because they still have a higher rate of out-migration (see Table 5.2), but also because of the extrinsic focus of their traditional socioeconomic system. The Iatmul were entrepreneurial geniuses, well-accustomed to transforming their advantageous geographic position into military and economic supremacy, partially by articulating Chambri commodities with Sawos valuables. Their position on the Sepik River allowed them to continue in this entrepreneurial role after the European intrusion, as missionaries, patrol officers, and explorers willingly provided them with goods in return for safe passage.[19]

The Chambri had no such geographic advantage, for few explorers penetrated the back swamps of the region until after World War II. They had, however, become skilled at surviving through adapting to the needs of their superiors, an ability they readily transferred to European administrators and entrepreneurs. In other words, the Chambri accommodated to the destruction of their monopoly on the production of specialized commodities by adopting a pattern of circular migration. They thereby acquired from Europeans what they had heretofore acquired from the Iatmul—the valuables necessary to pay for prestige and, now, also necessary to pay taxes. No longer able to sell their stone tools and mosquito bags to the Iatmul, they were probably more willing than their neighbors to be coerced through the Head Tax into selling their labor.

Conclusion: The Development of Barter Markets

Although the field notes of Margaret Mead and Reo Fortune occasionally refer to Chambri men accompanying their wives to barter markets and paying visits to their Hills trading partners, fewer and fewer of them assiduously maintained their exchange relationships.[20] The older men were preoccupied with rebuilding their burned-down villages,[21] while the younger ones were selling their labor to European entrepreneurs.[22] In either case, Chambri men had little occasion or desire to invest themselves in their trading partnerships, and allowed their women the task of acquiring subsistence goods. Since an incipient barter market had already developed during the exile at Kamanbo, it was a relatively simple matter to leave women in control of fish-for-sago exchanges once the Chambri returned to their island.

Table 5.2: The Rate of Out-Migration in Four Sepik Villages
(Percent)

Village	Never left	Currently away	Returned
Indingai	2	59	40
Tegowi	3	68	29
Avatip	27	35	32
Kanganaman	31	48	18

Source: Data were taken from Curtain, 1976. They describe the migrational histories of all adult males above the age of fifteen.

Thus, in both the Iatmul and the Chambri cases, women gained control of marketing when men found it necessary to separate the domestic from the political domains. Iatmul men had to establish their hegemony over their Sawos sago-suppliers while engaging in equal exchange with their Sawos shell-providers, a task they accomplished by adopting the division of labor I described earlier in this chapter. Chambri men, on the other hand, simply abandoned their trading partnerships with Hills men when their time became occupied with more immediately significant tasks—with either rebuilding their villages, or with earning, in a new way, the valuables they needed to play politics and pay taxes.

6

THE THEFT OF HISTORY:
COLONIAL ADMINISTRATORS
AND LABOR RECRUITERS

Although the Chambri found it a relatively easy matter to abandon their trading partnerships in order to earn the new European valuables they needed to play at politics and pay their taxes, they did not find it as easy to deal with Europeans as they would have liked. As one informant explained: "When the Australians first came we all thought, 'Man oh man! These are really Big Men!' But then we changed our thinking and hoped that they would go away. We liked the things they brought, but thought them rubbish men themselves." There is a tendency to interpret Melanesian Pidgin nouns metaphorically, but in this case I think my informant's use of *rabisman* must be understood literally as referring to individuals who will not or cannot pay their debts. In this chapter I discuss these European defaults from both a Chambri and a Western perspective and explain their effects upon the continued development of the regional socioeconomic system.

The Prince and the Pauper

All Chambri who have discussed the early years of European contact with me have invariably related a version of their Prince and the Pauper story. It is a long tale, whose several episodes each illustrate its dominant theme: an inquiry into the problem of interacting with those who do not behave as "equals" should, refusing to discharge the debts they owe to their compatriots. After summarizing the story's introductory sequence in the first paragraph, I present the last three episodes in their entirety for what they reveal about Chambri perceptions of early twentieth-century historical circumstances.

> During ancestral times there were two brothers, Namowi, the elder, and Wobowi, the younger. Wobowi had been tricked by his sister-in-law into incising her vulva with totemic designs. But Namowi thought that his brother had willingly performed the deed and, therefore, decided to kill him.

Namowi gathered together a ginger root, some tree sap, a saucepan, a spear, and half of a rattan door. He recited his "Mandonk" names,* and as he did so the rains and the winds blew up. The door moved up and down; the waters rose and covered the houses; and, finally, the door turned into a crocodile that swam to Wobowi's house and swallowed him.[1]

Wobowi had fortunately been carrying a stone adze and some *kina*, and these allowed him to cut through the belly of the crocodile. This was at Klinjambang.[2] Free at last, Wobowi met a tree kangaroo who offered his help after hearing Wobowi's story. This is how Wobowi arrived at Angoram: on the tail of a tree kangaroo. Because the creature described Angoram as "Wobowi's place," the two friends decided to live there.

Together they built a house and prepared sago. Just as they were constructing a men's house—having started to dig the holes for the carved posts[3]—Namowi arrived. He had heard that Wobowi was still alive, and had come to kill him.

Wobowi told Namowi that he had to excrete in the bush, but he actually was gathering all of the different kinds of red-juiced wild fruit.

"Why are you taking so long?" asked Namowi.

"I ate something rotten yesterday," answered Wobowi, who was placing the fruit in the post holes of the men's house.

As Wobowi descended into the first post hole to finish digging it, Namowi lowered the post into the hole, hoping to squash his brother to death. But Wobowi and the tree kangaroo had dug an escape tunnel off to one side of the hole, leaving Namowi thinking that the red-juiced fruits he had pulverized were his brother's bloody remains.

Arriving at Taway by canoe, Wobowi built two houses, prepared sago, and began to build a new canoe. Namowi, having once again heard that his brother was alive, continued in pursuit, accompanied now by his mother and his first wife.

When Namowi arrived at Taway, he did not recognize Wobowi, who had magically disguised himself. In his disguise, Wobowi asked Namowi why he had come. Namowi answered: "I've come to kill a pig and to prepare food because I've just killed my brother. What is your name?"

Wobowi replied: "I'm Andena, and you're Taway. How did you kill him?"[4]

"I killed him with a post," lied Namowi.

Wobowi invited his brother to sleep in one of the houses he had built. The old and young woman slept in the other. While everyone was asleep, Wobowi made magic over the canoe he had built.

*Mandonk is the name of an ancestral crocodile belonging to the Sekumbumeri clan of Indingai Village. When Namowi invoked his "Mandonk" names, he was calling upon the powers of his clan's ancestral totems.

He made the magic that undermines a canoe's structure—the magic of bat bones.*

The next day the two brothers set off for the ocean, Namowi and the women in the big, new canoe, and Wobowi in the old and small one. As they arrived near the mouth of the Sepik, Namowi asked Wobowi to gather mud and help him plug up the leaks in his canoe, but Wobowi ignored him. When they arrived near Manam Island, the big canoe broke into three pieces. Namowi and the women slept that night in the water, each holding on to a piece of the canoe. Finally, they shored at Wewak.

Wobowi, meanwhile, had arrived at the main village of the white men, where he announced that he was "a Big Man from New Guinea."

At this time, the king of the Australians⁵ did not know how to organize his workers. He didn't know how to ring the bell for lunch; he didn't know how to plant coconuts; he didn't know how to harvest coffee; and he didn't know how to run motors. Wobowi taught him all of these things.

When working for the king, Wobowi would take off his black skin. It had a zipper in it, and he could become a white man by taking it off. Whenever he bossed the workers, he would leave his black skin hanging from a nail in his house.

One day the king saw Wobowi's black skin hanging from the nail. He decided to try it on. When he wanted to take it off, he found the zipper stuck fast.

Since a black man could not be king, Wobowi married the king's daughter and became king himself. And this is why white men have come to Papua New Guinea with money and everything else. When Wobowi left Chambri, he took all of his knowledge with him. Now his descendants are coming back to teach us to do the things that pull in cargo.

And if you want to hear about Namowi, this is what happened after he shored at Wewak. He had carried two pieces of tree bark with him from the post he had used to try to kill his brother. With the bark in his basket, he walked from Wewak to Japanaut, from Japanaut to Nyaurengai, and from Nyaurengai to Kandingai. At Kandingai he met Parkemeri, who offered him soup. They spoke:

Parkemeri: "Eat."
Namowi: "Eat."
Parkemeri: "Soup."
Namowi: "Soup."
Parkemeri: "Me."
Namowi: "Me."
Parkemeri: "You."

*Bat bones were traditionally used as needles to pierce animal skins. Magical bat bones, it seems, can pierce wood as well.

Namowi: "You."

Parkemeri told Namowi—whose other name was Kwolim-bank—to search out Emosuie. Namowi did so, and the two of them anchored Chambri Island to where it now stands, Emosuie with a slab of stone, and Kwolimbank with the bark he had carried with him from Angoram.

Each of these three narratives, the story of Wobowi and Namowi, the story of Wobowi and the King of the Australians, and the story of Namowi, Parkemeri, and Emosuie, focuses on a different group of people who either maintain equality by discharging the debts they owe one another, or refuse to do so. The first, the story of Wobowi and Namowi, is an old tale to which the "King of the Australians" narrative has been attached. As such, it indicates Chambri attitudes toward the European intrusion by contextualizing later events within a myth about older relationships. The narrative is only one of many Chambri myths that relate conflicts between younger and older brothers (see Gewertz, 1979). Each of these stories expresses the contradiction between an ideological commitment to brotherly equality and the fact of age dominance.

Chambri brothers are supposed to be equal. By this I mean that the people think of all initiated males, except those who are linked by marriage, as either equal allies or equal competitors. Fellow clansmen, including biological and classificatory brothers, their sons, and so on, are allies who compete for status and prestige with other identically defined patriclans. Within each clan, however, certain individuals emerge whose ability to manipulate the clan's resources strategically within the affinal exchange system is of a higher order than that of their fellows. The Chambri call these clan leaders Big Men (*mabukan*) in recognition of their having achieved interclan power.

An older brother is more likely than a younger to achieve a position of leadership. He is initiated earlier and, in the past, had earlier access to crucial resources and relationships such as stone quarries and trading partnerships. Although primogeniture is not the rule, the elder generally inherits magical spells and ceremonial accoutrements from the father, who also designates him as his representative during affinal exchange ceremonies.[6] Today, in addition to an earlier access to many traditional resources, older brothers tend to receive a longer and better education, for families have a limited amount of money to spend on school fees.[7] These patent inequalities tend to erode the ideological assumption of fraternal parity. As a result, it has always been hard for Chambri to recognize the superiority of older brothers as merely the consequence of their head start in life rather than as a de facto license to power.

The conflict, as I have said, is typical of many Chambri myths, which invariably have younger brothers winning out in the end. What marks this

story as significantly different, however, is the scope of its action. Namowi
and Wobowi, either together or alone, visit Kalingala on the Korosameri
River, Angoram and Taway on the Lower Sepik, Wewak on the northern
coast, Manam Island off the northern coast, the Iatmul villages of Japanaut,
Nyaurengai, and Kandingai, and, of course, Australia. The dimensions of
this conflict for equality have expanded to include interactions through the
entire known world, including those between Wobowi and the king of the
Australians.

By placing the story of Namowi's first contact with Europeans within an
older myth about the relationship between older and younger brothers, the
Chambri are suggesting that the relationship between white men and Papua
New Guineans is analogous to that between male siblings. White men, like
older brothers, seem to have a de facto license to power. Yet, both should
be obliged to recognize their dependents as equals—older brothers because
their culture commits them to do so and white men because they have
promised to do so. Consider, for example, the following passage taken from
the migrational history of Yekirai, an Abelam who acted as a labor recruiter
during the 1930s.

> We used this approach to gain recruits: we would come to a
> village and have them line up. Then would follow a demonstra-
> tion of the trade goods we had with us. With a knife someone
> would cut bark from a tree. We would show them knives and
> tomahawks. Another man would take a torch made of dry coco-
> nut fronds, hold up matches and start a fire. Another man would
> have a razor and he would shave an onlooker's beard. Another
> would cut hair with a pair of scissors . . . .
> The villagers would be surprised and very impressed. He (the
> European recruiter) would go on to say:
> Yupela i salim ol pikinini i kamap bai ol i go wok kisim ol
> dispela samting kamap bihain, behain nau boi yu olsem tasol.
> [quoted by Curtain, 1978: 41–42]

The Melanesian Pidgin words quoted in the passage can be loosely translated thus: "If you send your sons to work, then later all of the good things
I've shown you will come to you." By law, a recruiter could not coerce
natives into going with him to work, for each had to "signify . . . [his]
willingness to be recruited" (League of Nations, 1926–27: 20). Many of the
natives who proved willing had profoundly misunderstood the nature of the
commitment they were making, for they believed that the recruiter's prom-
ises could only be fulfilled through the egalitarian interaction that characterized friendly male relationships. One Chambri informant, while explaining his father's reasons for encouraging him and his two brothers to
follow the recruiter, drew a comparison with child adoption. He said: "My
father thought that once we left for work, the recruiter would come right

away to exchange with him. He thought the recruiter was marking us as his sons, and that from then on he would return to help my father, as good friends should."

But the recruiter did not return right away to engage in exchange, and when the sons arrived home, they brought with them only a few of the wonders that the white man had demonstrated. Things were not as they should be, and many natives blamed the recruiters for unfairly and irrationally terminating the exchange relationships they had promised.

From the native perspective, the story of Wobowi and the king of the Australians is a simple wish-fulfillment fantasy with millenarian overtones. It is about an ultimate reversal of the ranks, when white men become black and black men become white; when New Guineans become Australian kings and kings become laborers; and when natives inherit their due from the white descendants of the ancestor they all share in common.

The third narrative, the story of Namowi, Parkemeri, and Emosuie, returns us to an earlier time when men, if not created equal, at least had the opportunity of becoming so through their actions—without having to change their skins. In the story, Namowi, who has been transformed into the Kandingai Iatmul, Kwolimbank, confronts Parkemeri, another Kandingai. Their conversation specifically eliminates all hints of inequality, for neither wishes to provide the other with a pretext for escalating their interaction.[8] They give each other a word for a word rather than a steel adze for a year's labor. And it is fitting that Parkemeri advises Kwolimbank to search out Emosuie, for we know that the dog-bat and the pig-man will become trading partners, maintaining their equality while they anchor Chambri Island, each limiting his gifts to the productive capacities of the other.

We also know that the Europeans arrived well after Chambri Island was fixed south of the Sepik River—whether Kwolimbank and Emosuie had a hand in its anchorage or not. Although I would not argue that the mythmaker understood the social processes at work at the time of the intrusion, the image of "fastening" or "anchoring" is nonetheless an accurate way of describing the changes that occurred.

The Male Dilemma: From Process to Organization

The European administrators and entrepreneurs who arrived in the Sepik not only induced the natives to engage in wage labor but also attempted to restructure indigenous sociopolitical relationships along Western lines. They brought with them the notion that peace and prosperity depended upon the maintenance of inviolate political boundaries, their model being the sovereign states of Europe. It was their belief that New Guineans should have the same aspirations, and they assumed that their task was to teach them how such a state could be achieved. Government, therefore, became the imposition of boundaries between village groups.

The Sepik peoples, however, had always lived with shifting coalitions that linked groups together against temporary enemies. Consider, for example, the migrational history of the Iatmul village of Yamanumbu, as L. W. Bragge recorded it:

> An ancestor called Mamandai is claimed to have brought his family from Kandingai in the past. His genealogy is clear and his period of migration is fairly positive. He was a fight leader of note,[9] and most of the present population of Yamanumbu can trace direct descent from Mamandai. In the period between the German departure and the Australian arrival, i.e., 1914 to 1923, Yamanambu was defeated by Avatip and Japandai and the village burned to the ground. The survivors fled to Japanaut, but re-established the village shortly after, and the land was not occupied by enemy forces during their absence.
>
> The Yaugusambi area between Yamanumbu and Japandai is the subject of a fairly hot dispute between these villages. The Japandais claim that this is where they hid the Nyaurengai people who were to become the Korogos after they were ejected from Nyaurengai.
>
> Yamanumbu and Japandai also hotly dispute the Wabiui waterway area with Sengo, as they had pushed Sengo out of this area through warfare until the establishment of Ambunti. [1974: page unknown]

Bragge's account emphasizes the flexibility with which the Iatmul held their sociopolitical boundaries: Kandingai became Yamanumbu; Nyaurengai became Korogo; Avatip and Japandai unite against Yamanumbu; Yamanumbu and Japandai ally against Sengo. The account also reflects Bragge's position as Assistant District Commissioner of the region, for he was committed to eliminating the very flexibility he describes. He hoped to be able to resolve land litigations judiciously once he had recorded the people's migrational histories—once he had learned who the "legal" owners of the disputed territory were. What he failed to understand was that the Iatmul never perceived the ownership of territory to be either permanent or permanently alienable. For them possession was nine-tenths of the law, but the remaining one-tenth promised restitution in time.

In other words, with the coming of the Europeans and the imposition of the Pax Australia, the Middle Sepik Iatmul, Chambri, Sawos, and Hills peoples were defined as belonging to particular cultural groups, living within particular and limited territories, and in specific and permanently bounded villages. No longer could Nyaurengai become Korogo, or Korogo cease to exist, because these peoples and places had been fixed on maps and recorded in census books. And the inequalities that existed between these peoples and places—the fact that Korogo has a population of over 850 while Indingai has a population of only 400, the fact that the Sawos live in the bush and the Iatmul on the river, the fact that Kwolikumbwi's mother was killed by a Suapmeri raiding party, circumstances that marked the temporary ascendancy of one person, village, or cultural group over another—had now become hierarchically fixed, and by foreigners who claimed the power to adjudicate objectively the disputes of those other than themselves.

This is not to say that the judgments of these administrators were unfounded. The indigenous political situation provided ample evidence of the existence of a status quo. The Iatmul, for example, were patently "princes of the Sepik," and showed every indication of having maintained their hegemony for a very long time. The difference between the indigenous situation and that which followed upon the European intrusion is simply this: no longer did power, status, and intergroup ascendancy have to be maintained at all, for Colonial Administrators had usurped this task. In other words, the equality of opportunity that structured relationships between groups of Sepik men was eliminated by the imposition of European political structures.

This equality of opportunity had made a potential reversal of the ranks a necessary complement to their actual arrangement. Anyone who defined himself as the equal of others was forced to demonstrate his equality. A leader's son, for example, was not guaranteed his father's position, any more than the father was guaranteed the continuing support of his constituents. Although they might fail in their attempts at equality, all Sepik men could count on others to justify the competitive social process that allowed them the promise of trying again.

But all of this changed once Europeans began to adjudicate land disputes. Maps were drawn. Censuses were taken. Peoples were fixed as belonging—immutably—to the bush or the river. Villages were ranked in terms of their degree of control; in terms of their labor potential,[10] in terms of their possession of desirable natural resources. And no longer was it possible for Namowi to change from a Chambri into an Iatmul without some European recording the transformation.

The Continued Development of Middle Sepik Barter Markets

The fact that Sawos could no longer hope to transform themselves into Iatmul had profound effects upon the continued development of Middle Sepik barter markets. The Iatmul, it will be remembered, were compelled to keep the Sawos villages trapped in a double bind—populous enough to desire a regularized supply of fish but small enough to pose no threat to

Iatmul hegemony over the river and its resources. This obligation was not compelling once the Europeans drew maps of the area, for the Sawos could no longer attempt to gain control of the territory assumed by European administrators to belong, inalienably, to those who had the best claims upon it.

One might expect the Sawos, with nothing to fear from Iatmul hegemony—the Australians having prevented the Iatmul from making periodic military incursions into Sawos territory—to inflate their fish-for-sago exchange rate. But the Sawos failed to take this advantage for demographic reasons. By the time of the European intrusion, Sawos villages had already expanded considerably.[11] A map of the area today indicates that what were once small and semipermanent hamlets have become permanent villages, and that several of them have subdivided. The hamlet of Torembi, for example, now consists of the villages called Torembi 1, 2, and 3, while Marap and Slei have each expanded into two separate settlements. Moreover, the mean size of Sawos villages had doubled over the last twenty years. While Sepik River villages are still considerably bigger than their Sawos counterparts (the former having a mean resident and absentee population of approximately 414 in 1977, and the latter a comparable population of just over half that size), it can no longer be said that the largest Sawos village is smaller than the smallest Iatmul settlement. Gaikerobi, for example, is over three and a half times the size of Tegowi (see table 6.1), and although Schindlbeck found certain Gaikerobi women still capable of autonomously supplying their large families with fish, it is unlikely that all of the sedentary Sawos would be able to do so (1980: 177–84).

Through the years, they have become increasingly dependent upon a regularized supply of Iatmul fish to support their expanding and increasingly stable villages, and today the Sawos are as dependent upon the Iatmul as the Iatmul are upon them.

The opposite is true of the Hills people, who obtained economic autonomy from the Chambri once the Australians began to place them on maps and record them in census books. Their independence was not achieved, however, until the mid 1960s, after they completed a descent begun by the Changriman in the early 1930s. Leaving their Hills hamlets, they gradually settled on the shores of Chambri Lake, a process I describe in detail in chapter 9. Unlike barter between the Sawos and Iatmul—where the European imposition of inalienable land rights stabilized the fish-for-sago exchange rate by trapping the Sawos in the bush—barter in the southern backswamps deteriorated once the Europeans persuaded the Hills peoples to descend from their hamlets. Their settlement in permanent villages on the shores of Chambri Lake at first necessitated an increased supply of Chambri fish to provision their now sedentary populations. But by the mid-

Table 6.1: The Population of Iatmul and Sawos Villages

Date of Census	Village	Iatmul Living in Village				Absentees				Totals
		Child		Adult		Child		Adult		
		M	F	M	F	M	F	M	F	
11–1–77	Japandai	65	51	51	64	29	8	5	2	275
11–2–77	Japanaut	96	84	87	86	31	19	15	20	438
11–2–77	Nyaurengai	75	55	31	22	32	10	8	4	237
11–2–77	Kandingai	142	128	110	92	50	19	13	14	568
11–2–77	Yentchamangua	96	86	77	62	44	15	12	7	399
11–4–77	Korogo	230	238	219	168	91	44	37	22	1,049
11–7–77	Suapmeri	106	95	66	57	75	36	17	20	472
11–7–77	Indabu	101	75	75	55	66	35	39	31	477
11–8–77	Yentchan	141	132	77	69	100	66	32	24	641
11–8–77	Parambei	259	205	152	134	173	93	61	45	1,122
11–8–77	Malingai	124	98	69	76	69	33	20	21	510
11–9–77	Kanganaman	241	207	149	146	146	90	54	53	1,086
11–9–77	Tegowi	67	48	36	30	39	24	12	7	263
11–9–77	Yamanumbu	70	62	84	71	35	18	38	20	406
									Total	7,943
									Mean	567.36
								Standard deviation		293.56

Date of Census	Village	Sawos Living in Village				Absentees				Totals
		Child		Adult		Child		Adult		
		M	F	M	F	M	F	M	F	
10–10–77	Sengo	114	90	76	52	37	8	6	5	388
10–11–77	Gaikerobi	193	170	126	152	105	52	35	35	868
10–11–77	Nogusop	95	95	90	79	40	12	11	5	427
10–11–77	Marap 1	79	87	68	71	7	3	3	—	318
10–11–77	Marap 2	63	69	61	86	1	—	—	—	280
10–12–77	Worimbi	107	101	94	84	14	1	1	—	388
10–12–77	Waniko	44	38	33	30	13	4	1	1	164
10–12–77	Kaimbiam	108	96	90	70	19	14	7	5	409
10–12–77	Miambe	35	31	20	17	6	1	1	—	111
10–12–77	Yakiap	38	38	32	24	5	3	—	1	141
10–12–77	Sarum	30	32	25	33	2	—	—	—	122
10–13–77	Slei 1	61	61	37	35	11	9	3	3	220
10–13–77	Slei 2	37	38	20	21	9	—	—	—	125
10–13–77	Namangoa	77	77	72	57	10	3	1	3	308
10–13–77	Torembi 1	138	101	81	83	—	—	—	—	403
10–13–77	Torembi 2	61	54	46	35	10	2	2	1	211
10–13–77	Torembi 3	63	62	36	44	—	—	—	—	205
10–13–77	Nambangoa	41	36	31	47	4	—	—	—	159
10–14–77	Yanget	56	66	41	54	4	1	1	1	221
10–14–77	Vagiput	31	39	40	35	5	1	1	8	153
10–14–77	Wereman	107	81	82	76	24	5	12	8	395
10–14–77	Maiwi	51	43	52	56	8	3	5	4	222
								Total		6,238
								Mean		283.55
								Standard deviation		165.08

Source: Figures were taken from the official government census records.

1960s, their descent had obliterated the essential boundary between fish-supplying and sago-producing peoples because Hills groups had learned to accomplish both tasks by themselves.

This process did not occur suddenly but had been developing ever since the Chambri exile, when the Chambri traded their knowledge of Iatmul customs for status and authority. While living at Kamanbo, the Chambri had taught their Mensuat and Changriman friends about the various customs of water people and had instituted an "Iatmulesque" barter market between their own and Hills women. Although this incipient barter market did not outlast the Chambri exile, it began the process of depersonalizing fish-for-sago exchanges—of disengaging subsistence transactions from personal friendships and obligations.

After the Chambri returned home to their island, fish-for-sago exchanges between them and the Hills people became a curious amalgamation of barter markets and trading partnerships. Few Chambri men regularly accompanied their wives to the bush, for many were away on plantations.[12] Those who remained, having become thoroughly convinced of the effectiveness of the Australian ban on warfare, no longer feared for their wives' safety and did not feel compelled to make the journey as protectors. Being no longer interested in bush products nor in need of political alliances, Chambri men ceased cultivating their Hills trading partners. They now undertook the trip to the Hills only as an occasional break in their routines.

Chambri women, on the other hand, made the journey whenever they needed sago. Together with their co-wives, sisters, sisters-in-law, or friends, they once again began visiting Garamambu, Kurapio, Milae, and Mensuat, journeying to all of the territories inhabited by those who had been the trading partners of their husbands or brothers. Being familiar with these men, they felt comfortable trading with them and their wives. The exchange rates they used were far more variable than those characteristic of Iatmul–Sawos markets, for they continued to be geared to the productive capacities of the barterers. Sago is harder to prepare in the dry season, when fish are most easily available, facts that I am told were initially reflected in their rate of exchange. But gradually, as Chambri women also became convinced of the effectiveness of the Pax Australia, increasing numbers of them began to abandon old friends in favor of the barter market located closest to their villages. Traveling to Kamanbo, the place where they had been exiled for so long, Chambri women began regularly to exchange their fish for the sago produced by the Hills women who had come to barter there as well.[13]

It was during this transitional time, when barter markets were developing from trading partnerships, that Margaret Mead and Reo Fortune worked among the Chambri.[14] Mead describes the coexistence of these two modes of exchange in *Sex and Temperament*, where she distinguishes between the barter markets of women and the trading expeditions of men (1963: 254).

Although Mead writes about trading partnerships, I suspect her information comes from native remembrances of things past, for nowhere in her or Reo Fortune's field notebooks is such an expedition described as if they had observed it. Moreover, they discuss the case of clan co-members who are surprised to learn that their "brother" has gone with his wife to a barter market, a situation that would not have occurred if he had been in the habit of visiting the Hills "resplendent" in his ceremonial accoutrements and carrying a large mosquito bag.[15]

Thus, in 1933 the acquisition of food—what Mead calls "the underlying economics of life"—was separated from "the minor war and peace that goes on all the time among the men" (ibid.). In other words, and as I suggested in the last chapter, the politics of affinal exchange was disengaged from subsistence-oriented bush markets.

But once barter markets became the dominant mode of Chambri–Hills exchange, why were they characterized by the barter style of Iatmul fish-wives? Why were the Hills women willing to accept Chambri condescension and an unfair exchange rate when political relations between their tribes had never been regulated by military hegemony? My guess is that they never would have done so unless the Colonial Administrators who were mediating native relationships had encouraged them to.[16]

In order to understand why I believe it to have been out of the question for the Chambri and their Hills barter partners to arrive independently at a one-to-one exchange rate, we must consider another aspect of the relationship between these groups of fish-suppliers and sago-producers. Not only had the Chambri "Iatmulized" certain of the Hills peoples when living at Kamanbo, but they had also begun incorporating them into their social and ceremonial organizations. L. W. Bragge was the first to record this when he wrote: "Changriman and Mensuat were heavily influenced by Chambri refugees who gave them several women in marriage. Most of these people have Chambri blood and speak the Chambri language. Ties of co-operation are close, and largely based on sago trade" (1973: page unknown). I must qualify Bragge's account in two respects. First, he exaggerates the genetic connection between the Chambri and these Hills peoples. Although some Changriman and Mensuat share Chambri blood, it is not true that most of them do. Second, while the Chambri did give three women to the Changriman and two to the Mensuat, they also received eleven in return, eight from the Changriman and three from the Mensuat. But what is significant about these marriages is not who gave how many women to whom; it is that, by marrying one another at all, the Chambri and the Hills peoples brought about a merging of the subsistence and the political domains.

This situation generated a minefield of paradoxes. Since marriage now linked the Chambri to their sago-suppliers, it was possible for Chambri men to achieve status and prestige by helping unrelated Chambri to fulfill the affinal debts they had incurred to Hills wife-givers. But how could this be? Were the Changriman and Mensuat, like other affines, to be periodically recompensed for wives and children? An affirmative answer would suggest that these Hills peoples were just like the Chambri, in which case were they fish-suppliers, or had the Chambri become sago-producers? A negative answer would suggest that Changriman and Mensuat wives were not valuable, perhaps not quite women. But were they men? And finally, if Chambri women bartered fish for sago in an Iatmul manner, by showing condescension for their barter partners at every transaction, how could the fathers and husbands of these sago-suppliers be treated as superior wife-givers?

North of the Sepik, Sawos men had been providers of both sago and shells to their Iatmul trading partners—a situation the Sawos found contradictory once the Iatmul began to demand a regulated supply of sago. But the Iatmul had managed to negotiate the transition from trading partnership to barter market by creating additional boundaries between social domains—by separating the inequality inherent in their hegemony over their barter partners from their equal relationship with Sawos shell-providers. The Chambri transition, on the other hand, produced a muddling of domain boundaries. During their exile, the Changriman and Mensuat had become both affines and barter partners, and the former position was behaviorally and conceptually incompatible with the latter.

It will be remembered from chapter 2 that the Iatmul occasionally married women from the bush. Let me recall Bateson's discussion of Mindimbit–Kwolawoli marriages to see if those involved experienced behavioral and conceptional difficulties similar to those I have described between intermarrying Changriman, Mensuat, and Chambri.

> Formerly, when the Kwolawoli were more powerful they had obtained a number of women from Mindimbit (I think as part of a peacemaking) and one of these women, Mambi, had never been "backed," i.e., no woman had been given in exchange. . . .
>
> The debate was then resumed on the subject of Mambi and continued until finally the Kwolawoli agreed to hand over a woman. The woman decided on . . . was a member of the wrong totemic group and in no sense the sister of the man who had married Mambi, but this did not concern Mindimbit, though they agreed that the Kwolawoli clans might quarrel on the subject. . . .
>
> A few days later a payment of valuables and a pig was taken to the Kwolawoli, but this may have been done solely to enable the Mindimbit to justify themselves in case of Government interference. [1933: 284–85]

Bateson's account can be easily summarized. When the Kwolawoli were powerful, they coerced the Mindimbit into providing them with women and refused to recompense them fully; once the Mindimbit regained their power, they forced this recompense from the Kwolawoli, paying bride-price only to appease the yet more powerful Australian government. In other words, these marriages reversed the expected relationships between wife-givers and wife-takers. Giving women, in this context, conferred neither political nor economic advantages, but rather indicated one's powerlessness. Thus, the marital alliances established between Mindimbit and Kwolawoli did not involve them in the politics of affinal exchange—or in fulfilling any mutual social obligations. They only intermarried when the relations of power between them were already known, so as to preclude one group's obligations to the other.

These relations of power were precisely what the Chambri were unsure of regarding their former trading partners from the Hills, and it is my contention that Iatmul-style barter markets would not have developed between these peoples had European administrators not encouraged their institutionalization. It is ironic that Gardi, in his description of a fish-for-sago barter market between Chambri and Changriman women, remarks that the participants seemed hostile to each other "as in the days of headhunting" (1960: 97). In fact, the Chambri were not hostile to the Changriman and Mensuat in the days of headhunting. The marketers who had their hands slapped by disgruntled Chambri fishwives were the same people among whom the Chambri had been exiled for nearly twenty years—the same people from whom their brothers or fathers had taken wives. Plainly something had occurred in the interim to alter profoundly the relationship between these two groups.

After their exile, those Chambri who had not engaged to sell their labor were aware that their position within the region had become ambiguous, particularly vis-à-vis the Parambei, Changriman, and Mensuat. The Iatmul group had vanquished them in warfare, and the Hills peoples had given them refuge. But now, with Australian support, the Chambri had the opportunity of reestablishing their autonomy within the area. Although they could no longer act as purveyors of stone tools and mosquito bags, they could sell their labor, earn valuable European commodities, and please their European protectors. They wished to ignore their experiences of the last twenty years, to "lose our memories altogether, and become Big Men again."

The Hills peoples, on the other hand, had been "Iatmulized" during the exile. They had no intention of forgetting the knowledge they had acquired from the Chambri, and the Changriman saw no reason why they should not inhabit the hamlet the Chambri had abandoned upon returning to their island. Aware of the Australian-imposed pacification through contacts with those Europeans who had arranged for the Chambri to return home, the Changriman were the first to abandon their hamlets in the Hills for permanent life at Kamanbo.

We know from Gardi's description of the "Chambriman" hamlet on the hill that their move was complete by the early 1950s. And we can assume that during the twenty years they were making the move their dependence upon Chambri fish steadily increased. They did not master the art of making and using canoes until the mid-1960s, but depended upon Chambri women to bring them fish "through the narrow channels in the swamp and over the lake" (Gardi, 1960: 98). Thus, the Changriman, having abandoned their small and scattered hamlets, increased their dependence upon Chambri fish in much the same way that the Sawos had augmented their need for Iatmul fish. There were, however, certain significant differences between these two settlement processes.

First of all, the Chambri had taken wives from the Changriman during their exile among them, and these women had not been transferred as part of the politics of subordination we saw in operation between the Kwolawoli and the Mindimbit, but rather as tokens in the politics of affinal exchange. The Chambri held no hegemony over the Changriman and, moreover, were obligated to them as wife-takers. At the same time, the Changriman were becoming increasingly dependent upon the Chambri as fish-suppliers.

The second difference between the settlement process that affected the Sawos and that which influenced the Changriman involves the point in time at which each people stopped migrating. The Changriman became committed to a sedentary existence only after the Europeans arrived. Indeed, the Administration encouraged them to adopt this life-style which "led many of [their kind] to leave the hills for new sites on the rivers" (Dye et al., 1969: 146). The Australians felt that they could control and civilize villagers more easily than they could bands of hunter-gatherers, for they could collect the head tax from settled peoples, and thereby encourage them to learn European customs on copra plantations. Aware that the Changriman were ready to descend from their hill hamlets, and convinced that the move would serve as an example to other Hills peoples, the Australians assisted them to settle permanently. They did this by encouraging the Chambri, who were confused by the conflicting obligations they owed to the Changriman, to adopt an Iatmul-style market. As one of my informants put it: "Markets were not something belonging to our fathers and ancestors. They came after we returned from Kambano, together with the Government."

One fish for one piece of sago must have seemed perfectly fair to the Australians, who were not aware of the complex social, political, and economic relationships that had caused this exchange rate to arise between the Iatmul and the Sawos. And this was fine with the Chambri, who were absolved of their conflicting obligations at the same time they could please their Australian protectors. That this exchange rate was not fine with the Changriman, nor with any of the other Hills peoples who had to work harder and longer than the Chambri to support it, will become clear in later chapters.

During the dry season, from July through September, Chambri Lake recedes, leaving mud flats which sprout a thick carpet of green.

During the dry season, when water levels drop as much as five feet, Chambri Lake is choked with fish that rise to the surface to seek oxygen.

Chambri women gather fish by the canoe-load during the dry season.

Women transport dried fish to barter markets.

Women produce sago by felling a palm, peeling back its bark, and then pulverizing its pith, from which they leach its carbohydrate.

Seated Iatmul women barter fish for sago produced by their Sawos counterparts.

Tambwi Kwolikumbwi, my Chambri father.

A Chambri men's house.

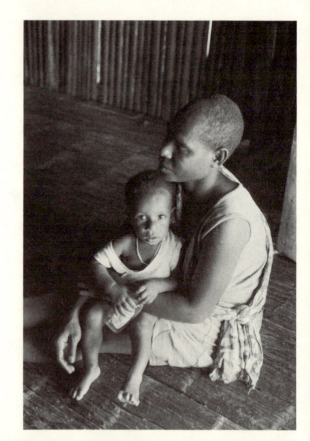

A Chambri mother and child.

Participant-observation during a phase of
male initiation.

THE RESTORATION OF HISTORY: WORLD WAR II IN THE MIDDLE SEPIK

If the European intrusion transformed egalitarian interaction into hierarchical control, World War II provided Middle Sepik peoples with the opportunity to reshift their sociopolitical relationships. In this chapter I discuss the suspension of Australian-imposed political and economic institutions and enterprises, focusing on what the Chambri and Iatmul peoples did when they temporarily regained control of their history, and how their actions affected the realization of Middle Sepik barter markets.

George Ellis and the Sambungundei Incident

On February 11, 1942, the civil administration of the Territory of Papua New Guinea, under attack by the Japanese, suspended its operation, thus temporarily ending nearly thirty years of Australian colonization. The District Officers, miners, missionaries, and other Europeans who had been working throughout the Sepik found themselves at loose ends. Their activities were no longer being supervised from Rabaul by the colonial administration, for that was where the heaviest fighting was going on, and they had no idea whether plans had been made for their evacuation. Gathering together at Angoram, they formulated escape plans, one involving the construction of an airstrip on the upper Karawari River just in case they should be evacuated by plane.

There were some, however, who refused to consider escape. George Ellis was one of these, believing anyone who abandoned the invaded territory to be a deserter. Stationed at Angoram before the war began, District Officer Ellis had hidden a large quantity of ammunition to fight off the invaders. He vowed never to leave his post, but to have his police "fight the Japs to the last man" (McCarthy, 1963: 216).

When Assistant District Officer Jim Taylor and Patrol Officer Charles Bates arrived at Angoram to help with the evacuation of those Europeans still in the Sepik region, Ellis responded with recalcitrance. He barricaded himself, together with forty native police, in the police station and refused to emerge. When Taylor and Bates armed themselves to force him out, Ellis ordered his men to fire at them. Taylor was shot in the groin. Bates and his men withdrew to Marienberg for medical assistance and to seek reinforcements.

Joined by the District Officer from Wewak and a number of natives who had been sworn in as special constables, Bates and his men returned to Angoram. They found Ellis dead in his house, having shot himself through the head after writing a suicide note to his family.

Ellis's police had abandoned him. Some of them had gone home to their villages, leaving their uniforms and ammunition at Angoram. Others, however, ran amok, killing and raping throughout the area. Their first white victim was a patrol officer, R. B. Strudwick, whom they shot as he was eating a meal at Timbunke. They then traveled up the Korosameri River in their stolen government launch, where they met and killed the three white members of the mining party that Strudwick had been supervising.

The renegade police were in possession of considerable ammunition and fuel, and could have continued their pillage for quite some time. Although there were initially only eight of them, they had persuaded nearly thirty Sepik villagers to join them, including several Chambri. Establishing headquarters on Sambungundei Island in Chambri Lake, these men traveled to neighboring villages to steal food and valuables and to rape women.

Their activities, however, did not last long, for the murder of white men was intolerable to the colonial government even during the extraordinary circumstance of the Japanese invasion. Patrol Officer John Mulligan and a large force of native constables finally defeated the renegades during a bloody battle at Sambungundei.

How can we explain the behavior of those Chambri and Iatmul who joined the renegade police to rape and pillage their neighbors and to kill the white men who stood in their way? Were they expressing the "latent hostility" they felt toward those they perceived as oppressing them (see Curtain, 1978: 17)? Was this hostility destined to "erupt once news became known that the Europeans were on the defensive in a major war" (ibid.)? In other words, were these police and their followers revolutionaries, who had gained consciousness of their position within the imperialist system that oppressed them?

I eliminate this possibility for several reasons. First of all, although the renegade police may well have felt latent hostility toward their European administrators, this motivation does not explain why they dispatched white and black men alike. Not only did they kill Europeans, but they also "ravaged a wide area, fomenting local uprisings at some points and caus[ing] serious disorders among the natives"(McCarthy, quoted in Curtain, 1978: 18).

Second, it would be farfetched to argue that they fomented these uprisings to overthrow imperialism or to demonstrate against oppression in the abstract. They themselves had begun to act as oppressors, stealing food, raping women, taking guns, steel tools, and whatever European-produced commodities they could acquire, and they did so because they wished to possess more of what Westerners had to offer.

A second explanation of the renegades' behavior is implied by Allen's contention that New Guineans recognized the Japanese as "nearer to . . . [themselves] in background and outlook than any other outsiders with whom . . . [they] had come in contact" (1976: 88). Could it have been that the police wanted to clear the Sepik region of inscrutable white men to make room for culturally cognate Japanese?

At first this explanation appears ridiculous, for it belies all that anthropologists know about the vast cultural differences between New Guineans and Japanese, and seems to be based on a naive tendency to regard those things which are unlike oneself as similar to each other. But when we reflect upon the cleverness of Japanese propaganda, we are forced to conclude that their insight into the New Guinean world-view was quite sophisticated. Consider, for example, the following pamphlet distributed by the Japanese among literate New Guineans:

> Just now times are hard, but as soon as we have finished off the whites . . . we will send many ships laden with cargo and you will have all the clothes, shoes, blankets and firearms, canned food in abundance and all the utensils you desire. The white skins are cowardly, they ground you down and exploited you but we will treat you as men. We are mighty and we are your friends and your ancestors. [quoted in Allen, 1976: 87]

If New Guineans responded favorably to the Japanese—if they recognized them as being like themselves—it was because the Japanese promised them what they wanted—namely, access to European goods.

This desire for cargo is, in fact, how my Chambri informants explain the activities of the renegades and their followers. Ambunowi, for example, who remembers those Chambri who joined the police, describes them as "boss-boys who decided to steal everything and kill everyone once the white men had gone away," and explains their actions as a means of acquiring Japanese cargo. Taplambun, another Chambri who remembers these men, agrees. He describes them as "humbugging the whole area over women and food."

> They would go into a village, steal the food and rape all of the women, and then go back to Sambungundei. This all took place before the war, when many Chambri believed that the Japanese

would bring us the cargo that the Australians had held on to. That's why some of the men went over to the police. They had to take many heads so that the Japanese would know their power.

But why did the renegade police, assuming that they wanted cargo, decide to pillage and murder their way through the Sepik, raiding villages that could provide little or nothing of what they desired? How can we understand Taplambun's association between power, raiding, and the acquisition of goods? Why would Sepik men assume that by taking many heads they could persuade the Japanese to provide them with cargo? The connection between these activities and events is illuminated by Bateson's description of the male ethos among the Iatmul:

> Running through this plexus of cultural details we can clearly see the general position of head-hunting as the main source of pride of the village, while associated with the pride is prosperity, fertility and the male sexual act. . . .
>
> Closely linked with these emphases upon pride . . . is the development of the spectacular side of head-hunting. Every victory was celebrated by great dances and ceremonial which involved the whole village. The killer was the hero of these and he was at the same time the host at the feasts which accompany them. Even the vanquished assented to the beauty of the dances, as appears from a text collected in Mindimbit describing the typical series of events on a raid:
>
>> (After the fighting) they leave off. Then he (the killer, standing in his canoe and holding up the head which he has taken from the enemy) asks "I am going to my beautiful dances, to my beautiful ceremonies. Call his name." (The vanquished reply) "It is so-and-so that you have speared." (Or the victor will say) "This one is a woman" and they (the vanquished) will call her name (and they will cry to the victors) "Go. Go to your beautiful dances, to your beautiful ceremonies." [1958: 141]

This apparently sympathetic response on the part of the vanquished village is only comprehensible as part of a general sociocultural commitment to egalitarianism—to the possibility of turning the tables and having the victor become the vanquished. Those who are celebrating the beautiful dances and the beautiful ceremonies know that they may well be mourning tomorrow, for they live in a world in which it is understood that a head will be taken for a head.

This commitment to egalitarianism helps us to understand why the rebel police ravaged native villages and killed white men in cold blood. They were not revolutionaries trying to wrest capital away from their oppressors. Nor were they madmen who reverted to "savagery" in a time of trouble and anxiety. Rather, they were demonstrating that they were the equals of those they attacked and of those they expected to bring them cargo. They fully anticipated reprisals, for reprisals are part of what is necessary to remain men among men. In other words, they were reestablishing themselves as Sepik warriors and anticipating that the Japanese—cognizant of their powers—would engage them in reciprocal exchange in a way that the Australians had not.

Japanese Massacres and the Chambri Lake Intrusions

Of course, the Iatmul living on the Sepik River never did acquire the abundant cargo that the Japanese propaganda had promised. Instead they frequently found themselves caught in the crossfire between Japanese and Allied Forces. At the Iatmul village of Timbunke, for example, ninety-six men and one woman were massacred early in 1944 by natives from other Sepik villages acting under Japanese orders. Several Timbunke had previously assisted the Australians to find a small Japanese garrison that had been stationed in the area. In response to this betrayal, the Japanese sent word to the Timbunke that a gift of pigs was expected in compensation. Arriving at the exchange site designated by the Japanese, the Timbunke found fifty natives waiting for them, all of whom were armed with clubs and knives. The Japanese emerged from their hiding place in the bush to help the armed natives tie the Timbunkes' arms together. This done, they set their henchmen upon the helpless people, bayonetting or machinegunning those who survived the clubbing and knifing.

A similar incident could have occurred at Avatip, when a party of one hundred Japanese soldiers arrived there, led by the same Iatmul leader who had organized the Timbunke massacre. Curtain reports that the Avatip, some of whom had been helping the Australians, were convinced that what had happened to the Timbunke would happen to them. They decided to take the offensive. After two days of fasting to appease their *Tambaran*, or ancestral spirits, each Avatip man took his stone dagger, singled out a Japanese soldier and, at a given signal, attacked (1978: 21).

Other Iatmul, however, were not so brave, and preferred to seek refuge from the war in the back swamps of Chambri Lake. These were the men and women who migrated to the islands of LukLuk, Arinjone, and Timbunmeri. They had found that the Sepik River was no longer a desirable location now that Japanese, and not they, controlled its advantages.

LukLuk and Arinjone had always served as temporary fishing and gathering sites for groups of Iatmul, Chambri, and Hills people. During the war, however, Iatmul from Nyaurengai built a permanent village on LukLuk, as did some Japanaut Iatmul on Arinjone. But the most significant reshifting from the Chambri point of view occurred when a group of Kandingai moved from their village to inhabit Timbunmeri Island.

Unlike LukLuk and Arinjone, which were permanently inhabited before the war, Timbunmeri's history seems to have been one of violent intrusions and expulsions, as certain groups attempted to establish permanent villages on it and others prevented them from doing so. In fact, except for the respite provided by Western law and order between 1925 and 1944, the use of Timbunmeri—or Kabano, as the Chambri call it—has always been contested by contingents of Chambri, Hills, and Iatmul men. It is an island rich in sago palms and hardwood trees but, more importantly from the Chambri perspective, it rises from the lake close to the rivulets they must use to travel to the Sepik Hills. Those in control of the island, therefore, would find it possible to attack Chambri marketing parties destined for the bush. For this reason the Chambri, although themselves never intending to inhabit Timbunmeri, have preferred that no other group does so.

In 1944, however, with the Australians gone from the region, several clans of Kandingai Iatmul, who had been forced from their homes by hunger after the Yentchamangua Iatmul blocked access to the sago market at Torembi,[1] were invited by the Chambri *Luluai*,* Wapiyeri, to move to Timbunmeri Island. The Yentchamangua had taken advantage of the Japanese invasion to rekindle old hostilities, and Wapiyeri felt he had to help his "brothers," the Kandingai, out of a difficult situation.[2] The Kandingai were all too willing to accept his invitation, for they had come to realize how unsafe the Sepik River was during this time of Allied-Japanese fighting.

Given the amount of time and energy that had been spent by Chambri to keep Timbunmeri free of intruders, one wonders how Wapiyeri could so easily invite the Kandingai to take refuge there. When I asked Wapiyeri this question, he said, "Just as Kwolimbank helped Emosuie to anchor Chambri Island where it now stands, so I helped the hungry Kandingai to sit down and feed themselves. It's the custom among brothers to act in this way."

Not satisfied with this answer, I asked him why he had chosen to help his Kandingai brothers at that point in time. He responded with a lecture on the nature of brotherhood, using the following story as an illustration.

> A long time ago, when I was young, Mepan, a Mensuat woman from the Sepik Hills, was killed by Chambri *changuman* [sorcery]. It was Yarapat's line of fathers who worked the magic, causing a snake to come up from the ground and bite the woman. But they didn't do it on their own account. No, Yambimun, Bania,

---

Luluais were villagers appointed by the Australian administrators to coordinate local-level political concerns with those of the colonial government.

Klimbandi, and Kamentengin, all men of Mensuat, had requested that they do so.

Well, Yarapat's line of fathers waited for a long time for the Mensuat to pay them a pig for their troubles. But the pig didn't come. So, when they saw Yambimun's dog, left at Chambri by his master, they killed and ate it.

Walinakwan and Wusuai went to Mensuat to tell the father of the dog what Yarapat's line had done. His stomach became hot, and he came to Chambri to cool it. But Yarapat's line denied ever having seen his dog. So Yambimun returned home to Mensuat to form a fight party, having decided to cool his stomach through war.

The Mensuat killed Amen and Mngilailin, both of whom belonged to my men's house. They didn't have their heads cut off, though, because this wasn't a real war, just a cross.

Suwangan's ancestor was looking out of his window at all of the action when Salande, a Big Man from Mensuat, speared him through the hand. There were many injuries that day. Eventually Andisok, Ambunowi's ancestor, extended a stick outside of his window to which he had attached some *kina*. The *kina* tabooed the fighting as soon as Bania, the Mensuat leader, took them.

Some time later, my father started to think about the good Chambri men who had been killed by the Mensuat. The more he thought about them, the more he worried. So he went to visit his good friends at Kandingai. He offered them many *kina* if they could help him revenge the dead Chambri.

The Kandingai filled three canoes with warriors. They decided to wait for the Mensuat near to where the grass grows thickly, close to the bush hamlet. As the Mensuat were leaving one morning to kill some wild pigs, the Chambri and Kandingai ambushed them. They killed three Mensuat before the bushmen even knew what was happening. After they had enough killing, Marikumban and his Kandingai friends, Kaliomeri and Kambo, fled to the Kamanbo rivulet near Timbunmeri, where they slept peacefully until dawn.

The story describes an incident where the Kandingai helped the Chambri against a Hills group, the implication being that Wapiyeri repaid his father's debt by giving Kandingai refuge on Timbunmeri. When I asked him if this was an appropriate reading of the story, he said: "No, the Kandingai were like older brothers to us. It would have taken many things to repay them. But before the white men came back after the war with Japan, we thought we could do it."

Among the many things done by the Kandingai were: assisting the Chambri in most of their minor hostilities since the turn of the century;[3] helping the

Chambri free Timbunmeri from its previous inhabitants, the Manabi; and cooperating with the Australians to convince the Chambri to return from a twenty-year exile in the Hills. The Chambri debt to them was considerable, but the Chambri did not accept it with equanimity.

Committed to an ideology of egalitarianism, the Chambri chafed under Kandingai patronage but were unable to do much about it, given their small population and their peripheral situation within the regional socio-economic system. When Wapiyeri invited the Kandingai to stay on Timbunmeri, however, he believed that he and his people were finally to emerge as a major power within the Sepik. Considering their long-term subservient position as commodity-suppliers to the Iatmul, their opportunity to assist the Kandingai must have seemed all the more sweet.

Unfortunately, what the Chambri believed would be a temporary stay—a visit they thought would reverse the direction of Kandingai–Chambri dependency by placing them in the unaccustomed role of patrons—turned into a permanent situation. The postwar Australian administration decided that the Kandingai had genuine claims upon the island and deserved to remain permanently settled there, thus sanctioning and in fact perpetuating what had been achieved only through a suspension of the colonial presence. So long as Australia administered the area, the political processes through which villages migrated from territory to territory remained closed.

Wapiyeri feels misused by both the Australians and by his former Kandingai allies, but not because they have betrayed his confidence. His own story of "brotherhood" is, after all, rife with treacheries: the Mensuat pay to have their own woman ensorcelled; Yarapat's relatives are not compensated for their services; Wusuai and Walinakwan betray their people to the dog's Mensuat owner. What disappoints Wapiyeri, rather, is his incapacity to reply adequately to the Kandingai and Australian betrayal. About the former he asks: "I paid them for their assistance when I invited them to Timbunmeri. Why are they troubling us and ruining everything by staying on our ground and in our water?" And about the latter he says: "Since the Australians have fastened our customs, we can no longer behave like men." In other words, Wapiyeri recognizes that his open-ended social interactions have been permanently transformed into a hierarchically organized system in which a reversal of the ranks is out of the question. Self-regulation and autonomy have been eliminated for the sake of peace and stability.

The Realization of Chambri Lake Barter Markets

It was not until the Australians returned after the war that the Chambri realized they had a problem on their hands. The Iatmul had always been so vociferously committed to their Sepik River villages that it was thought impossible for any of them to choose life on islands in the back swamps, where those they called *numanki*—that is, incompetents—lived.

If life in the lake region initially appealed to the Iatmul as an escape from Japanese-Allied crossfire, after the war it became a means of remaining insulated from the new Australian administration. The Iatmul and Chambri who lived there were not as closely observed as were their river-dwelling counterparts (that is, not until St. Mary's Mission was built on Chambri Island in 1957). Thus, they could hold their ceremonies in peace: scarifying, initiating, divorcing, practicing polygyny, and, sometimes, allowing their young men to earn the right to wear black paint in the traditional manner—through the taking of a head, or through the ritual slaughter of an infant acquired from a neighboring people.

Moreover, the Iatmul realized that life on Chambri Lake could be supported in a familiar manner, for fish were easily available and sago could be obtained through barter. This is why Wapiyeri was so pleased to help the Kandingai by inviting them to Timbunmeri. They had been deprived of their access to the Torembi sago market and were hungry for their favorite food. By bringing them to Timbunmeri, Wapiyeri reasoned that he could assist his friends without imposing upon his own people.

The Kandingai, after all, could acquire sago just as the Chambri did, in exchange for fish with the Hills peoples. By inviting the Kandingai to Timbunmeri, the Chambri could acquire status without having to expend any effort, or so Wapiyeri reasoned.

What he did not realize, however, was the degree to which the Iatmul migration into the lake region would drastically transform the nature of the relationships between groups of fish-suppliers and sago-producers. Having developed from individualized male-dominated trading partnerships during the Chambri exile, when the refugees traded their knowledge of Iatmul customs for status and autonomy, barter markets evolved during the pre–World War II years (see Mead, 1963), when Chambri men left their villages to work on plantations for European entrepreneurs. But they were only fully realized within the lake region after the Iatmul moved in. Then the markets became completely depersonalized, with Chambri and Iatmul women mingling to exchange fish with their counterparts from the various sago-producing hamlets.

By the time World War II ended, the major back-swamp barter market was near Changriman. Mali, Bisis, Chambri, and Iatmul women would meet there to exchange their produce at a rate which had been customary between Iatmul and Sawos and which the Australians encouraged as manifestly fair: one fish for one piece of sago. But circumstances were not the same as they had been between Iatmul and Sawos, particularly because the Iatmul migration doubled the number of water people from whom the Hills women could obtain their fish. They had no intention of supplying these additional women with sago. Why should they? They could easily obtain sufficient fish from either the Iatmul or the Chambri, and the government's reinstated pacification policy eliminated the possibility of military coercion. They could do as they pleased, and it certainly did not please them to prepare enough sago to satisfy twice as many water people.

With the Kandingai competing for Hills sago, and with exchanges set at a one-to-one rate, the supply of fish far outweighed the Hills women's demand, and the Chambri frequently returned from market expeditions without having made the exchanges they had counted on. They told me that their children "cried of hunger for sago"; that "sago was our strength and the Kandingai pulled it from us." Whether exaggerated or not, their fear is understandable, for they were experiencing a profound transformation in the nature of the social relationships that regulated their subsistence economy. No longer could they count on their friendships with the Hills people to insure that they received the sago they needed. For the first time in their history, the Chambri were competing for their subsistence and the Hills people had a choice of friends.

The Chambri could not respond to these changed circumstances in a traditional manner, through the payback system illustrated by Wapiyeri in his story about brotherhood. They had no hope of eliminating the Kandingai from Timbunmeri through warfare, for they were no longer regulating their own lives. Rather, they appealed to the outside authority of Australian judges, hoping to persuade the law that their claims upon the island were the more justified.

L. W. Bragge's patrol reports are preoccupied with land cases, and particularly with disputes between the Kandingai and the Chambri. Throughout his tenure as Assistant District Commissioner of the East Sepik District, between 1971 and 1974, the Chambri and Kandingai were actively disputing ownership of Timbunmeri. Indeed, they had been arguing over the island ever since the Kandingai clans decided to settle permanently there rather than return to the village they inhabited before the war.

These are the bases of both sides' claims: The Kandingai argue that they purchased the island from the Manabi, the island's original inhabitants, after they helped the Chambri defeat this people in war. The Chambri counter this assertion by insisting that the shell money paid by the Kandingai to that remnant of Manabi living among the Mali, Garamambu, and Changriman was not meant to purchase land rights, but rather to establish barter markets—that to acquire sago from these bush-peoples, the Kandingai had to pay for their markets, like "a man must pay for his wives."

The Chambri brought their grievance before the Land Titles Commission several times during the 1950s, and each time the authorities decided in Kandingai's favor;[4] the island, they argued, had been duly purchased and now belongs to the Kandingai Iatmul. The Chambri do not accept this decision and believe that the newly independent government of Papua New Guinea will eventually reverse it. To this end, Patrick Yarapat, an influential Chambri leader, has compiled, in Pidgin, a collection of evidence bearing on the case. This consists of a variety of data which Yarapat divides into the following eight categories: the Chambri forefathers who owned territory on Timbunmeri Island; the men's houses that were built there; the people who died there; the subdivisions of land and water that prevail there (since these would only be known by people familiar with the island); the destruction wreaked by the Kandingai upon Chambri property found there; the islands and rivulets used illegally by the Iatmul throughout Chambri Lake; and the confrontations between Kandingai and Chambri since the former moved to Timbunmeri.

Those items in the last category are perhaps the most revealing as they contain reports of actual behavior. For example, consider the following two events. According to Yarapat, the first of these occurred in 1957, and the second in 1969.

> Suwangan, Woliop, and Yembon [all three men were of Kilimbit] went to find crocodile eggs near Timbunmeri. Kandal and Malisupwan of Kandingai met them and asked them: "Why have you three come inside this water of mine?"
>
> The three of them answered: "Whose child are you that you can ask us this question?"
>
> Malisupwan replied: "I'm the child of Mevan."
>
> Suwangan said: "Sorry too much, but I think your mouth talks for nothing. I know Mevan, and this is not the place his ancestors come from [literally, "this is not the ass ground of his family"]. And this is not his water either. He belongs to Kandingai. Your father took you and brought you inside my boundary mark. The men of Yentchamangua killed you something no good, and they raped your mothers, and they destroyed your canoes inside the Kingisu rivulet. Your fathers ran away together, and stay here at Kabano now. All right, I'll teach you. Your fathers weren't doing well. They stayed inside the bush, and ate bark of the bamboo and sugarcane, until Wapi got them and brought them here. You can't ask us questions about why we're here. We're the ones who should be asking you these questions."
>
> Malisupwan agreed: "Yes, I understand. My father told me this story. We are Kandingai. We came to stay in your waters, to eat from your waters, and to live on your ground within your boundary mark. We belong to the Sepik, to Nyaula. We're of the habit of acquiring food wherever we can get it, of stealing fish belonging to another water. Yes, you're right, for a long time ago my father told me about this ground and water of yours. I have heard your talk before."

Kaviwon and John Wasi went to market with Mali. Yawa of Kandingai spoke to the women of Mali: "Why do you give sago to the women of Chambri?"

A woman from Mali replied: "We don't know your women. We only know Chambri women. If you want to market you must go to your own bush, to the Torembi bush. You can carry fish and tobacco and go to the women of Torembi, and they'll give you sago. You belong to another region. We only know the women of Chambri in order to change fish for sago."

All the women began to fight, until Kaviwon and Wasi stopped them. Kaviwon then said: "In the past, our fathers and ancestors didn't market as we do now. Headmen would meet, that's all, in order to change sago and fish for their own families. When the government came, then we all began to market together. If the women from Mali want Kandingai fish, it's all right, they can get them. But they must scrub enough sago for everyone."

All of the conversations Yarapat has summarized take the same form. Men from Chambri, engaged in visiting trading partners, or seeking crocodile eggs, or cutting down hardwood trees, or some other activity, come into contact with Kandingai men from Timbunmeri; the Kandingai challenge the Chambri's right to be where they are, or to be doing what they are doing; and the Chambri demonstrate—calmly, reasonably, and successfully—that it is the Kandingai who should be worried about rights of access and use, for none of their Iatmul ancestors were born on the island on which they, their descendants, now live.

Kaviwon's reputed last statement to the women of Mali is the only indication in Yarapat's body of data of the real issue at stake in the Kandingai–Chambri land disputes, namely, the competition between the two groups of fish-suppliers for the limited supply of Hills sago. That Yarapat does not directly confront this issue is not surprising, for Australian judges found it impossible to adjudicate problematic socioeconomic relationships unless they were translated into questions of land and resource ownership. Thus, the problem of sago-supply becomes transformed into the question of conflicting land claims, and Yarapat argues that the Chambri have more right to Timbunmeri than the Kandingai.

As an example of this transformation, consider maps 4, 5, and 6, a series of drawings executed by Yarapat to illustrate Chambri land claims. He drew these maps in my presence, rejecting the first two as inadequate but pleased with the accuracy of his final version.

Yarapat may have felt his first try to be inadequate because it is such a fine illustration of Chambri political processes prior to the European intrusion. On map 4, he arranges villages and hamlets in complementary opposition, distinguished from one another only by their names and allies. He makes no attempt to depict their actual geographic locations. The world

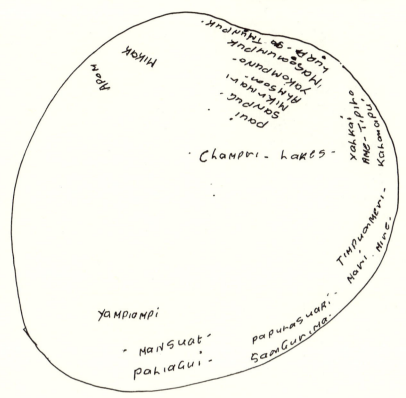

Yarapat's First Map

this map portrays is one in which the tit-for-tat payback system prevails—where equal men and the groups they represent regulate themselves through egalitarian competition.

Map 5 begins the transformation completed in map 6. Both of these drawings roughly depict the actual locations of islands within Chambri Lake. Map 5 distinguishes these from the Sepik Hills hamlets that are located in the upper portion of the page (Mensuat, Sanguriman, etc.). And map 6 relates these lake and hills settlements to the Iatmul villages on the right-hand side of the page (Sarmpote, Yamanumpu, etc.), and to the Korosa-meri hamlets on the left and upper portion of the page (Watakataui, Sapi-kantui, etc.).

On map 6, Yarapat indicates the boundary line between Iatmul and Chambri territories with four small *x*'s. His indifference to the Chambri–Hills boundary suggests that this map, like the first one, expresses political concerns, but differently. On map 4, Yarapat distinguishes groups by their

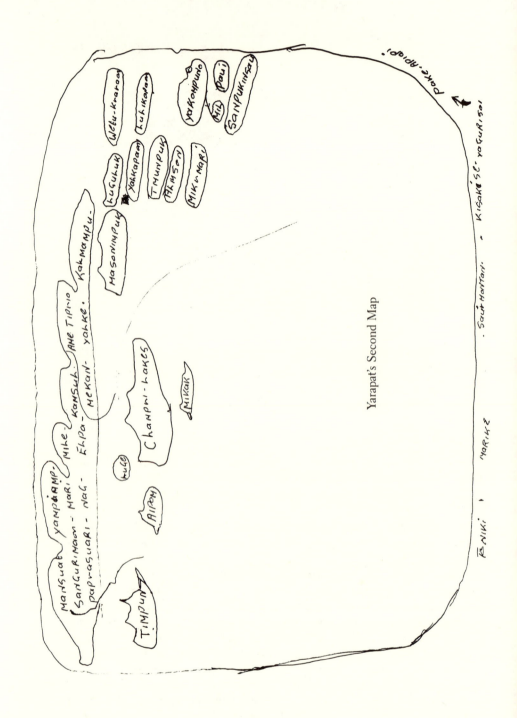

Yarapat's Second Map

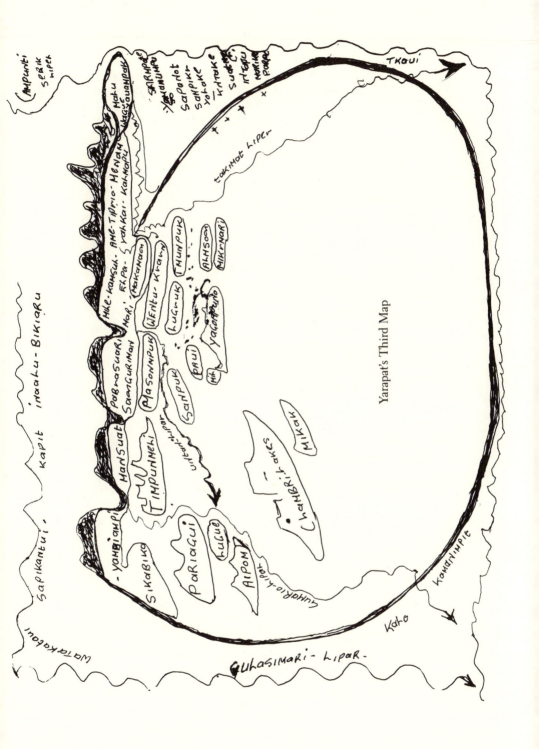

Yarapat's Third Map

names and allegiances, while on map 6 he contrasts their particular and limited territories. And while we know that political alliances have shifted through time according to historical circumstances, Yarapat's boundary marks can only be changed by external judges. Indeed, he explicitly drew the maps to help these judges decide future land cases in favor of the Chambri, indicating the degree to which the Iatmul have penetrated into lake territory. Map 6, he argues, describes the "true" and "traditional" territorial boundaries, as those in power should maintain them.

His argument would never convince Wapiyeri, who had hoped that World War II would reestablish the flexibility of egalitarian interaction throughout the Sepik. Wapiyeri had been one of the three Chambri men to join Ellis's renegade police. Returning to Chambri Island at night rather than camping out on Sambungundei, he was never apprehended by the Australians. Ironically, he was subsequently appointed their Luluai.

Wapiyeri's expectation—that World War II would inaugurate the permanent reinstatement of egalitarian interaction—was not borne out by events. The Australians returned to the region and institutionalized the transformations that had occurred in their absence, sanctioning and perpetuating a fish-for-sago exchange system that could not support those who depended upon it. The Iatmul had moved into the lake to stay, for the Land Titles Commission recognized the validity of their claims.

Wapiyeri had been mistaken in his assumption that he could reverse the direction of Kandingai–Chan.bri dependency by extending an invitation to Timbunmeri. He was just as mistaken in his assumption that the Japanese would engage him in equal exchange once they learned to respect his power. His error on both counts was to suppose that the Australians would never again return to transform the flexible and open-ended social relationships that had been reestablished in their absence into static and hierarchically organized social structures. In essence, he had bet on the wrong side.

FROM SAGO-SUPPLIERS TO ENTREPRENEURS: THE ACCOMMODATION OF CHAMBRI WOMEN

Recently I had the privilege of escorting a member of Papua New Guinea's parliament around New York City. Matias Yambumpe is a Chambri who was president of his Local Government Council before being elected to the House. He has had a long career in government, has traveled widely, and has been living in the capital city of Port Moresby for many years. New York, however, amazed him. As we stood together on the roof of the World Trade Center, after ascending 107 floors in seconds, I remembered that Margaret Mead had written about Mr. Yambumpe's father, Walinakwan, in *Sex and Temperament*. She described him as

> beautiful, a graceful dancer, a fluent speaker, proud, imperious, but withal soft-spoken, and resourceful. In addition to his first wife, who had been given him as a child by his mother's clan, two other women had chosen him as a husband. He was a fortunate man. All three of his wives could plait mosquito-bags, and Wali-nakwon was therefore in a fair way to become a rich man. [1963: 253]

Mr. Yambumpe, the second son of Walinakwan's first wife, is also a fortunate man, as I shall show in this chapter. But his good fortune was earned by engaging in activities very different from those which preoccupied his father—activities his father would not have thought possible. Neither of Mr. Yambumpe's two wives, moreover, has ever woven a mosquito bag. The second, a woman much younger than her husband, does not even know what one looks like, because all of them have been sold by now to museums or tourists. And although Mr. Yambumpe is also a fine speaker, the words he uses would be incomprehensible to Walinakwan, for they frequently refer to international economic policy, to money, to development, and to education.

There have, in other words, been tremendous changes in the Middle Sepik over the past twenty-five years, and in this chapter I discuss some of them, focusing on the transformation of barter into money markets and the development of regional political organizations. I do not argue that the Sepik peoples—the Chambri, Iatmul, Sawos, and Hills—are now living totally new lives, for this is not the case. Nor do I wish to apply the anthropological cliché about continuity in change, for it is a distortion of the historical process. Walinakwan would not have understood many of his son's concerns, and Mr. Yambumpe has lost much of his father's knowledge.

The perspective I feel best elucidates the changes that have occurred throughout the Middle Sepik was suggested to me by Mr. Yambumpe himself, as he tried to come to terms with the subway trains, the bridges, the buildings, and the people of Manhattan. He said to me: "This strength is not something you made. And it's not something that your fathers made. It's something that was made slowly; it comes to you from your distant ancestors, each building upon what came before. Your ancestors did not have these things themselves. They were more like Papua New Guineans than you are. This means that we, too, can expect these things to come to Papua New Guinea some day."

Although I would not agree with Mr. Yambumpe's unilinear evolutionary conclusion that subway trains and so on could be expected to develop in New Guinea, I think his general point well founded. He realizes that just because we Americans have subways and skyscrapers doesn't mean that our ancestors knew about these developments when they settled the country. Our strength—to use Mr. Yambumpe's term—is dependent upon our ancestors' activities, but it can not be explained by them. In other words, we must learn to separate the consequences from the causes of change if we wish to learn about the process through which change comes about.

Descent from the Hills

The most important change experienced by the Chambri in recent years has been the descent of their sago-suppliers from the Sepik Hills to the shores of Chambri Lake, a move which effectively destroyed all fish-for-sago exchange south of the Sepik River. Bragge's descriptions of these migrations all reveal the same general pattern:

> In 1970 Mensuat established a permanent village on Peliagwi and are now living there. There is some resistance from Wombun, but this is tempered since Mensuat is a major sago-supplier. . . .
> Later the Changriman group settled with Chambri refugees living at Kamanbo and thus they settled at their present village site in 1950. . . .

> At present the Mari groups consist of Big Mari, Small Mari,
> Milae, and Kurapio Hamlet. . . . Big Mari and Milae are sixteen
> miles apart in a straight line, with Small Mari and Kurapio lo-
> cated between them. Milae set up its permanent camp in 1970.
> Without law and order enforcement these small groups would be
> in constant danger—Milae for example is on land claimed by
> Garamambu. . . . Kurapio is in a similar position, being a thorn
> in the side of the hard pressed Kandingais at Timbunmeri. [Bragge,
> 1973: pages unknown]

Thus, over a twenty-year period, each of the Sepik Hills hamlets has moved
closer to the lake, with Changriman leading the way and the others following suit.

They moved for a variety of reasons: out of curiosity; out of a desire to
acquire the European goods they knew were more easily accessible the closer
to the river one was; because they were no longer afraid to do so, having
learned to put their faith in the Australian ban on headhunting; because
life nearer the water seemed easier and sweeter; because they were afraid to
disobey the white men who wanted them to move so that they could be
counted more easily and so that something called "development" would
proceed; because the missionaries who reached them convinced them of
the damnation that would befall if they did not make themselves accessible
to God. For all of these reasons, it seemed best to move, and so they slowly
made their way down from the hills to build Sepik-like houses on the uninhabited islands in the lake, or on the shores of the hills in which they
used to live.

Bragge, it will be noticed, did not provide a migrational history of the
Garamambu. He did not do so because in 1966 the jurisdiction of Garamambu fell to civil servants stationed at Ambunti, while he administered
the Iatmul, Chambri, Sawos, and remaining Hills peoples from the patrol
post at Pagwi. Nevertheless, the Garamambu have figured extensively
throughout Chambri history, both as sago-suppliers and as military allies,
and their gradual descent from their mountain hamlets may serve as an
example of the process that brought all the Hills people to the shores of the
lake. I think we might also regard the socioeconomic effects of that migration as typical.

McCarthy mentions the Garamambu in his autobiographical *Patrol into
Yesterday*, an account of his experiences as an administrator of the colonial
government. In 1930 the Garamambu asked him to help halt attacks made
upon them by their (now dispersed) neighbors, the Kamchua. At first he
thought the Garamambu "a timid people" who were being troubled by "a
wild tribe, sometimes friendly and sometimes hostile and their mood, at
any given time, could not be depended upon" (1963: 60). Along with six

police, two officers, the occupants of some thirty Chambri war canoes, and numerous Garamambu—now "painted and plumed and fully armed . . . no longer the timid shy folk of yesterday" (ibid.)—McCarthy set off to make peaceful contact with the wild Kamchua. Unfortunately, he failed to do this, for one Kamchua man was shot by the police, and the tribe was wiped out after successive raids by the Garamambu and other groups before they could be pacified. What McCarthy's patrol did initiate, however, were friendly relationships between the government officials stationed at Ambunti and the Garamambu.

These relationships convinced many Garamambu that life atop their mountain was insufficient; that the only way to integrate themselves adequately within the new Australian-run government was to become more accessible to those Europeans who were to be found, in increasing numbers, down below. This government, after all, seemed favorably disposed toward them. As one old Garamambu man put it: "They [the government officers] were our good friends. They helped us finish off the Kamchua, and so we called them our ancestors."

Numerous Garamambu men began to migrate to plantations; others worked for the prospectors who began to search their mountain for gold; and others decided to establish settlements on the shores of Chambri Lake. It is to the activities of these last individuals that the Chambri attribute the breakdown of their fish-for-sago exchanges with the Garamambu, particularly to the following events, transcribed from the account of a Chambri man who participated in them.

> After we destroyed the Manabi [see chapter 5] some Garamambu were living on Timbunmeri while others moved to Simandung-wan. Chambri had also built houses and *haus tambaran* at Timbunmeri, near to where the Kandingai now live. We were all angry with a Garamambu who was playing around with an Indingai woman. Our fathers worked poison on a pig and some tobacco and then gave them to the Garamambu.* Garamambu smoked the tobacco and it awakened their blood so that they wanted to fight with Chambri. One Garamambu came to where the Chambri were staying. They called this man Təpwi. He was returning to his house when he met Tive of the Mangembit *haus tambaran*, and he cut Tive's head off altogether and then ran away with it.
>
> The Big Men of Chambri met and talked and did magic. They took away all of Garamambu's strength. Some Chambri were afraid because Garamambu lived on top of a mountain and had bows and arrows. Two groups went to Kurapio and two groups went to

---

*By "working poison" my informant means that magical names were recited over the food and tobacco in order to imbue these substances with ancestral powers.

Mepen.[1] The [patrimoiety] Nyeminimba held the shields and the [patrimoiety] Nauinimba held the spears because it's right for mothers to protect their children.[2] They fought mostly with Təp-wi's clan. Soon they changed positions and Nauinimba held the shields and Nyeminimba held the spears. They surrounded Təp-wi's house so that those inside couldn't run away. But Təpwi turned himself into a fly and escaped. Eventually they set fire to his house and everyone inside of it died. The Garamambu heads were gathered and put in string bags. The Chambri went back to their camp and sang all night at Timbunmeri.

The subsequent two episodes of the Chambri–Garamambu hostilities appear in chapter 2, where I describe the events that led to the death of the Garamambu leader, Kwaremanki, who was brought by Kanda, his Chambri partner, to be killed with honor at Indingai Village (see pp. 41–42).

I estimate the death of Kwaremanki to have occurred around 1929, a few years after the return of the Chambri from their exile at Changriman. The Təpwi incident happened considerably earlier, around 1905, when the Chambri were in retreat from the Parambei, during their brief stay on Timbunmeri Island. These dates reveal that the Garamambu wanted to live on the shores of Chambri Lake before McCarthy contacted them in 1930, but that the Chambri did not approve of the migration. One Chambri man explained his people's adamancy in the following way: "If we allowed the bush-people to move down below, they would not take our fish unless we begged them to."

What the man meant is this. (1) As trading partners, the Garamambu and Chambri interacted reciprocally; each had trading friends among the other people, and both could use the products provided by their partners. (2) With the advent of barter markets, however—when the one-to-one exchange rate that had evolved within the sociopolitical context of the Sepik River and its northern floodplain was applied south of the river, between the Chambri, Iatmul, and Hills peoples—this reciprocity was undermined. The Hills peoples could acquire the fish they needed from either the Chambri or from the Kandingai on Timbunmeri, and they were unwilling to insure that their old friends were supplied with sufficient quantities of the carbohydrate. (3) But once the Hills peoples descended to the shores of Chambri Lake—once they could fish for themselves on a regular basis, having mastered canoe technology and use—there was no need for them to supply anyone with sago. They only had to return to the sago-rich valleys between the Sepik Hills to prepare enough for themselves, for fish were now as easily available to them as they were to the Chambri and Iatmul.

That Chambri men were not particularly perturbed by the destruction of their fish-for-sago exchange system must be explained within the context of modern political alliances, particularly those expressed within the Local Government Councils. These councils, which were instituted by Australian administrators at the same time that the Hills people settled on the shores of Chambri Lake, became significant to those Chambri leaders, including Matias Yambumpe, who wished to gain regional political power and economic prosperity for themselves and their people.

Local Government

The numerous cultural and linguistic groups found within Papua New Guinea—over seven hundred in all—have led administrators to urge that local government, where leaders could sensitively comprehend the socio-economic lives of their constituents, be adopted throughout the country. The Local Government Councils were established, each representing a number of Australian-imposed census districts. The Chambri, the Hills peoples, the Middle Sepik Iatmul, the Sawos, and certain groups of southern Abelam were incorporated within the Gaui Local Government Council, the first two cultural groups as members of the Chambri Lakes Census Division, and the other groups as members of the Main River, Burui-Kunai, and Sepik Plains Census Divisions, respectively. The Gaui Council meets once a month at the subdistrict patrol post of Pagwi to administer various government allocations designated for locally significant projects.

Garamambu was originally a member of the Chambri Lakes Census Division within the Gaui Council, but in 1966 it was reclassified and now belongs to the Upper Sepik Census Division within the Ambunti Council. Looking at the map on page 9, the reasons the Garamambu had for wishing membership within the Ambunti Council will become clear. After many of them moved down from their mountain to live at the village of Yerakai, located just southeast of Ambunti, access to this administrative center became eaiser than access to Pagwi. Moreover, Ambunti, as a district headquarters, has always had many more employment opportunities than Pagwi. My general impression from talking to many Garamambu men is that all of them have spent a considerable amount of time working for the government at Ambunti. This fact suggests that the desire to earn money has had a profound importance in restructuring local sociopolitical relationships. If I had not enquired about the Garamambu while living among the Chambri, I would never have guessed that the two peoples had once been in close contact (see table 8.1).

The desire to earn money has figured considerably in Chambri participation in local government as well. Consider, for example, a few excerpts from the Indingai Village Book, a record kept by Australian patrol officers

Table 8.1: The Number of Intervillage Visits, May 1974–April 1975[a]

			Into Indingai		
Changriman	*Mensuat*	*Milae*	*Mali*	*Garamambu*	*Iatmul*
22	16	16	8	0	5—Nyaurengai
					1—Kandingai
					4—Suapmeri
					1—Kanganaman
					1—Kaminimbit

			From Indingai		
Changriman	*Mensuat*	*Milae*	*Mali*	*Garamambu*	*Iatmul*
8	70[b]	0	0	4	3—Timbunke
					23—Kanganaman
					12—Paramber
					3—Kaminimbit
					1—Tegowi

[a]The data include all visits that lasted one night or more.
[b]The high number of Indingai visits to Mensuat is explained by the presence of a sago store on the island of Peliagwi, where the Mensuat now live. Indingai, journeying to buy sago at the store, will frequently stay overnight with friends.

of their trips to Indingai which was left at the village to encourage responsibility and leadership among the villagers.

10/7–9/60:[3] Endeavored to stir up interest in coffee and coconut planting. Lack of ground would rule out any large scale plantings of the latter and coffee should be concentrated upon re: cash crop. 10/11–18/61: Coffee and copra production were encouraged. Deputations were brought to me by both the men and women to have Yambumpe recognized as the popular leader. He is very sincere and has done a lot in the coffee and native artifacts field and the people were told that they could make their choice when the L.G.C. was established. 12/5/61: Yambumpe of Indingai, Mindik of Kilimbit and Yampur of Wombun have apparently been selected as a sort of Business Committee for Chambri, to lead the people in Agricultural Development. All are sincere types, who are keen to do something. Long talk with them at Ambunti re: pitfalls of getting mixed up in politics at village level and usurping position of officials. Appeared to understand all this. Also told that agricultural leaders should be actual leaders in work too and should have bigger and better coffee etc. plots than anyone else. . . . 4/4/62: Yambumpe and others in office today. Deposited £187/11 in a society account known as Chambri Island Trading. Initial order sent to B.P.'s. People intend to operate trade store. . . . Villages of Indingai, Wombun and Kilimbit involved. 9/8–9/64: Arrived Tuesday. People in mourning for death of Kilimbit, ex-Tultul and leader. Election deferred 'til tomorrow.* 9th-Yambumpe elected overwhelmingly. People keyed up with fruition of their desire of several years to join L.G. work. Talked with various people stressing necessity of hard work as prerequisite for prosperity and welfare. 9/18/69: Councillor Mathias Yambumpe returned unopposed. 6/5/71: Mathias, L.G. Cr. of Indingai charged with debt-arbitration accepted by all. The Archimedes motor currently at K. Dowrie's store for repair is communally owned.[4] After its repair Mathias will repay all shares if share holders so desire and take over full ownership of the motor. . . . 9/17/71: G.C. election held. Mathias Yambumpe re-elected unopposed.

It is clear that Mr. Yambumpe, ignoring the patrol officer's warning to avoid politics on the village level, found local government more profitable than cash cropping. Neither coffee nor copra is now harvested at Indingai, and Mr. Yambumpe, one of the shrewdest and most powerful men of the Middle Sepik, was the president of the Gaui Local Government Council before he was elected to Parliament in 1976. He, along with Australian administrative officers, encouraged the Sepik Hills people to move down to the shore, persuading them that neither economic development nor local government could succeed if they persisted in living like "bush spirits." To grow strong and rich they must "become men," build permanent villages, grow coffee, and be counted in the census of the Gaui Council. The Sepik Hills people took this advice, moved from their mountain hamlets, and promptly began charging money for their sago.[5]

Mr. Yambumpe gained knowledge of European customs while working from 1954 to 1956 as a copra cutter at Talasea, New Britain, and as Chambri's business advisor after he returned home. His sophistication and astuteness are, at times, startling. In September 1968, for example, a patrol officer wrote of him:

> Arrived to conduct a survey of Samugude [*sic*] Island for luxury hotel. Much time expended in explaining advantages of such a move but to no avail. Cr. Yambumpe being the stumbling block— he wants the people themselves to construct a hotel or some sort of building!!! No amount of talk on my part can get him to change his mind. The actual line and compass survey was still done, however, and the pertinent information for land investment report gathered. It is unfortunate that the Cr. can't see past the end of his nose; it appears that once again the people have missed out on a good thing due to their own stupidity. Have been waiting for over an hour now for the men to mark the ground. This man Yambumpe is not a Councillor's bootlace—the sad fact is that the

---

*The election described here was the first Gaui Local Government Council election.

people seem to think he is something out of the [the next two words were illegible]. [Indingai Village Book]

If the patrol officer had bothered to find out why Mr. Yambumpe was adamant against the hotel scheme, he would have discovered in his antagonist, not stupidity, but a rather remarkable penetration. Mr. Yambumpe's main concern *was* to protect the integrity of his people. He feared that if tourism came to Chambri on a large scale neither wealth nor status would come of it, but rather "white men would become rich while the Chambri would lose their good customs." They would become underlings to white bosses, and no longer would be able to escape back to their villages when tired of being misunderstood. "It is one thing when we work for white men in towns," he said when I questioned him about the incident. "Then we can come home again. But when the white men move into our villages, where can we go then? Tourism is all right. It's good when people come to buy our carvings. But we, ourselves, want to be in charge, so that we, and not some strange white men, can earn the profits."

My impression of Mr. Yambumpe during the monthly Gaui Council meetings I attended was that he, and he alone of all the councillors, could see far past his nose, and that the only similarity between him and a councillor's bootlace was that he managed to keep the other councillors tied up in knots. At the July 1974 meeting, for example, the topic under discussion was the allocation of money for the following year. Yambumpe wished to propose a project and changed seats with the vice-president to do so. After the vice-president recognized him, Yambumpe began by avowing his own devotion to the work of the council, reminding the councillors of the gravity of their own responsibilities. He told them that the queen of England had a book in which the councillors' names were listed and exhorted them to take their work seriously. Far be it from him to make himself a party to any action that would reflect badly on the reputation of the council. However, the Chambri people had been asked to accumulate $5,000 to pay one-third of the cost of lengthening and improving Kilimbit's airstrip to allow tourists to fly directly from Wewak to Chambri.[6] (The money referred to throughout this chapter is in Australian currency.) The Territory Airlines Limited had volunteered to defray two-thirds of the cost, $10,000 in all. Yambumpe assured the councillors that the Chambri could find the money they needed elsewhere—that taking Gaui Council money really was not necessary. If they couldn't raise it by working, they could take a loan from the World Development Bank. But he suggested that it would not look good if he, Gaui's president, did not exhibit sufficient faith in the council, and so he was willing to let Gaui allocate $5,000 for Kilimbit's airstrip during 1975. No councillor objected. No one suggested that World Development

Bank loans have to be repaid while council funds need not be. And several of the councillors applauded Mr. Yambumpe's altruism.

Mr. Yambumpe rarely "misses out on a good thing because of stupidity." But there is little doubt that his first commitment is to his own people. Why, then, it may be asked, did this sophisticated and shrewd politician encourage the resettlement of the Sepik Hills people when he must have suspected that their access to the lake would destroy the bartering system upon which his people had depended?[7]

The answer to this question lies, I believe, in the relative lack of developmental potential in Chambri territory. According to a land research report by the Commonwealth Scientific and Industrial Research Organization, the Chambri land system has "no agricultural land use capability" (Haantjens et al., 1972: 182). The report also states that "land reclamation does not appear feasible, or would not produce good land" (ibid.). Moreover, the Chambri seem to be indefinitely limited to water transportation, for their area has been deemed "unsuitable for road construction" (ibid.). The Pagwi Fishery Project "provides a significant means of entry into the monetary sector for a large number of river Sepik [and Chambri] who, apart from fishing, have little alternative means of earning a living" (Philpott, 1974: 38).

Thus, because the Sepik area remains "out of the mainstream of [economic] development" (Philpott, 1972: 37), progress has come to be measured by villagers in terms of isolated economic benefits, such as the number of water tanks, aid posts, outboard motors, classrooms, and roads in an area. Local government councillors are expected to transform tax money into projects that will directly benefit their constituents. Philpott, in his study of economic development in the Sepik River Basin, argues that "local government has a vital role to play and we would like to see the Councils more effectively integrated into the total planning process" (ibid.). He insists that "the people need to be able to make their ideas and plans known however unrealistic some of their demands may be" (ibid.). Philpott ignores the fact, however, that "grass roots participation" can become extremely competitive. Will a rivulet be dug this year, or will a road be built? Will Torembi have two classrooms added to its school, or will Changriman's aid post be rebuilt? Where will the five available water tanks be placed, at Chambri, at Japandai, at Yangit? And since Kandingai had its rivulet dug last year, shouldn't Yentchamangua have its dug this year? These are the kind of questions that concern the villagers of the Middle Sepik, not only with respect to necessary improvements, but also in comparison with other villages within the Gaui Council. Under these circumstances, a councillor who is incapable of satisfying his constituents' craving for tangible benefits will quickly lose their support and be replaced by another representative.

Mr. Yambumpe was aware that if he were to acquire for the Chambri the benefits they demanded from him as their councillor, he had to have an adequate power-base within the Gaui Council to sway the vote on important matters. Which villages could compose this power-base? Certainly the Nyaula would never vote as Yambumpe desired, for the Kandingai Nyaula were involved in land litigation with the Chambri over Timbunmeri Island. The Parambei Iatmul have felt no allegiance with the Chambri since the Parambei wars and still resent the ascendancy of a member of the tribe they vanquished to the council's presidency. And the Sepik Plains and Burui Kunai Sawos speakers, who never were allied to the Chambri in the past, see their own developmental needs as quite different from those of the water-people. This left the Sepik Hills people, but the only way to obtain them as allies within the council was to transform them from bush-people to water-people—from the children of bush spirits to men—from sago-suppliers to entrepreneurs interested in acquiring a developmental policy identical with that of the Chambri. Thus, in order to assure their prosperity, the Chambri were forced to make a sacrifice. They relinquished their fish-for-sago exchange in return for political viability.

The Women Accommodate

Those Chambri, however, who were the most concerned about gaining regional political viability within the Gaui Local Government Council did not relinquish much themselves. Chambri men had not been concerned with procuring subsistence goods since they abdicated their trading partnerships with the Sepik Hills peoples some thirty years before. It was the women who were in control of the fishing and marketing, and it was the women who had to accommodate to the destruction of the fish-for-sago exchange system.

While Iatmul women were still paddling their fish-laden canoes up the Sepik's northern tributaries to the Sawos barter markets, Chambri women began to undertake another kind of marketing expedition, to the patrol post of Pagwi and to the towns of Wewak and Maprik. There they sold their fish to migrant laborers, government employees, and natives without fish of their own but with enough money to acquire some from the Chambri.[8]

The market price of fish varied with the distance to the market from the fishing grounds. At Wewak, for example, one smoked fish cost ten cents; at Maprik the price was two for ten cents; while at Pagwi ten cents would buy two to three fish, depending upon their size (see Seiler, 1972: 106). Clearly, the attraction of higher market prices was offset by the costs of travel to, and of upkeep in, the large market towns. In 1973, for example, to go from Chambri to Pagwi and back cost each fish seller between four and eight dollars, while the round trip from Chambri to Maprik cost between six and ten dollars. While on selling trips most fish sellers consumed their own produce which they supplemented with market-bought tubers, rarely spending more than thirty cents per day. Those who journeyed to Wewak spent considerably more. Their round trip by motorized canoe and truck cost each fish seller between fourteen and eighteen dollars, while food took another fifty cents to five dollars per day.

The women migrated approximately once a year, frequently during the dry season, after they had smoked and put by great quantities of fish. Generally delegating one or two sellers to market fish belonging to co-wives, sisters, and sometimes sisters-in-law, the women reduced the costs of travel while leaving a sufficient number in the village to care for children and tend to husbands, fathers, and brothers.

At each market town long-term Chambri migrants built squatter settlements that could be utilized by visiting marketers. At Pagwi a motorboat driver for the government built a native-style guest-house behind his rented, government-built home to accommodate those Chambri with business at the patrol post or those wishing to sell fish at the market. At Bainyk, a suburb of Maprik, four Chambri migrants built a larger settlement consisting of two guest-houses on land belonging to Numakum villagers. The Numakum were afraid that, if houses were not built on their land, the Bainyk Vocational School would take possession of it. They therefore encouraged the Chambri to build, after receiving a token payment of ten dollars. At Wewak, ten migrants who wished to live semipermanently in town to sell artifacts to tourists cooperated to build Kreer Camp. In 1974 it was a large settlement, with numerous women's houses and three small ceremonial houses. The Kilimbit lived toward the west, the Wombun toward the east, and the Indingai in the center of the camp, duplicating the spatial arrangement of the three Chambri villages.

A woman's decision to visit a particular market was more dependent upon whether she was on good terms with those migrants who semipermanently inhabited the various squatter settlements than it was upon her pecuniary interests. For example, Indingai marketers felt so ill-at-ease staying at the Kilimbit and Wombun-dominated Bainyk settlement that one Indingai finally established another camp close to Maprik High School.

Seventy-four women went to Pagwi, Maprik, or Wewak in 1974 to sell fish, staying with friends and relatives for periods ranging from one day to more than eight months (see table 8.2). Those fifty-three who were present while I was administering an economic survey early in 1975 indicated that they earned $1,263.00 through the sale of fish in the towns (see table 8.3).

The Chambri also earned money by selling fish to the government. In November 1973, the government of Papua New Guinea, concerned to

Table 8.2: Frequency of Trips by Indingai Women to Market Towns during 1974[a]

Month	Town	No. of Marketers Leaving Village[b]	Range of Time Spent in Town (Days)	Average Time Spent in Town (Days)
January	Pagwi	3	3–7	5
	Maprik	2	5–14	9.5
	Wewak	2	7–21	14
February	Pagwi	2	6–9	7.5
	Maprik	1	5	5
	Wewak	0	—	—
March	Pagwi	3	2–9	6
	Maprik	1	8	8
	Wewak	3	12–45	29
April	Pagwi	4	4–14	9.3
	Maprik	1	6	6
	Wewak	1	14	14
May	Pagwi	4	1–14	10
	Maprik	0	—	—
	Wewak	2	18–22	20
June	Pagwi	3	5–14	9.6
	Maprik	6	7–12	10.1
	Wewak	1	90	90
July	Pagwi	0	—	—
	Maprik	6	13–30	24.5
	Wewak	5	22–245 +	71.4 +
August	Pagwi	5	2–14	9.6
	Maprik	11	8–90	28.2
	Wewak	1	75	75
September	Pagwi	4	2–6	5
	Maprik	1	14	14
	Wewak	0	—	—
October	Pagwi	0	—	—
	Maprik	3	18–39	32
	Wewak	4	14–60	28
November	Pagwi	3	14–37	21.7
	Maprik	1	25	25
	Wewak	3	21–112 +	54.3 +
December	Pagwi	1	7	7
	Maprik	0	—	—
	Wewak	0	—	—
Total		87		

[a]The data for the months May–December were collected by the author through observation, while those for the months January–April were reconstructed from conversations with informants.
[b]Number of women going to town two times = 8; no. of women going to town three times = 3; no. of women going to town four times = 2; percentage of de jure female population (15 years. +) making marketing trips = 79.

Table 8.3: The 1974 Earnings of the Fishwives of Indingai Village

Number of fish sellers	53
Amount of money earned from fish sales	$ 1,263.00
Range of money earned per person	$ 3.00–100.00
Mean amount of money earned	$ 29.00
Standard deviation	19.09

Source: The data in tables 8.3, 8.6, and 8.8 were collected from the 108 non-migrant Chambri males and females, above the age of fifteen, who were present while I was administering an economic survey early in 1975.

stimulate self-sufficiency in food production, initiated a fisheries project to supply protein-lacking inland villages with Sepik and Chambri fish (see Philpott, 1974: 38–40). The project had operated actively for only four months, when the freezer boat belonging to the Department of Agriculture, Stock and Fisheries broke down. Twenty-five Indingai (eighteen women and seven men)[9] sold 392 pounds of smoked fish to the government during this four-month period, earning approximately twenty-four dollars in all.

Chambri women also earned a small income through the sale of produce, including betel nuts, lime, plaited carrying baskets, mussels, tortoises, eels, water-lily seed-pods, and wild fruits (see table 8.4), bringing the total 1974 income of Indingai women through the sale of fish and market produce to just over $1,700. They spent just over $1,600 of this income on sago (see table 8.5).

Chambri women purchased most of their sago at a money market held on Saturdays at Indingai Village. This market was established by the Catholic priest who headed St. Mary's Mission School. He wished to provide the native teachers he employed—who had no land rights at Indingai and could not, therefore, grow their own gardens—with a source of cheaply purchasable food. The market, therefore, not only attracted Mali, Mensuat, and Changriman saleswomen—who came to sell their sago from their homes at Kurapio, Peliagwi, and Kamanbo, respectively—but also Chambri and Iatmul women who wished to sell produce to the teachers. Thus, Indingai's money market was attended by women from Suapmeri, Indabu, Kanganaman, Parambei, Kaminimbit, LukLuk, Arinjone, and Aibom, all of whom were interested in selling pumpkins, watermelons, coconuts, tobacco, yams, taro, sweet potatoes, betel nuts, and other items to the mission employees or to other monied natives.

Although Chambri and Timbunmeri women sold their produce at this market, they were primarily there as purchasers of sago. Generally bought by the block, each cost between forty cents and a dollar, depending upon its freshness and the season. Newly prepared sago was more valuable than dried-out blocks, and the price of both went up during the dry season, when

Table 8.4: The Earnings of Indingai Women at the Indingai Native Market,
March 1974–February 1975

Date	No. of Sellers	Range of Earnings ($)	Total Earnings ($)
March 30, 1974	6	.30–8.70	22.20
April 13, 1974	10	.10– .80	3.00
May 11, 1974	8	.20– .50	4.80
June 10, 1974	12	.20–1.20	6.00
July 19, 1974	10	.20–1.50	5.00
August 17, 1974	10	.30–2.70	16.00
September 14, 1974	14	.30–1.50	11.20
October 12, 1974	11	.30–1.60	8.80
November 11, 1974	7	.20–3.00	8.40
December 21, 1974	5	.30–2.00	6.50
January 15, 1975	7	.30–1.20	7.20
February 15, 1975	8	.10–1.20	3.50
		Total	102.60
		Mean	8.55
		Estimated standard deviation	4.955
		Approximate amount earned per year	445.00[a]

[a]Figure derived by multiplying the twelve-week arithmetic mean by fifty-two and rounding off to the nearest dollar.

it was difficult for the Hills women to find enough water to wash the edible starch out of the pulverized pith, and when it was difficult to negotiate the weed-choked rivulets to get to Indingai's market.

My Sepik Hills informants told me that they earned more from the sale of sago than from any other industry. The Mensuat of Peliagwi Island established a sago store in which blocks of sago were displayed with price tags for the benefit of visiting customers from Chambri, Timbunmeri, and occasionally Aibom. In August 1974 the store took in $58.30; in November 1974 it took in $17.90; and in February 1975 it took in $38.40, indicating that approximately $458.40[10] was earned by the Mensuat over a one-year period from their sago store alone. Their annual sago revenue was much higher, of course, because most of their sales were made at Indingai market.

Additional Means of Earning Money

The migration of the Hills people to the shores of the lake and the subsequent collapse of the fish-for-sago bartering system made circular migration between Chambri and town-based money markets an economic necessity. It seems, in fact, that Chambri women reestablished the one-to-one ratio

Table 8.5: The Amount of Money Spent on Sago by the Women of Thirty-five Households, July 1974–February 1975[a]

Month	Expenditure Range per Household ($)	Total Expenditure ($)
July	.50–7.00	61.70
August	1.00–9.50	89.20
September	1.00–8.30	78.80
October	1.00–10.00	71.50
November	.30–6.20	64.71
December	0–6.00	56.30
January	1.00–12.20	89.10
February	.50–6.00	79.20
Total		877.20
Mean		73.10
Standard deviation		11.61
Approximate yearly expenditure		1,619.00[b]

[a]The figures presented in tables 8.5, 8.9, and 8.10 must be taken as estimates of the amount of money that would be spent if all adult Indingai were living in their village throughout the year. Because of the phenomenon of circular migration, with artifact and fish sellers leaving their village for up to eight months, the number of purchasers of sago, trade goods, and market produce varies from week to week. It is therefore impossible for me to correlate absolutely Indingai earnings with Indingai expenditures, for many of the 108 non-migrants in my economic survey had been absent from their village while the sago, trade-store, and market studies were in progress, and many of the 84 individuals, migrants early in 1975, had been living in Indingai for long periods during 1974.

[b]Figure derived by multiplying the eight-month arithmetic mean by twelve and rounding off to the nearest dollar.

of fish to sago by selling enough fish and market produce to purchase their sago requirement.

Interestingly, Chambri men had no idea of how much was spent on sago annually—undoubtedly because women purchased most of it with their own money. This was not because men had no money of their own, but rather because they spent what they had in other ways. Indeed, the 1974 incomes of Chambri men were considerable. Here I discuss the various means they used to acquire money before describing the different uses to which Chambri men and women put their funds.

Philpott, in his socioeconomic survey of Sepik riverine settlements, wrote that among the Chambri: "Artifacts are considered to be a major industry— the people have evolved a distinctive style much in favor with the tourists. Fishing is of lesser importance" (1972: 251). My observations of Chambri economic activity confirmed Philpott's opinion, for, as tables 8.3 and 8.6 indicate, the total revenues earned through artifact sales surpassed those earned through fish sales.

Artifacts, including carved masks and spears, plaited baskets, and bead

Table 8.6: The 1974 Earnings of the Artifact Sellers of Indingai Village

	M	F	Total
Number of artifact sellers	34	49	83
Amount of money earned from arti- fact sales ($)	1,523	543	2,066.00
Range of money earned per person ($)	2–228	2–50	2.00–228.00
Mean amount of money earned ($)	43.51	11.31	25.00
Standard deviation ($)	48.44	11.84	22.42

and seed ornaments, were sold in three different contexts. The first, and most common, was at artifact markets set up for tourists visiting Chambri. They arrived at Chambri once or twice a month in motorboats, stayed for a few hours, and then returned to the air-conditioned, fully equipped tour- ist ship *Mareeba* that was docked at Pagwi. Before leaving, the tour-guides informed the Chambri of when the next group of tourists would arrive and asked them to arrange the market along with a performance of traditional songs and dances. Troupes from the three Chambri villages took turns en- tertaining the tourists and each was paid approximately thirty-five dollars for performing these "sing-sings." The money was divided among all the performers, including anyone who lent shell and feather decorations to the performers. Each individual usually received only about fifty cents for his efforts. The artifact market, on the other hand, was much more lucrative, for the tourists were interested in taking home souvenirs from each village they visited. Carved masks sold for between two to fifteen dollars, spears for about ten, baskets for three, and the ornaments vary from fifty cents to two dollars.

The second occasion for the sale of artifacts occurred when European entrepreneurs, including some missionaries, visited to buy large quantities of carvings for shipment to Australia and the United States, or to replenish their stocks in the artifact stores they operate in Papua New Guinea towns. These entrepreneurs usually refused to offer more than two dollars per carv- ing. In this way, they managed to acquire not only small carvings ordinarily valued at this amount, but also larger masks worth five and ten dollars each, from craftsmen anxious to make a sale. An artifact dealer would spend as much as five hundred dollars in one afternoon, purchasing carvings that would return him ten times that amount on the urban tourist market.

Finally, some individual Chambri journeyed to Pagwi, Maprik, or We- wak to sell artifacts to hotel guests and other European residents. Eighty- three Indingai men and women went to town in 1974 in hopes of selling their carvings, baskets, and jewelry (see table 8.7). They, like the fish sell- ers, lived with town-dwelling relatives or at the Chambri section of Kreer Camp. Each night they went to one of the hotels to display their carvings

Table 8.7: Frequency of Trips by Male[a] Artifact Sellers to Towns during 1974[b]

Month	Town	No. of Sellers Leaving Village[c]	Range of Time Spent in Town (Days)	Average Time Spent in Town (Days)
January	Pagwi	0	—	—
	Maprik	1	6	6
	Wewak	3	12–15	13
February	Pagwi	0	—	—
	Maprik	2	12–20	16
	Wewak	4	8–24	19
March	Pagwi	1	7	7
	Maprik	2	7–14	10
	Wewak	3	5–25	15
April	Pagwi	0	—	—
	Maprik	0	—	—
	Wewak	1	7	7
May	Pagwi	1	1	1
	Maprik	1	60	60
	Wewak	6	18–105	36.2
June	Pagwi	1	5	5
	Maprik	1	18	18
	Wewak	4	7–180	103
July	Pagwi	2	3	3
	Maprik	2	30	30
	Wewak	2	17–245v	131
August	Pagwi	0	—	—
	Maprik	5	3–20	13.4
	Wewak	1	7	7
September	Pagwi	0	—	—
	Maprik	1	14	14
	Wewak	2	5–9	7
October	Pagwi	1	30	30
	Maprik	3	16–39	23.6
	Wewak	3	7–19	13.3
November	Pagwi	0	—	—
	Maprik	2	25–31	28
	Wewak	2	90–112v	101v
December	Pagwi	0	—	—
	Maprik	0	—	—
		0	—	—
Total		53		

[a]Although Chambri women sold artifacts too, they never journeyed to the towns exclusively to do so, but would combine their fish- and artifact-selling excursions.
[b]The data for the months May–December were collected by the author through observation, while those for the months January–April were reconstructed through conversations with informants.
[c]Number of men going to town two times: 4; no. of men going to town three times: 4; no. of men going to town four times: 2; no. of men going to town five times: 1; percentage of de jure male population (15 yrs. +) making artifact-selling trips: 44%.

for the tourists' inspection, or they sold them door to door in the expatriate residential neighborhood. Hotel managers did not discourage the artifact sellers, for their guests enjoyed the "primitive display." The highest price for carvings could be obtained in the towns, but the cost of transportation and food often completely consumed all profits. The figures in table 8.6, therefore, indicate gross earnings; net earnings, minus the transportation and food expenditures of the travelers, were approximately six hundred dollars less.

Another village-based industry that occasionally brought in money was the sale of crocodile skins. However, in 1974 this formerly lucrative industry was in decline. Overkilling in the past had depleted the crocodile population, and a minimum size requirement had been imposed by the government. Moreover, there was a native-imposed taboo against slaughtering large specimens believed to contain spirits of ancestors. During 1974 only two Indingai men sold crocodile skins to a Papua New Guinean entrepreneur who paid $86 for one skin and $45 for the other.

Ten Indingai men and women earned $710 from the sale of livestock in 1974—$575 for the sale of pigs, $120 for a bull, and $15 for chickens.

Except for the bull, which was sold to Kanganaman villagers, the livestock was bought by fellow Chambri involved in affinal exchange ceremonies.

Finally, seventy-five Indingai received monetary gifts from relatives who were migrant laborers, either mailed to them at irregular intervals or brought home by the migrants during their Christmas vacations (see table 8.8).

It should also be mentioned that, although the two Indingai owners of outboard motors were absent while I administered the economic survey, one as a teacher at a nearby mission school and the other on a short vacation in Wewak, they earned approximately $200 in 1974 by transporting Chambri villagers to Pagwi and other Middle Sepik villages. This $200 is their gross return, for each had to pay for repairs to his motor. Their expenditures amounted to over $50 a piece. A third Indingai—a government employee stationed at Pagwi—purchased an outboard motor in mid-1974

Table 8.8: The Monetary Gifts Received by Indingai from Migrant Laborers during 1974

	M	F	Total
Number of individuals receiving monetary gifts	32	43	75
Total amount of money received ($)	1,158	1,157	2,315.00
Range of monetary gifts received per person ($)	2–275	2–400	2.00–400.00
Mean value of gifts received per person ($)	36.19	26.91	31.00
Standard deviation ($)	66.06	59.56	62.03

and earned approximately $150 in hiring fees. But the earnings only partially paid for the motor, and when it broke down late in 1974 its owner had no funds for repairs.

Major Expenditures

The $7,900 earned by Indingai in 1974 through the sale of artifacts, fish, crocodile skins, livestock, produce, and through gifts from migrant laborers, commissioned sing-sings, and motorboat hiring fees was not all disbursed on sago. The data presented in tables 8.9 and 8.10 specify the other major expenditures of Indingai during a comparable time of one year.

The money spent at St. Mary's Mission store, run by the priest stationed at Indingai Village, bought various household items, such as mosquito nets, knives, straw mats, blankets, frying pans, saucepans, kerosene lamps, folding chairs, pressure stoves, clocks and radios; food, including rice, flour, salt, biscuits, bread, tinned mackerel, goose and beef, milk powder, sugar, candy, soda, and peanuts; clothes, such as trousers, skirts and shorts, singlets and "laplaps" (a yard of material wrapped around the body and fastened at the waist); fuel (kerosene and petrol); and miscellaneous items, such as cigarettes, tobacco, matches, lighters, flints, writing tablets, stamps, pens, fishhooks, dyes, and religious songbooks. I collected my data by stationing a research assistant close to the store with instructions to record the amount of each expenditure, the items purchased, the name of the purchaser, and the village in which he lived. The people were most cooperative for they wished to discover how much money the store made.

The Indingai native market brought together people from surrounding villages to purchase each other's surplus produce. Both I and a research assistant recorded the number of sellers present from each village and attempted, with varying success, to ascertain the amounts of money they earned at the market. These data were then supplemented by asking Indingai how much they had spent and what they had bought. Betel nut, betel pepper, sweet potatoes, yams, taro, coconuts, native tobacco, and pottery were regularly purchased. During the dry season, watermelon and pumpkin were favored items.

Most large purchases made by Chambri entailed the conjoining of clan resources. Such purchases might be of a large canoe, a shotgun, or an outboard motor. Thus, the government employee I referred to earlier would not have been able to spend $350 for a secondhand outboard motor unless he had been financially assisted by his clan leader. As this laborer was stationed at Pagwi, he expected that his taxiservice would always be available to villagers returning from selling trips in Maprik and Wewak. However, when the motor broke down and the laborer found himself without enough

Table 8.9: The Amount of Money Spent by Indingai at St. Mary's Mission Trade Store during One Week of Each Month, June 1974–November 1974[a]

Week	No. of purchasers			Expenditure Range ($)			Total expenditure ($)		
	M	F	Total	M	F	Total	M	F	Total
June 16–23	38	52	90	.20–15.58	.10–1.50	.10–15.58	38.42	26.71	65.13
July 15–21	48	59	107	.30–5.00	.10–4.50	.10–5.00	60.38	26.52	86.90
August 21–28	25	27	52	.10–10.00	.10–.90	.10–10.00	22.95	19.25	42.20
September 23–29	28	47	75	.40–16.80	.10–3.00	.10–16.80	45.38	17.46	62.84
October 21–27	38	53	91	.30–19.50	.10–3.30	.10–19.50	33.97	16.35	50.32
November 18–24	63	42	105	.10–2.55	.10–.90	.10–2.55	19.17	20.10	39.27
Total							220.27	126.39	346.66
Mean							36.71	21.07	57.78
Standard deviation							13.80	4.10	16.17
Approximate yearly expenditure							1909.00	1096.00	3005.00[b]

[a] The figures do not include my expenditures, the expenditures of the mission teachers and employees, or those of my research assistants.
[b] Figure derived by multiplying the six-week arithmetic mean by fifty-two and rounding off to the nearest dollar.

to pay for the repairs, he again sought money from the clan leader. This time, however, he was refused. The clan leader would lend no more money until his initial investment had been returned, and as I left the field the outboard-motor owner was seeking help from unrelated clans.

Among the miscellaneous items which are purchased from other natives are bird-of-paradise plumes, the skins of tree kangaroos and cassowaries, seasoned wood (such as iron wood) for carvings, string bags, pigs, and poultry. I estimate that Indingai villagers spent approximately $175 on such items in 1974. The string bags were bought from the Sawos speakers at Sepik River markets, the wood and the fur and feather valuables were purchased primarily from the Garamambu and Milae during marketing expeditions to their villages, and the pigs and poultry were bought from other Chambri.

Indingai spent approximately two hundred dollars on beer. Purchased at Pagwi, Kaminimbit, or Parambei, a carton of beer costs between six and nine dollars.

Finally, in 1974 Indingai villagers owed approximately $982 for council, church, and school-committee taxes, and for primary and secondary school fees. Only a portion of the money was paid, however, for the schools, particularly at the secondary level, are very lenient about collecting fees, and the school-committee taxes are considered an unnecessary burden by most villagers. Moreover, as the president of the Gaui Local Government Council at the time these studies were done came from Indingai, he rarely exercised his prerogative to incarcerate tax defaulters. I estimate, therefore, that about five hundred dollars was spent by Indingai for taxes and fees in 1974, while another thirty was repaid to the World Development Bank which had lent a group of Indingai villagers a thousand dollars in 1971 to purchase ten head of cattle.

Conclusion: The Division of Labor

At first glance, table 8.11, which summarizes the expenditures and revenues of Indingai villagers over a one-year period, indicates a relatively balanced budget, with men and women having earned what they needed to support themselves now that their fish-for-sago exchanges had become mediated through money. A closer look at the data that comprise this table presents a somewhat different picture, however, for they reveal that Indingai women spent most of their incomes on subsistence products, while Indingai men purchased luxuries or made capital investments.

Consider, for example, table 8.12, a breakdown of the number of individuals who purchased particular items at St. Mary's Mission Trade Store. Twenty-five percent of all the women who shopped there over the six-week study period purchased either fish or rice, while only 9 percent of the men

Table 8.10: The Amount of Money Spent by Indingai at the Indingai Native Market during One Market Day of Each Month, March 1974–February 1975[a]

Date	No. of buyers			Expenditure range ($)			Total Expenditure ($)		
	M	F	Total	M	F	Total	M	F	Total
March 30, 1974	6	11	17	.20–.60	.10–2.00	.10–2.00	3.70	6.10	9.80
April 13, 1974	4	8	12	.10–.80	.10–.80	.10–.80	1.78	3.59	5.37
May 11, 1974	4	10	14	.20–.50	.10–.50	.10–.50	1.25	2.51	3.76
June 10, 1974	6	17	23	.20–.60	.10–1.00	.10–1.00	2.84	3.66	6.50
July 9, 1974	6	7	14	.20–.80	.10–1.10	.10–1.10	2.90	4.80	7.50
August 17, 1974	7	11	18	.10–.70	.10–2.30	.10–2.30	4.86	5.15	10.01
September 14, 1974	5	9	14	.10–.80	.10–2.50	.10–2.50	4.90	6.30	11.20
October 12, 1974	5	6	11	.10–.80	.10–3.20	.10–3.25	3.60	4.54	8.14
November 16, 1974	4	8	12	.10–.60	.10–1.00	.10–1.00	3.14	4.40	7.54
December 21, 1974	5	6	11	.10–.50	.10–.50	.10–.50	1.62	3.78	5.40
January 25, 1975	5	9	14	.10–.70	.10–1.50	.10–1.50	3.54	5.10	8.64
February 15, 1975	3	10	13	.10–.80	.10–1.50	.10–1.50	4.68	5.19	9.87
Total							38.81	55.12	93.93
Mean							3.23	4.59	7.82
Standard deviation							1.39	1.04	2.15
Approximate yearly expenditure							168.00	239.00	407.00[b]

[a]The figures do not include the sago purchases that were made at the Indingai native market, nor do they include my purchases, the purchases of mission employees, and those of my research assistants.
[b]Figure derived by multiplying the twelve-week arithmetic mean by fifty-two and rounding off to the nearest dollar.

Table 8.11: Summary of Indingai Expenditures and Revenues for a One-Year Period

Revenues

Item	Amount ($)		
	M	F	Total
Artifact sales	1,523	543	2,066.00
Fish sales	0	1,263	1,263.00
Crocodile skin sales	131	0	131.00
Market produce sales	0	445	445.00
Sing-Sings	220	200	420.00
Livestock sales	520	190	810.00
Gifts from migrants	1,158	1,157	2,315.00
Motorboat rentals	350	0	350.00
Totals	3,902	3,798	7,700.00

Expenditures

Item	Amount ($)		
	M	F	Total
Food and transportation costs	700	400	1,100.00
Sago expenditures	0	1,619	1,619.00
Trade-store expenditures	1,909	1,096	3,005.00
Market expenditures	168	239	407.00
Outboard motor purchases and repairs	450	0	450.00
Miscellaneous purchases	100	75	175.00
Beer purchases	200	0	200.00
Loan repayment	30	0	30.00
Taxes and fees	200	300	500.00
Totals	3,757	3,729	7,486.00

Table 8.12: The Number and Kind of Trade-Store Purchases Made by Chambri Men and Women during One Week of Each Month, June–November 1974

Item	Number of Purchases	
	Men	Women
Biscuits	52	42
Soap	33	43
Packaged cigarettes	65	9
Rice	19	55
Tinned mackeral	22	47
Kerosene	21	46
Tobacco	30	24
Bread	18	22
Batteries	25	9
Tinned meat	16	12
Sugar	14	12
Soda	18	4
Peanuts	15	5
Matches	16	1
Writing paper	9	8
Salt	4	8
Detergent	5	6
Trousers	9	2
Pencils	7	3
Petrol	9	0
Margarine	5	3
Stamps	5	3
Cotton material	3	4
Newspaper for rolling cigarettes	5	2
Envelopes	1	5
Flashlight	4	2
Candy	3	1
Coffee	1	3
Prayer book	2	2
Flashlight bulb	2	1
Nails	2	1
Rubber	1	2
Skirts	1	2
Cake	1	1
Flour	1	1
Milk	1	1
Mosquito net	0	2
Pans	0	2
Pins	1	1

Table 8.12 (*Continued*)

Razor blades	1	1
Sharpening stone	0	2
Shoe polish	2	0
Sleeping mat	1	1
Tea	1	1
Tinned duck	0	2
Towels	2	0
Diaper pins	0	1
Hat	1	0
Hooks	0	1
Knives	0	1
Paint	0	1
Ruler	1	0
Sandpaper	1	0
Shirts	0	1
Swimming trunks	1	0
Thread	0	1
Toilet paper	1	0
Toothpaste	1	0

were interested in acquiring these basic foodstuffs. Over 17 percent of the men, on the other hand, bought filter cigarettes or soda, while only 3 percent of the women acquired these superfluities. Moreover, men spent over 48 percent of their yearly incomes on trade goods, while women used only 29 percent of their revenues at the store, and generally to supplement the cheaper foodstuffs they acquired themselves through fishing, foraging, and marketing.

These figures substantiate the assertion that Chambri men, concerned to attain political viability within the Gaui Local Government Council by bringing the Hills people down from the bush to act as Chambri constituents, did not have to relinquish much. They had not been engaged in subsistence-oriented trading relationships with the Hills people for some time, having abdicated control of marketing once they became involved in earning the valuable playing pieces they needed to engage in the politics of affinal exchange.

In the next chapter, I return to a consideration of this form of local-level politics, describing how leaders have negotiated the transition from shells to shillings within the affinal exchange system, and explaining the consequences of their initially successful accommodation—consequences which may make it necessary for Mr. Yambumpe's sons to modify their father's political strategies as profoundly as he had to change those of Walinakwan.

9

FROM SHELLS TO SHILLINGS: THE ACCOMMODATION OF CHAMBRI MEN

Although many anthropologists have emphasized the tenacity with which Papua New Guineans have maintained traditional customs in the face of significant technological and structural changes wrought by the coming of Europeans, most agree that the movement from stone to steel, from subsistence to sale, and from limited currency to universal money has created contradictions within traditional sociopolitical systems that must result in new modes of organization. Epstein, for example, working among the Matupi at a time when the people still employed two distinct forms of currency—Australian money for European-type transactions with employers and store owners and shell money for initiation and bride price transactions—found that political authority and wealth were no longer concurrent in the hands of the older Big Men (1963: 207). These had, in the past, been the persons to whom many others were beholden. But the affluence of young migrant laborers, as measured in cash, had created a power vacuum by allowing the younger men to satisfy personal and private desires without the assistance of their elders. Lacking extensive networks of indebtedness upon which their authority had formerly been based, the Big Men's influence now extended only to the members of their local matrilineages.

The contradictions within Matupi society appear, therefore, to have resulted from the inability of the political system to accommodate the capacity of its younger members to spend money for personal ends without establishing social obligations. Although all ceremonial transactions were still made with shell currency, the younger men had "developed aspirations which [could] no longer be satisfied within a traditional politico-economic framework" (ibid.: 214), and they had begun to look toward national rather than community politics as a means of acquiring power. Epstein asserts that "many [young] Matupi would perhaps be happy to see the end of shell money, but insofar as they continue to pursue traditional activities [for the payment of bride-price and for proper obsequies of kinsmen] and remain linked by ties of interdependence with Tolai or other groups who insist upon the use of *tambu*, the need for shell-money persists" (ibid.: 210).

Epstein's analysis of Matupi socioeconomic organization is illuminating because he demonstrates that Australian currency and shell money had different social values. The use of the former allowed individuals to fulfill personal and private desires without establishing social indebtedness, whereas the use of the latter established the social and ritual obligations upon which power relations were traditionally based. It is important to recognize, however, that the contradictions built into the structure of modern Matupi were not the product of the introduction of Australian currency per se but rather resulted from an inability to incorporate the newly emerging, autonomous wage-earning population into traditional networks of dominance and subordination. The Matupi did not succumb hands down to the powerful and all-purpose currency introduced by Europeans but, rather, involved themselves in new money-making relations which became incompatible with traditional sociopolitical goals. Their actions held consequences of which they were not aware.

In this chapter I describe three examples of affinal exchange among the Chambri. The first was recorded by Reo Fortune before Australian money was adopted for bride-price transactions, and the second and third by me after shell valuables had been eliminated from traditional exchange relationships. They provide an interesting contrast to Epstein's discussion of Matupi exchanges because they demonstrate that the Chambri initially incorporated the wage-earning population within the accepted relations of dominance and subordination and developed a functional identity between Australian money and traditional shell valuables. Thus they maintained their political system essentially intact in the face of changed circumstances. Nevertheless, as the third case indicates, it was precisely by maintaining a nexus of traditional social relations and values that the Chambri created new circumstances with which they are today finding it difficult to contend.

The Tanum Affair

Fortune's account of the Tanum Affair is the story of a Big Man's attempt to extricate himself intact from the numerous demands of his various wives' kin.[1] My data indicate that Tanum had five wives, only four of whom were mentioned in Fortune's story. The first, Sabwe, bore Ndumanduma, while the second, Toremanunk, bore Kundungwi. These men, their father, their mothers' brothers, and various related and unrelated supporters took part in a drama involving incest and agnatic rivalry that was resolved, only temporarily, by Tanum's astute manipulation of his rapidly disintegrating networks of control. Below I summarize Fortune's account of the major events. (See figure 9.1 for the cast of characters.)

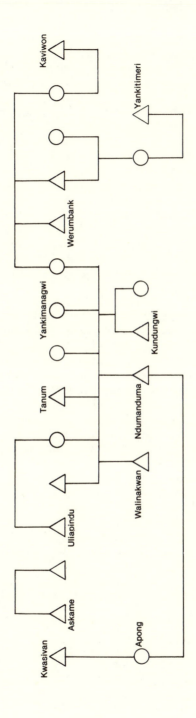

Figure 9.1.　The Cast of Characters in the Tanum Affair

The girl, Apong, had become Ndumanduma's wife through the assistance of Askame, Tanum's co-resident in the Yangaraman men's house, who had paid most of her bride price. The rumor had it, however, that Tanum had seduced his daughter-in-law—that he had "made the first hole in this woman."

No one mentioned this seduction until Kundungwi "went in after," and made the girl pregnant.

Ndumanduma, the lawful husband, fled to his matrilateral kinsmen at Indingai's Boroboroman men's house, refusing to speak to his father out of shame.

Kundungwi, also in need of support, convinced his matrilateral kinsmen from Kilimbit to join him at Yangaraman, where everyone concerned was to gather.

At Yangaraman, after everyone had assembled, the mood was volatile. They all were waiting for Tanum to return from a marketing expedition, but could not wait in silence. Hostile accusations were exchanged, and Askame demanded his valuables back from the girl's father.

Finally, Tanum's canoe was seen approaching the village. All conversation stopped as Tanum drew quietly towards the shore. He ignored the assembled men and ascended to his house on top of Chambri Mountain.

Various supporters of each son climbed the mountain to speak to Tanum, but they all returned without having done so.

At dusk, Tanum ran down the mountain carrying a bundle of spears, hurled them at Ndumanduma's mother's brother, who was sitting in Yangaraman, and then returned to his house.

The young wife, who had been hiding in the bush, was found by Kaviwon, a brother-in-law to Kundungwi's *waus*, and brought to Tanum's house.

Tanum interrogated her: "Why did you get yourself pregnant when your father's sister [Ndumanduma's mother] has not yet her mourning off [is still being mourned]? You hung up your *bilum* on the head of Ndumanduma [you married him]."

Yankimangwi, Tanum's fourth wife, joined in: "We've no *tarebon* to pay for you and Kundungwi. You two must pay for yourselves."

At this point the girl's patrilateral grandfather entered the house and said: "You can have your pay back and we'll take back the girl."

Tanum replied: "I don't want to discuss Apong, but the girl to be initiated and cut."

He was referring to his daughter, Kundungwi's full sister, who was soon to be initiated by Kundungwi's *waus*. He wondered whether these men would still sponsor the ceremony.

After much discussion of this topic, Tanum descended the

mountain to join the others in Yangaraman. He addressed the assembled body, ending with the statement: "I've put all my wealth into Ndumanduma, the child of my first wife. It stays for Ndumanduma."

The next morning Tanum was seen chasing Apong with a spear in his hand.

In the evening Tanum convinced Fortune to accompany him to Boroboroman, where Ndumanduma's *waus* had gathered. He intended to fight these men if they insisted upon returning the valuables Askame had paid for Apong.

Kwasivon, Apong's father, accused Fortune of helping Tanum. He said to Tanum: "You wouldn't get her [Apong] back if you hadn't a white man with you."

Fortune tried to explain that he was on no one's side, but the men were not interested in his words.

The next day, a deputation of Kundungwi's *waus* and their supporters returned with Kundungwi to Tanum's house. Tanum was not at home, and so they talked to his wives. Various of them said: "All the mothers of Kundungwi are now old—not one young one. Kundungwi has put us in a bad way. You said, 'Soon all the mothers' brothers of Kundungwi in Kilimbit will take Apong to Kilimbit.' This talk you attributed to us, it was not so—it was not our talk. You were lying. We would not say such a thing of you, all who are of one house."

Tanum entered the house and walked straight toward the women, apparently not seeing the deputation or Kundungwi at all. Finally he addressed them: "You may have said that I didn't pay much for my wife—but her son, Kundungwi, is at all times finishing my wealth. They all [speaking of the deputation] did not kill a pig to give to their sister when her child was cut [initiated]. They did not help her to pay for her child. What does all their talk and speechifying matter?"

After much desultory discussion, the deputation rose to leave, with one final parting comment: "But in view of the outrageous beliefs and talk you've had and circulated regarding us in this matter, of course we cannot help you or cooperate in the initiation washing ceremony of your child."

The next day, Tanum and Walinakwan, his third wife's son by another marriage, set off for the Olimbit men's house in Kilimbit. They carried with them a long rope of yams and a *kina*. While Tanum waited in Olimbit, Walinakwan delivered the yams to Uliapindu, his mother's brother, and the *kina* to Werumbank, Kundungwi's *wau*. He was accompanied by Tanum's wives who had also walked to Kilimbit.

Werumbank flew into a rage when he saw the party approach his house, and took a finely woven *bilum* from his cache of valuables. He planned to give the *bilum* to his sister, thereby nullifying the peace offering he felt sure she was carrying to him. His classificatory daughter's husband, Yankitimeri, managed to wrest the *bilum* from him, and return it to its place among his other valuables.

Werumbank addressed the members of Tanum's deputation: "The quarrel of your people you turned on us. We didn't do what Kundungwi did. Keep your quarrel and do not turn it on us again. . . . Yesterday I told Walinakwan that he could take over our relationship. He could kill a pig and get currency from our sister's sons, and see to the initiation of the daughter of Tanum."

But Yankitimeri had already removed the totemic leaves that Werumbank had placed in his doorway to mark his anger at his sister, her husband, and their children. By removing these leaves he indicated that their quarrel had been resolved.

Later that day, Tanum placed a *kina* in the Yangaraman men's house to repay Askame for having thrown spears there.

He ignored Ndumanduma and his *waus* completely.

The Tanum Affair is the story of five different sets of relationships, each pivoting around the aging Big Man. It describes the relationship between Tanum and his sons, between Tanum and Ndumanduma's *waus*, between Tanum and Askame, between Tanum and Apong's agnates, and between Tanum and Kundungwi's *waus*. The first set can be easily misread as the paternal counterpart to oedipal jealousy. In this sense, Tanum steals the woman his sons both covet in retaliation against the threat he believes they offer to his prowess.

But Tanum is no preemptive Laius, and, if Kundungwi and Ndumanduma were a threat to Tanum, the nature of the threat must be understood in Chambri terms and within a Chambri sociopolitical context. To make these terms and this context clear, consider the fact that nine out of eleven of Tanum's siblings were female. Tanum and his brother, Wundan, the first two born to a father who was himself the last born, received many shell valuables from their sisters' husbands in bride-price and other affinal exchanges. They were the last of a once larger clan and used these valuables wisely, to establish extensive affinal connections throughout Indingai and Kilimbit. Tanum, as I have mentioned, married five women. Wundan married two. And they lavishly displayed their wealth by compensating their wife-givers whenever the occasion called upon them to do so. Moreover, Wundan and Tanum also helped unrelated individuals to pay their affinal debts. Indeed, they contributed part or all of the valuables used in bride-price payments by eleven of the seventeen Indingai men, ten to fifteen years their juniors, whom I know about.

But something happened between the time Wundan and Tanum made their mark on Indingai society and Fortune's observations of the Tanum Affair—something to undermine their power base and erode their control over affinal exchanges. These exchanges had been dependent upon a surplus of valuables. Their seven wives had woven mosquito bags. Their sisters brought them bride wealth. And they had direct and inherited access to a quarry from which they could produce valuable stone adzes. But within a short time, their fortunes suffered a severe reversal. The Iatmul ceased to trade valuables for Chambri commodities. Tanum's sisters' sons completed their initiations and brought their mothers' brothers fewer valuables. Wundan's one daughter died before she could earn her father a bride-price. Tanum's own daughters were still too young to be married. And Wundan, who was rumored to be the manipulative intelligence behind his clan's successes, died a premature death.

Tanum was left to care for his own family, and for Wundan's as well. And no one trusted his ability to conjoin sufficient resources to manage the affairs of his clan. His sons and nephews were clamoring for wives. Indeed, Wundan's eldest son married a woman rumored to be promiscuous, having decided to accept the status of a "rubbish man." But Kundungwi and Ndumanduma wanted something better than this, and both threatened to abandon their father and take up residence with either their matrilateral kin or with unrelated friends who would welcome their clientage.

The Melanesian Pidgin word used to describe a person's allegiance to one or another social group is *bisnis*. A man is said to belong to a clan because his is the *bisnis* of the clan. When he wishes to transfer his allegiance he can simply move his *bisnis* elsewhere. And an individual wishing to increase his status has the option of making a business deal with the power-seeking headman of a wealthy clan.

Both Ndumanduma and Kundungwi wished to make such a deal. But Tanum's dilemma did not end there. Not only was he failing to manage the business of his own clan, but he was also incapable of maintaining the networks he had established with unrelated individuals. He had assumed these extrafamilial affinal debts, the sign of any true Chambri leader, when his resources matched his aspirations. Now they had to be abandoned. And there were others ready to snatch them up.

Askame was one of these, at least insofar as Ndumanduma was concerned. Askame contributed most of the valuables used to purchase Apong from her father's family, and he would be the one to maintain affinal exchanges with her group. Since prestige for both a Chambri clan and its leader is achieved by paying affines large bride-prices, by overcompensating brothers-in-law for their contribution of foodstuffs during rites of passage celebrated for sons, and by assisting unrelated clan members to do the same, Askame's successes signified Tanum's failures. Ndumanduma had become

Askame's client, and there is bitter irony in Tanum's statement to the men of Yangaraman, that he had "put all of [his] wealth into Ndumanduma, the child of [his] first wife," for Askame had stolen this child from him.

I think we are now in a position to understand Tanum's seduction of Apong. This act would have been considered highly irregular by the Chambri, provided that they recognized Apong as Tanum's daughter-in-law. That they did not is indicated by two facts. First of all, Fortune reports them as commenting that Tanum wished to steal Ndumanduma's bride, not that he seduced his daughter-in-law. Second of all, many of my informants insisted that I place Ndumanduma on Askame's genealogy, for "he had been adopted by Askame at the time of his marriage." By seducing Apong, in other words, Tanum was showing his abdication of responsibility for both his son and the girl. Both had become the business of another.

We are also in the position of understanding the relationship between Tanum and Ndumanduma's *waus*. It will be remembered that Tanum compensated Werumbank and Askame but ignored his first son's matrilateral kinsmen. Since Askame had already assumed Ndumanduma's affinal debts, why should Tanum be interested in these men? He certainly would win neither status nor power by acknowledging his incapacity to maintain relationships with them. Better to ignore them entirely.

Kundungwi's *waus* were another matter, for Tanum had not yet lost this son. Indeed, the story Fortune tells can be read as Tanum's attempt to maintain Kundungwi's business, a task demanding that he keep Kundungwi's *waus* duly compensated. Throughout Fortune's notes, the relationship between Tanum and Werumbank emerges as paramount, precisely because it was so tenuous. And this is why Tanum was preoccupied, not with Apong's pregnancy, but with the forthcoming initiation ceremony of his young daughter, Kundungwi's full sister. The question on his mind was whether Werumbank and Kundungwi's other *waus* would assume that he was incapable of repaying their affinal assistance. Would they mount the ceremony, and give him a chance to emerge again as a man able to pay his debts, or would they write him off, before the fact, as an incompetent rubbish man?

Thus, Tanum's reputation was riding on the successful completion of his daughter's initiation, a fact which raises two questions in my mind, the first of ethnographic interest and the second of narrative importance. Throughout Mead's and Fortune's field data they note several young women receiving the hundreds of half-inch vertical cuts in rows down their backs, buttocks, and upper thighs that mark initiated Chambri from mere children. This is curious, because generally the Chambri do not initiate girls. Indeed, I was told that they do so only when mothers' brothers are sufficiently wealthy to sponsor more than their expected share of initiations, and that to initiate nieces is a sign of an extremely well-off man. Werumbank was such a man, which is why Tanum was preoccupied with fulfilling his debts to him. If he could manage to repay Werumbank for sponsoring the initiation of this girl, then his reputation within Chambri society would be reestablished. But this does not explain the relatively high number of female initiations. Could it be that these initiations were attempts by Chambri men to maintain the system of affinal exchange intact in the face of the high rate of labor migration on the part of their young men? Were they initiating women because there were few men left in the village to be initiated?

The statistics I presented in chapter 6 indicate as much, for a considerable number of young men were absent from their homes during 1933, probably for the purpose of labor migration.[2] It is in relation to this fact that we must pose the second narrative question: how could Tanum, a man who had lost his luck, expect to compensate Werumbank adequately? Where would he acquire the necessary valuables? Would a migrant clansman be returning in time to help him?

We must not forget, however, about a second major change in Tanum's world. The year 1933 not only saw a rise in the rate of labor migration, but it was also the year when two anthropologists arrived to study the Chambri. Tanum's activities were observed and recorded by Reo Fortune and Margaret Mead, and my guess is that he expected Fortune to assist him in acquiring the valuables he needed. Certainly the Chambri suspected as much, for Kwasivon accuses Tanum of using the white man, and presumably his resources, to pay his debts. Fortune and Mead were living on Tanum's land and may well have been paying him rent. Certainly I did as much for my Chambri hosts when I lived among them.[3]

If this was so, then Tanum must have been fully aware of how fortunate he was. Without the congeries of certain atypical circumstances—namely, the high rate of male labor migration and the visit of two American anthropologists, he would never have had the opportunity of reemerging as a significant force within Chambri society. His was the chance of a lifetime, and he meant to make the most of it. No wonder he was concerned to insure that Werumbank and his brothers would mount the appropriate ceremony. No wonder he went out of his way to humble himself before his son's *waus* by presenting them with yams and a *kina*. If they pulled out of the ceremony after he had apologized to them, then the wrong and the shame would have been theirs.

Werumbank and his brothers were miffed, they said, because Tanum and his wives had accused them of plotting to take Apong to Kilimbit. They planned to retaliate against these rumors by calling off the initiation ceremony of Tanum's daughter "in view of the outrageous beliefs and talk [Tanum and his family] had and circulated regarding [them] in this matter." They had not done what Kundungwi had done, that is, impregnated a brother's wife, and they were not to be accused of sanctioning his behavior.

How are we to understand Werumbank's outrage at what he insists was a false accusation? Were his moral sensibilities offended? Did he recognize Kundungwi's deed as incestuous and was he upset that anyone might think him a party to such immorality? I think not, for nowhere does Fortune describe him, or anyone else for that matter, as objecting to the multiple seduction of Apong. Werumbank was upset not because of his relation to an immoral Kundungwi, but rather because Tanum knew that Werumbank wished to assume the role of wife-taker to Apong's family.

I am now able to summarize the relationships that were negotiated throughout the Tanum Affair:

1. Tanum had lost Ndumanduma to Askame, an unrelated patron who had assumed Tanum's position as wife-taker to Apong's agnates.

2. Werumbank, a Big Man from Kilimbit, wished to win Apong from Askame, in order to assume the position of wife-taker to her agnates and defeat Askame at his own game.

3. Tanum, who had been overlooked throughout these negotiations and counternegotiations as a rubbish man, hoped to reemerge as a significant power within Chambri society by using his newfound resources to reenter the game. His first step was to coerce Werumbank into acting as a *wau* should, thereby stymieing Werumbank's designs upon Apong's family. His message to Werumbank was clear: I am no longer to be ignored. Don't negotiate for Apong's family without taking me into consideration. I have slept with the girl too, and I may yet reassume Ndumanduma's debts.

4. Werumbank and his brothers, by publicly displaying their outrage at Tanum's "false accusation," conceded that he had, indeed, reemerged as a significant contender for social status. And when Werumbank's son-in-law removed the totemic leaves from his father-in-law's doorway—before Werumbank accepted the *kina* offered in recompense by Tanum's deputation—the message he was sending to Werumbank was straightforward: you can no longer afford your anger, for Tanum is able to manage his affairs once again.

The nature of intermale interaction exhibited between the participants in the Tanum Affair marks no departure from that which we discovered in the examples of affinal exchange I presented in chapter 4. In this case, as in the others, we see an illustration of Chambri politics as a process in which fortune and foolishness provide opportunities for clever men to establish shifting networks of dominance and control. From all of the examples we learn that social groups tend to disintegrate when their leaders overcommit themselves to extensive extrafamilial exchanges. This collapse may be precipitated by an Iatmul exchange partner, who cannot maintain the level of reciprocal exchange set by a demanding, overcommitted Chambri leader; it may also result from a group's incapacity to find wives for its members; or it may be caused by extraordinary and unpredictable circumstances, such as the destruction of the Chambri commodity market by intruding Europeans. Whatever its cause, large and wealthy Chambri groups are inevitably redefined as nonegalitarian and hence defined out of the game, which goes on among the "equals."

The Case of the Masilai Stones

In preceding chapters I argued that Australian Colonial Administrators transformed what were essentially fluid and egalitarian interactions between groups of Chambri and Iatmul into a static and hierarchically arranged social organization. They recorded groups of peoples in census books and placed them on maps demarcating land boundaries, which resulted in a structure of inequality among these indigenous groups that undermined their socioeconomic interactions. In the case of those interactions based on balanced reciprocity, this structure of inequality precluded the possibility of a reversal of the ranks. In the case of fish-for-sago barter where the fish-suppliers maintained a one-to-one exchange rate through military sanctions, the structure of inequality institutionalized social and political domination. But in the case of the politics of affinal exchange, the Australian-imposed structure of inequality had no effect whatsoever, at least not initially.

Administrators allowed Chambri and Iatmul men to remain as preoccupied as they wished with local-level politics. Since the politics of affinal exchange were limited in significance by the native preference for village endogamy, government officials were uninterested in it. They had been contending, after all, with intertribal warfare, and whether or not men like Tanum won status within villages like Indingai seemed of little significance to them. It was therefore completely possible for the Chambri and the Iatmul to continue playing their old game, a game that remained dependent upon the imposition of an egalitarian specification, although it had come to be played with shillings rather than shells.

Consider, for example, the affinal exchange that occurred on October 1, 1974, after David Wapi, a young Chambri man whom I had hired to assist me in maintaining a daily migrational record of all persons entering or leaving the village of Indingai, came to my house to request an advance on his salary. He wanted his next fortnight's $A10 to help his father, Wapiyeri, pay for the food they planned to give to those of their affines whom they had invited to observe the decoration of two stone monoliths named Koromeri and Wumbrianmeri.

There are over 125 stones on Chambri Island that are considered dwelling places of ancestral spirits and consequently bear names. In former times these *masilai* stones served to mark the burial places of a clan's headhunting victims. The stones are repositories of clan strength, and when one of David's affines deprecated the powers of Koromeri and Wumbrinameri, he provoked David's agnates to mount the decorating ceremony to vindicate the stones' potency.

Seven men from two different patriclans decorated the two stones with their totemic leaves in a ceremony lasting only a few minutes. They then adjourned to a party at the house of Yarapat, Wapiyeri's father's father's father's brother's son's son's son's adopted father's son. Arriving there, they found that Wapiyeri had arranged fourteen pairs of coconuts in a semicircle. Next to each pair, he had placed an aluminum bowl containing approximately three pounds of rice, two small tins of mackerel, and one trussed turtle. Wapiyeri, I was told, had donated the food on behalf of "the family." He was going to give it to his *kandere* (affines) who would, in turn, "buy back their mothers' milk."

As the fourteen *kandere* collected their food, each threw some money down on a mat that had been placed on the floor for this purpose. The contributions ranged from $A.50 to $A2.00, amounting to $A15.60 altogether. Wapiyeri did not think this was enough, and so Yarapat, as "half family, half *kandere*," brought the sum up to $A20.00. He did this shilling by shilling, while orating to the assembled hosts and guests about his generosity. Kubusa, he said—the affine who had deprecated the *masilai* stones—had not come to the party. Wapiyeri did not have the strength to pull him, even with Chambrinamak's (my) help. But, he, Yarapat, was a truly strong man, and would force Kubusa's attendance at the next possible occasion.

It is my contention that the Case of the *Masilai* Stones had as little to do with the offense Wapiyeri took at Kubusa's deprecation of Koromeri and Wumbrianmeri as the Tanum Affair had to do with Apong's seduction. Many Chambri women are seduced, and many men take offense at the insults of their neighbors, but only occasionally do they mobilize for and against one another around such incidents. More frequently they let the matter rest, primarily because they have neither the resources nor the allies to do anything else. What both of these cases had in common, and what frequently instigates affinal compensations of all kinds among the Chambri, was a competition between two or more leaders for control of the affinal prestations of related or unrelated individuals. In the Tanum Affair this competition took place between Werumbank and Askame over Apong's agnates, and it was Tanum's purpose to stymie both men's designs. In the Case of the *Masilai* Stones, the competition involved Wapiyeri and Yarapat over the position of wife-giver to Kubusa.

Figure 9.2, which makes the relationships between these antagonists clearer, indicates that both Yarapat and Wapiyeri had given women to Kubusa. Both were therefore entitled to receive recompense from him. But the situation had been complicated by two past events, the marriage of Wapiyeri's younger brother to Kubusa's full sister, and the adoption of David's "uncle" by Yarapat's father.

Saimeri's marriage was considered highly irregular. He was warned against marrying Tsinsowinamak, his father's brother's daughter's daughter, for such an alliance would produce a situation in which two intermarrying clans were simultaneously wife-giver and wife-taker to the other. And when Saimeri died a premature death, his brothers were convinced that Kubusa's ancestors were responsible. They felt it wise to sever affinal connections

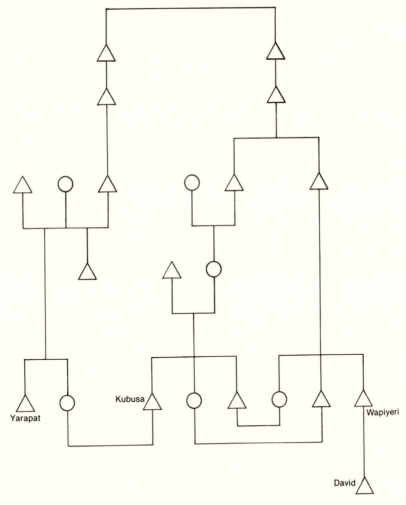

Figure 9.2. The Antagonists in the Case of the *Masilai* Stones

between their group and Kubusa's, saying that these wife-takers had begun to "eat up our strength," and it was no longer worth the affinal recompense to send women to them.

But Kubusa did not give up his claim as wife-taker. He insisted that Saimeri's clan provide him with a woman, for he was ready with a large brideprice. David's agnates, somewhat troubled at the thought of passing up a large affinal prestation, but more afraid of losing their patrilineal substance to Kubusa's ancestors, found the perfect solution. They encouraged Yarapat to give his sister to Kubusa, for although there was no biological relationship between his and David's clan, David's agnates freqently referred to Yarapat and his sister by sibling terms. Yarapat's father had married the widowed mother of one of David's uncles, and was called "father" by this uncle. By extension, David's agnates viewed Yarapat "as if he were one of our family." I suspect that the close connection between Yarapat and David's agnates was emphasized by the latter because they wished to retain some degree of control over Kubusa's family's affinal prestations and at the same time they wished to escape any supernatural retribution brought on by Saimeri's inauspicious marriage. Yarapat was young, and his clan was neither large nor wealthy, and by marrying his sister to Kubusa, David's agnates thought they could maintain the best of all possible solutions—control without commitment.

But times changed, and so did the fortunes of all three of these interrelated groups. By 1974, Yarapat and Kubusa had become the two most important men living in Indingai Village, while David's family had declined in power and significance. Kubusa's sons, one a corporal in the army and the other the owner-operator of a motorboat taxi service to and from Pagwi Patrol Post, supplied their father with the money he needed to establish and maintain extensive networks of extrafamilial affinal relationsips.[4] Yarapat, now the owner of the most elaborate house in Indingai Village, had close connections with Matias Yambumpe, at this time the president of the Gaui Local Government Council. He was Yambumpe's unofficial liaison officer, entertaining visiting dignitaries, including Papua New Guinea's first prime minister, Michael Somare (who came to Yarapat's house-opening party), and generally upholding Yambumpe's rule throughout the three Chambri villages. He did this through eloquent and persuasive discourse, backed up by rumors of his ability to ensorcell those who disobeyed him, and by his maintenance of a network of extrafamilial affinal relationships nearly as extensive as Kubusa's.[5] How he maintained these networks remains a mystery to me, for Yarapat should not have been a wealthy man, dependent as he was upon his own hard work at artifact and crocodile skin sales to earn his money. Be this as it may, the Chambri I spoke to thought it fitting and proper that the families of Yarapat and Kubusa should intermarry for, as one informant put it, "in-laws should be able to fight each other equally."

Wapiyeri did not agree. His formerly large and powerful clan had become denuded of its constituents by age, death, and labor migration. He was old. His brothers were dead. And his sons had abandoned him, moving to We- wak, Madang, and Port Moresby to seek their fortunes in the towns.[6] He lived in his once grand but now crumbling house with his three old wives, a daughter-in-law, and David. His absent sons sent him little money and rarely visited home. And when I hired his one remaining son, he hoped to be able to use the salary I provided to reestablish himself within Indingai, perhaps by coercing Kubusa into recognizing him once again as an affine "to be fought with equally."

The Case of the *Masilai* Stones was not Wapiyeri's first attempt to rees- tablish himself as a power within Indingai society. He had also tried to earn capital for investment in affinal transactions by selling an old and formerly sacred carving to a European entrepreneur. Unfortunately, his scheme was blocked when six different Indingai men claimed ownership of the carving. At the debate which ensued, one claimant argued: "My grandfather pro- vided the wood from which the carving was made; it's mine as much as it's anyone's." Another insisted: "My grandfather owned the adze used to carve it; if it hadn't been for my family the carving wouldn't exist." As it turned out, Yarapat persuaded them all to have the artifact declared national cul- tural property, thereby preventing anyone from trying to turn it into ready cash. Wapiyeri did not, however, recognize the equitability of Yarapat's so- lution to the problem of the carving's ownership. When discussing the in- cident with me he said: "Yarapat ruins everything of mine. He's a man who brings ruination to everything." What he had ruined, both in the case of the carving and in that of the *masilai* stones, was Wapiyeri's chance to play successfully the politics of affinal exchange. On both occasions Wapiyeri had been proven incapable of managing his affairs. Even with David's sal- ary of $A10 per fortnight, his clan had become "less than equal," and hence unable to play the game of status and prestige except, perhaps, as a client of others.

Magic, Science, Religion, and Money

Before the destruction of the Chambri commodity market, when shell valu- ables were still acquired in exchange for stone tools and mosquito bags, the egalitarian specification upon which the politics of affinal exchange de- pended was ultimately imposed by the Iatmul. Iatmul trading partners who could not satisfy the demands of Chambri Big Men would opt out of their reciprocal trading relationships and begin patronizing less demanding part- ners. Thus, a Chambri Big Man's networks of extrafamilial affinal relation- ships could expand, but only to the point allowed by his Iatmul trading partners.

After the Kamanbo exile, the Iatmul no longer supplied the Chambri with shells or regulated their use of them. Since the Chambri had nothing to offer the Iatmul in exchange for the valuables, few new shells entered their economy. During the Tanum Affair, in fact, Werumbank and Askame were establishing and maintaining their affinal relationships with the shell valuables they had managed to horde during the years of exile.

If the Chambri had not substituted shillings for shells, this situation of scarcity would have strangled the Chambri affinal exchange system, resulting in a rigidification of patron–client relationships. Tanum, for example, would not have reemerged as a significant contender for social status unless he had been able to acquire valuables from someone—probably from Fortune. Moreover, leaders would have been forced to limit their networks of control, being without the shells necessary to do otherwise. The affinal exchange system would have wound down to a static halt, mother's brother's daughter's marriage would probably have increased, and a Big Man's power would no longer have been based on his control of extrafamilial affinal relationships.

Once the substitution of shillings for shells had been made, however, it again became unnecessary for Big Men to regulate themselves. Kubusa and Yarapat relied, as had their ancestors, upon an external source of the valuables they needed. The difference was that, whereas their ancestors had sold commodities to their Iatmul friends, Kubusa and Yarapat sold artifacts, crocodile skins, or labor to an impersonal and European-dominated market. Although they had managed to negotiate the change from shells to shillings intact, without destroying the affinal exchange system that regulated their sociopolitical lives, the success of their conservative adaptation held consequences of which they are only now becoming conscious.

As an indication of these consequences, consider the following series of incidents. During my second field trip, Rudolph, the son of Scolastica Wusuai, returned home from Maprik High School with a badly ulcerated sore on his leg. Since it was causing him considerable pain and preventing him from walking around, Scolastica decided to ask Andrew Yorondu, a Chambri shaman, to work his "*yuli*" magic.

Yuli is the Chambri word for dog, and Yorondu's *yuli* magic, which he inherited from his father, involved chanting the totemic names associated with certain mythological Chambri dogs over a collection of the patient's totemic leaves. The chant is believed to imbue the leaves with the dryness of a dog's tongue, a dryness that is transferred to the patient's sore by applying the leaves as a bandage. Yorondu has had considerable success in curing ulcers with this magic, and Scolastica paid him two *kina* for his trouble. (The *kina* referred to here are the official currency of Papua New Guinea, not the shell valuables.)[7]

When the sore began to hemorrhage that night, Yorondu was called in again for an emergency consultation. He brought more magically endowed leaves with him, but when these did not stop the bleeding, I was asked to do so in the European manner. Working together, the three of us managed to stop the hemorrhaging with cotton gauze, but when I offered to treat Rudolph with penicillin, both Scolastica and Yorondu refused my offer, explaining that Rudolph's illness was not curable through Western medical techniques since its cause was "something belonging to us alone."

The next day, when Rudolph was still no better, Scolastica asked Father Padlo, the pastor of the local Catholic church, to cure her son through prayer. The Father agreed to come that afternoon. Arriving at Scolastica's house with his Melanesian Pidgin Bible, a relic of the true cross, and a plastic ketchup bottle full of holy water, he enjoined us all to be good Catholics, asked Francis, Rudolph's father, to read a passage from the Bible, and then squirted the holy water on each of us and throughout the house.

Scolastica was sure that this religious cure would work, but just to be sure, she decided to take her family to sleep in her husband's brother's house that night. She made me promise to tell no one where she was, just in case the malevolent ghosts might hear my talk and follow her to her family's temporary abode.

When Rudolph was still no better in the morning, Scolastica became desperate. Her troubles had doubled during the night, for her eight-year-old daughter, Angela, had come down with malaria and was burning up with fever. Scolastica knew that she had to meet her troubles head-on, and so she sent word to three Iatmul shamans living on Timbunmeri Island, to come to Chambri to cure her children.[8]

The Iatmul shamans arrived the next day. They brought several varieties of leaves with them, over which they chanted their own equivalents of the *yuli* magic. One made a few small cuts in Angela's forehead with a razor blade, and another rubbed the powerful leaves over her body, and then over Rudolph's leg. The third, who had taken a mouthful of water, sat with his eyes closed, thinking the water full of curative powers. His thinking done, he spat the water over us all, while shouting an Iatmul name of which I never learned the meaning. Scolastica paid them twenty-eight *kina* and a pig for their services, hoping that their powerful magic and her high pay would put an end to her troubles.

Unfortunately, her troubles continued, for neither child appeared any better the next morning. Reconsidering her rejection of Western medical techniques, but not trusting in my ability to use them adequately, Scolastica paid for the motorboat taxi-service to Pagwi, where she took her children to the medical aid post. With the help of chloroquin and penicillin, both

Angela and Rudolph recovered rapidly. Their cure had cost Scolastica over sixty *kina*.

Sixty *kina* is an unusually large amount of money for a Chambri woman to control. But, then, Scolastica is an unusual woman. She is Matias Yambumpe's youngest sister and has been managing the trade store he established at Indingai Village.[9] The money she used to cure her children was the money paid into Matias' store by Indingai who purchased beer, cigarettes, tinned fish, or other items. Her husband, Francis Wusuai, was a motorboat driver for the government when I was first in the field, but he had lost his job and seemed to be at loose ends during 1979. He was being paid to help members of Matias's clan construct a house that they hoped would serve as a hotel for visiting European tourists. The Chambri I spoke to thought this highly inappropriate work, for Francis was not a member of Matias's clan, and should not have been receiving money from him. They said: "Francis Wusuai has confused things. He should be giving money to Matias, for he married Matias' sister, not vice versa."

In my discussions with Scolastica, Francis, and other Chambri about the illnesses of Rudolph and Angela, five causes emerged: (1) Francis's affair with the wife of the late Clement Kongai; (2) My research assistant's abduction of Francis's clan-brother's daughter; (3) The elopement of Kanbo, a young Chambri woman, with a teacher at the Mission School; (4) The remarriage of two Chambri after both abandoned their spouses without gaining the approval of their families; and (5) Scolastica's successes at running her brother's trade store. What is most interesting about these reputed causes—each a conflict situation believed to have provoked concerned ancestors to seek revenge—is that only three out of the five bear any connection to Scolastica, Francis, or their families. And yet they are all indicative of the same essential conflict. My Chambri informants, it would seem, in discussing the causes of Rudolph's and Angela's illnesses were describing a more general concern.

What the five conflict situations have in common is this: they all involve the establishment of relationships that undermine the affinal exchange system—relationships that preclude the expected exchanges between wife-givers and wife-takers and consequently prevent enterprising individuals from gaining control of these exchanges. Francis's affair with Kongai's wife, for example, may have provoked her dead husband's ghost to wreak revenge upon Francis's children, but it had not convinced anyone alive to seek retribution.[10] Francis had no intention of paying compensation to the woman's agnates or to members of her dead husband's clan, arguing that the affair "is my business and no one else's."

Nor did Godfried Yangim, my research assistant, regret taking Julie Kubusa as his second wife. He says he was forced by his family to marry his first wife and sees no reason why they should prevent him from taking someone he likes better as a second. But since neither he nor his agnates have any intention of paying the bride-price necessary to acquire the woman he likes legally, they all fear supernatural retribution. Godfried has, so far, avoided this by moving from Indingai to Wewak, where he and Julie support themselves by selling artifacts to the tourists. Although he visits his first wife at Indingai quite frequently, he is always careful to leave before Julie's ancestors have time to make him sick.

Kanbo has not been so lucky, for she became seriously ill with stomach cramps and fever shortly after eloping with a teacher she met at Indingai's Mission School. She returned home to Chambri to receive a native cure that required the compensation of wife-givers by wife-takers. Unfortunately, her husband's family knew nothing of the Chambri and their customs and had no intention of sending the appropriate sum of money. Because of this, every Chambri I spoke to assumed that Kanbo would die.

Sickness had not yet struck the two Chambri who had abandoned their spouses to marry one another, but everyone was sure that it eventually would. The ancestors of four clans had been outraged by their behavior, after all. The two newlyweds were not living on Chambri Island when I was last in the field, having built themselves a temporary house on Peliagwi Island. Rumor had it that they did not plan to return to Chambri, but to become "bush *kanakas* with the Mensuat."

Finally, there is the case of Scolastica's successful management of her brother's trade store, which may serve as the archetype of all the aforementioned conflict situations, for it illustrates most clearly the systemic consequences of the adaptive substitution of shillings for shells. Unlike the Matupi, the Chambri found it relatively easy to incorporate the newly emerging, wage-earning population into the accepted relations of dominance and subordination, so long as they were willing to convert those wages into the exchange items that signified their social status. Thus, Wapiyeri purchased rice and tinned fish to present to his wife-takers in return for the currency which now indicated wife-taking status.

The willingness to convert money into food, and to give currency in affinal exchanges, marked an individual's commitment to the sociopolitical system in which he participated and to the culture he shared. This commitment was easy to make—indeed, it was impossible not to make—as long as money was earned away from the village, and the ongoing nature of Chambri political manipulations limited the choice of emigrant wage-earners to staying within the village and conforming to clan obligations, or leaving the village permanently. In other words, as long as valuables were externally supplied and regulated, the wage-earning population had to convert their resources for use in socially acceptable networks of dominance and subordination in order to be admitted back within their villages.

This situation has changed, for Chambri now hire other Chambri to perform nontraditional wage-labor, such as Scolastica's management of her brother's trade store, or Francis's employment by his brother-in-law's agnates to build a tourist hotel, or Kubusa's hiring of several young motorboat drivers to run his taxi service, or another Chambri's use of paid laborers to care for the herd of cattle he has established on a small island in Chambri Lake. These employer-employee relationships have transcended patron–client and affinal ties and have confused the accepted relations of dominance and subordination, allowing wife-takers to employ wife-givers, and patrons to sell their labor in order to earn the money necessary to maintain their rapidly disintegrating networks of extrafamilial affinal relationships. Young men no longer define social success in terms of these traditional patron–client relationships, but rather in terms of the new employer-employee condition. It is not that they refuse to be incorporated within traditional relations of dominance and subordination, but rather that the nature of these relationships has altered. Five years ago, young Chambri males would have thought an investment in a large affinal exchange to be the best of all possible business deals. Today they rarely pay bride-prices for their wives, believing that their money is better invested elsewhere, even if only in buying beer to throw a party for their contemporaries. With the Catholic Father's help, they marry whom they like, and if their parents object, they simply move from Chambri to one of the towns, where they believe their chances of finding employment are better anyway.

Those young men who were encouraged to seek work in the town in order to earn money which their agnates could then introduce into local-level political networks have begun to marry non-Chambri wives—wives whose agnates are unwilling to engage their affines in affinal exchange. And even more problematic, young Chambri women, who have been forced to journey to Wewak in order to sell their fish for the money they need to purchase sago, have begun to marry non-Chambri husbands and to bear non-Chambri children (see table 9.1).

Table 9.1: The Frequency of Exogamous Marriage at Indingai between 1974 and 1978

	Indingai	Kilimbit	Wombun	Sub-Non-Chambri	Total	Percentage of Exogamy	
						Extravillage	Non-Chambri
Indingai							
M	5	2	1	7	15	20	47
F	5	2	1	3	11	27	27
Totals	10	4	2	10	26	23	38

Thus, the consequences of the adaptive substitution of shillings for shells have been destructive of the very relationships Chambri elders hoped to maintain, and the texture of life within the three Chambri villages when I was last in the field can only be described as anomic. No one is sure any longer who is beholden to whom, or of how to establish and maintain social relationships. Everyone is afraid of supernatural retribution, and I saw more shamanism during one summer than I had seen during the entire period of my previous fieldwork. The question of whether the situation will stabilize with time, as employer-employee relationships become firmly established, is a moot one, for the substitution of shillings for shells has not been the only change with which the Chambri have had to deal, as we shall see in the next chapter.

10

SALVINIA MOLESTA:
THE DESTRUCTION OF
AN ECOSYSTEM

In the last analysis, Chambri men lost control of their affinal exchange system by losing control of their women. Forced into the towns by the transformation of sago-suppliers into entrepreneurs, Chambri women have begun to marry men they meet there—men whose agnates are uninformed about and uninterested in the politics of affinal exchange. When the practice of tribal exogamy was limited to young Chambri men—migrant laborers who took wives from the areas in which they were working—their elders could act as if nothing was amiss. Indeed, Chambri Big Men considered these women's agnates fools, for why else would wife-givers not demand to be compensated in affinal transactions? But now that Chambri sisters and daughters have begun giving themselves in marriage to non-Chambri, the affinal exchange system appears doomed. Bride-prices are infrequently paid and children are rarely bought back from their matrilateral relatives. Female exogamy, moreover, means the end of Chambri autonomy, for the children of Chambri women are growing up speaking foreign languages.

In the recent past even these out-marrying Chambri women would probably have returned to their villages once sickness or other commonplace life crises convinced them that their ancestors were displeased at their marriages. Now, however, their return seems unlikely, not because Chambri brothers and fathers have lost more control, but rather because there is little for these women to come home to. Of late the Chambri have been experiencing a major environmental crisis, which has resulted in the eclipsing of marriage as a prime topic of concern by the problem of simple food gathering.

Salvinia molesta *in the Sepik*

During the high-water season of 1979, 90 percent of Chambri Lake was covered by a floating water fern, originally from South America, called *Salvinia molesta*. The spongy fern grows so thickly that both canoes and fish traps are severely hampered by the barrier it forms. Since the Chambri are sedentary hunter-gatherers who grow no crops but subsist entirely by fishing, the effects of the fern have been catastrophic.

The Catholic priest stationed at St. Mary's Mission in Chambri Lake, concerned to provide the East Sepik Provincial government with proof of the seriousness of the environmental crisis, asked three literate Chambri to keep a record of the food consumed by the people living in all three Chambri villages over a two-day period. According to this record, the 691 Chambri living at home managed to catch only 76 fish on May 3 and 4, 1979, not enough to support them. Instead of fish, they ate coconuts, wild greens, store bought foods, and whatever sago they still had on hand. They had not been able to acquire sago from the Sepik Hills peoples for some time, for most of the Mensuat and Changriman had once again ascended to their hills hamlets, where they tried to fulfill their protein demands through hunting. What good was their access to the rich fish resource of Chambri Lake when *Salvinia molesta* made these fish inaccessible? Far better to return to the mountains, where marsupials, cassowaries, and other game were still available.

The Chambri themselves had prepared the sago on which they were subsisting, and access to the limited number of palms located on or near Chambri Island became their paramount concern. One sorcery trial that I witnessed was most interesting in this regard. The son of a man from Kilimbit had been hit by a car while he was selling carvings in Wewak. Although the accident victim was well on the way to recovery in the hospital, his father publicly declared that his son was destined to die of his injuries. The old man argued that his sister's husband's brothers had ensorcelled his son in order to gain control of the grove of sago palms that the boy was eventually to inherit. If his son were to die, then these men's children, born of the boy's paternal aunt, would inherit the palms. Since there were seven other patrilineally related heirs, the old man's argument made no sense to me until I realized that his sorcery accusation was not meant to disenfranchise his sister's children. He knew that they had no chance of inheriting the palms. What he wished was the disenfranchisement of his sister, whose clan status gave her the right to use the palms to feed her family. The old man hoped that by arousing the sympathies of his covillagers he would be allowed to keep the palms for himself. There were few of them, and he was afraid that he and his agnates would soon be without the life-sustaining food.

No one is sure how the fern was first introduced into the area. It is known that since 1971 it has spread throughout the Middle and Lower Sepik, covering over 79 square kilometers of the Sepik River and its connecting tributaries, lagoons, and lakes, and affecting the subsistence of nearly 35,000

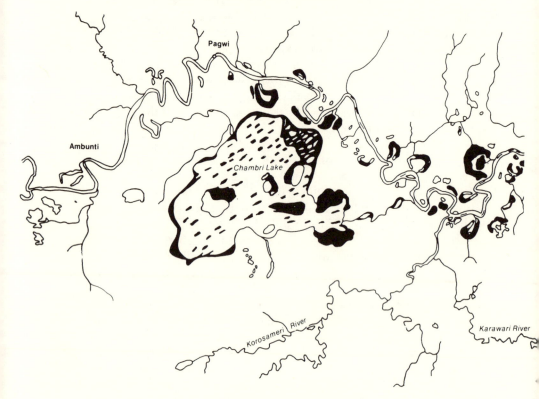

Salvinia molesta in the Sepik

people (see map 7). Because the Sepik provides it with nearly perfect grow-ing conditions, the fern has spread rapidly, doubling in size every 2.2 to 11 days.

Mangi Pinang, a man from Angoram,[1] describes the plight of his people in a letter to the editor of the *Post Courier*:

> In 1973, the year in which the weed was first seen in my la-goon,[2] people became curious about its presence and the rate at which it was spreading. . . .
>
> The two methods [the people have found to rid themselves of the infestation] are blockage and burning. The blockage system is used during the wet season while the other is used during the dry. . . .
>
> [But] the lagoons are covered over [again] in a matter of weeks and the Sepik River is being used again as a salvinia weed dump which carries a never ending string of salvinia weeds to be depos-ited at Kopar, the mouth of the Sepik. . . .

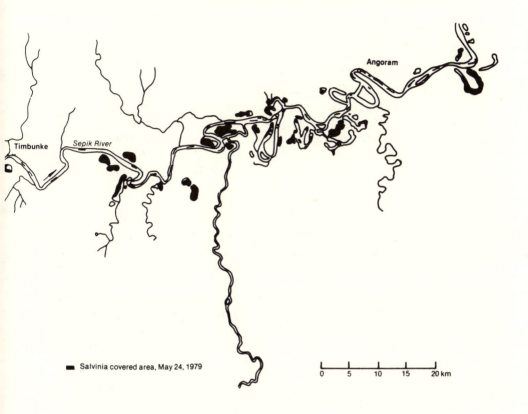

Angoram

Timbunke   Sepik River

■ Salvinia covered area, May 24, 1979

0   5   10   15   20 km

As the lagoons have become covered, fishing either by nets or spears has become impossible.

Water transport is the only means of transport around the area but the presence of the weed has made it difficult for the Sepik River people, especially those from lagoon areas, where canoeing has become almost impossible. . . .

People have been restricted from paddling their canoes out of the villages by themselves because of the fear of being trapped among the weeds in the middle of the lagoon.

There have been many cases where people have been trapped and left helpless until nightfall, when rescue teams were sent out.

Starvation is not impossible. People in areas like mine have been really affected. Their hours of food collection have been restricted and [they] have been left without fishing grounds.

Sago making has become impossible because of the distance to get to sago swamp areas. . . .

> Who can rescue these people, with more complex knowledge
> and skills to fight the menace? [1979: 4]

The Government of Papua New Guinea, alerted to the problem, hired
D. S. Mitchell as a consultant to the Office of Environment and Conservation. (It is to him that I owe the photographs of *Salvinia* and map 7.) In
his report on the incidence and management of *Salvinia molesta* in Papua
New Guinea, Mitchell has suggested three possible methods of eradicating
it. The first involves spraying the affected areas with herbicides, probably
paraquat or AF101 (a new herbicide developed by the Alan Fletcher Research Station, Ministry of Lands, Queensland, Australia). Unfortunately,
these herbicides are toxic, and the degree to which they will injure other
aquatic organisms is unknown. The second method, biological control,
involves introducing an insect, either the grasshopper *Paulina acuminata*,
the weevil *Cyrtogagous singularis*, or the moth *Samea multiplicalis*. These
insects have not been particularly successful in reducing the *Salvinia* infestation in Botswana and Sri Lanka. Moreover, they may not limit themselves
to a diet of the fern but may learn to consume the wild greens upon which
many Sepiks depend. As one of my Chambri informants put it while discussing the possibility of biological control: "If you, Deborah, could learn
to eat our native foods, why can't these insects?" Finally, the third method,
mechanical and manual removal, is prohibitively expensive and seldom
successful against large areas of *Salvinia*.

Referring specifically to Chambri Lake, Mitchell writes:

> Chambri Lake obviously provides a special problem, as there is
> relatively little flow [of water] through the system from the river,
> and there is no possibility of a substantial proportion of the weed
> being swept out of the system through the lower channel. . . .
> Repetitive chemical control of large areas on the lake would be
> prohibitively expensive but it may be possible to alleviate the sit-
> uation around particular village sites by the use of booms and
> judicious application of herbicides. In the long term the most cost-
> effective means of control for this area would be the introduction
> of biological control organisms. [1979: 42]

Whether alleviating the situation around particular village sites would
allow the Chambri to acquire the fish they need is questionable. And certainly such limited mobility would prevent the continuation of an economy
based on the exchange of fish for sago, whether or not the exchange is
mediated through the acquisition of money. Thus, the prognosis is grim,
and many Chambri feel helpless in the face of it. By the time I arrived
there, almost 50 percent of the population had fled to the town of Wewak.[3]
The remaining people, many of them old and all weakened by their low-

protein diet of coconuts, wild greens, and sago, recognize that their culture and society may never recover.[4]

Of Missionaries, Ferns, and Ambiguous Categories

When I returned to Papua New Guinea during 1979 my plan was to investigate the validity of the ontological concept of sex roles. I suggested in my research proposal the need to abandon this concept and adopt a more systemic approach. In particular, I wished to study the social changes wrought by the increased earning and spending capacities of Chambri women. I had heard from Chambri friends writing to me in the United States about "a no-good grass," but I did not understand the seriousness of the situation. In any case, once I arrived in the Sepik, I abandoned my research design, not only because it would have been impossible to carry out under the circumstances, but also because I felt morally and scientifically obliged to study the present condition—to collect any information which might help the government to alleviate this disaster.

Once I returned home, I found myself in the extremely privileged position of trying to find a framework to interpret this change rather than suffer its effects with the Chambri. My job became to analyze the social processes associated with the introduction of *Salvinia* as objectively as possible. To this end, I found interesting the following two passages, the first from Mangi Pinang's Letter to the Editor, quoted earlier, and the second from an anonymous newspaper article.

> Since 1973 the people have been wondering how and why these weeds came into the areas.
> The most popular conclusion held among many villages, especially my village and the next, was that because the people had disobeyed God's commandments God sent this weed into the area to make people suffer and be punished. [1979: 4]

> Sepik River villagers are using the water-weed salvinia as a weapon.
> They are planting the weed to destroy fishing grounds during family or village disputes.
> A parliamentarian, Mr. William Eichorn (Angoram), said yesterday hundreds of fishing grounds and gardens have been destroyed.
> "The weed is one of their most lethal weapons."
> "But they don't realize the damage it's doing to the river," Mr. Eichorn said.
> He confirmed a recent Food and Agriculture Organization consultant's report that starvation was facing villagers along the

Sepik River if control measures were not taken immediately. [*Post Courier*, 1979: page unknown]

Thus it appears that the villagers in and around Angoram have accepted God's retribution with neither the patience of Job nor the obedience of Abraham. They have become neither passive nor penitent, but have responded to this manifestation of divine will in a peculiar manner—not, it seems, by disavowing their polygamous marriages, nor by attending church more frequently, nor by abandoning their "pagan" beliefs in sorcery, but rather by destroying one another's fishing grounds through weed warfare.

Although I never witnessed the Chambri planting the fern in the dead of night in their enemies' fishing grounds, they assure me that this has frequently happened. Indeed, they attribute its presence in Chambri Lake to a Kandingai Iatmul named Sui, who they say planted it inside Chambri territory to rid the lake region of its rightful inhabitants. The Chambri's response has been to return parts of Sui's harvest to Kandingai and Timbunmeri waters.

No Chambri I spoke to, however, blames any indigene for the fern's initial introduction into the region. Instead, they refer to a Catholic priest stationed at a mission at Timbunke, who owned a tropical fish tank. He is said to have disposed of the fern in the Sepik River after it had overgrown his tank. Their story possesses considerable verisimilitude, for as Mitchell informs us:

> *Salvinia* was first positively identified in Papua New Guinea early in 1977 when it was seen on fish ponds at Bulolo and Wau.[5] Specimens were collected from the Sepik River at Angoram in May 1977 and subsequent enquiries among the local villagers revealed that it had first appeared there in 1975. From the plant's pattern and rate of growth, it can be deduced that the weed was probably introduced into the Sepik somewhere upstream of Angoram in 1971 or before, possibly near Pagwi. It is also present in bomb-holes in Wewak.
>
> The plant has been spread principally as an aquarium plant and has been seen in an ornamental pond at a Madang hotel in 1977 (T. Petr, pers. comm.) and [in] aquari[um] shops in Lae in 1973 (D. Sands, pers. comm.) and in Port Moresby in 1975 (I. Johnstone, pers. comm.) and May 1979 (A. Haines, pers. comm.). [1979: 10]

Whether or not the Timbunke priest purchased the fern from one of these shops as a botanical curiosity is unknown to me, but it seems likely that someone brought the fern to the region in this manner. What is significant to an understanding of the social processes associated with the *Salvinia* infestation is the Chambri perception of its introduction, particularly their insistence that a priest was to blame.[6]

In chapter 1 I discussed another recent introduction into Sepik waters, *Tilapia mosambica*, the ubiquitous fish called *makau* by Sepik natives. This fish escaped from experimental breeding ponds into the Screw River, arriving in Sepik waters at just the time when Bishop Arkfeld was making a tour of the region. Bishop Arkfeld is a highly respected and popular clergyman who pilots his own plane and whose landings on native airstrips are stirring events in the lives of village inhabitants. Whether encouraged in their belief by local priests anxious to win converts or not, the Chambri and many of their neighbors assumed that Bishop Arkfeld had brought *makau* with him to insure that "his children" would never be hungry. Thus, there is a precedent within Chambri historical memory for the introduction into their region of aquatic organisms by Catholic priests.

Unlike Mangi Pinang from Angoram, however, most of the Chambri I spoke to do not attribute the introduction of either *makau* or *Salvinia molesta* to the state of their souls. They never told me that Bishop Arkfeld rewarded them because they were good or that God, through the agency of the Timbunke priest, punished them for disobeying his commandments. They are quite accustomed to disobeying both the commandments of their own and of the white man's ancestors when it suits them, and I think it an accurate generalization to say that they have adopted an extremely pragmatic attitude toward these ritual lapses. Their pragmatism was first brought home to me when my Chambri brother broke the postpartum taboo against working after his wife bore him a son. Rather than remaining in the men's house as he was supposed to do, he mended the ladder to his wife's house. When I asked him about his actions, he said: "If the baby cries tonight I'll know that I did wrong. But since you gave me money yesterday, it will be easy for me to hold the ceremony to appease my ancestors." This does not mean that my Chambri brother was incapable of distinguishing between the wrongness of his actions and his ancestors' disapproval, but rather that he could not conceive of being incapable of rectifying his wrongs through his own initiative.

The Chambri adopt the same pragmatic attitude toward the commandments of the white man's powerful ancestor, Jesus Christ. During one case of Chambri divorce, for example, the local Catholic priest attempted to convince the participants that what they were doing was wrong. He entered the house in which the compensation was taking place without being invited and lectured all those present about Jesus' displeasure at divorce. He said that he, as Christ's representative among the Chambri, was compelled to tell them that they would all go to hell if they insisted on engaging in sinful behavior. The woman and her ex-husband had been married in church, before God, and they were committing a mortal sin by divorcing one another. All those who were helping them to do so were also in a state of sin and had better mend their ways before God's final retribution.

Many of those engaged in the divorce proceedings were upset by the priest's words and may have feared the hell-fires he promised. But when he left the house, Anton Bascam, a man from Kilimbit spoke: "Why does this white man think he can enter this house without knocking? When we wish to enter his house, we must knock on his door and wait for him to let us in. He says, 'Come in,' and then we do so. But sometimes he says, 'I'm busy now, come back later,' and then we must listen to what he tells us and go away. Why does he not do the same when he wishes to come into our houses? Instead, he breaks his own rules—the rules of God—and comes in when he wishes to. This man is incorrect (*kranki*). He does not represent Jesus well. Jesus wishes us to be happy, and so we are compensating these good men here. This priest doesn't understand anything about Jesus. He breaks Jesus' rules, and so we can too."

Bascam's casuistry may not be doctrinally sound, but it does demonstrate the Chambri tendency to value those precepts we take to be moral absolutes only if they can be used flexibly, as justifications for pragmatic action.[7] Contrarily, they tend to reject or ignore moral principles when they become impediments to socially acceptable actions. Although Mangi Pinang may have been thoroughly converted to Christian thinking, the Middle Sepik people I know well would find it difficult to believe that God would introduce *Salvinia molesta* to punish them for their pagan behavior. This is not to suggest that they would doubt his power to do so, but rather that they would deny the gravity of their crimes. In other words, the relationship between their crimes and God's punishment would remain unclear to them, because they have been behaving no more sinfully than usual.

Nothing in Chambri experience has prepared them for *Salvinia molesta*. Although they have experienced environmental crises—particularly periods of flooding and drought—they have attributed these events to ancestral displeasure and have dealt with them accordingly, through compensations and sacrifices.[8] But until recently, they have never had difficulty accommodating to anything that white men have introduced. Indeed, they have viewed European commodities as providing wonderful, if not miraculous, opportunities to play their political games all the more intensively.

Within the last few years, however, increasing numbers of Chambri men have begun to sense that their lives are out of control, particularly because their women have started to marry foreigners. And as if to provide cosmic verification of these suspicions, *Salvinia molesta* appeared on the scene. It is my contention that Chambri men are expressing their fears of lost social control by blaming a priest for the introduction of the pernicious fern, and that they are engaging in weed warfare in an attempt to regain that which they have lost.

My argument hinges on Chambri perception of the priest who ostensibly introduced the fern. As a celibate male, he possesses a gender identity that to many Chambri and Iatmul appears ambiguous. One Chambri man expressed this ambiguity in the following manner:

> The nuns say that they are married to Jesus. This I understand because Jesus is a powerful ancestor who had many wives. But the priests I don't understand at all. They're married to whom?—to the nuns?—to each other?—to themselves? They must be men who are also women, and they must play with themselves at night. They say that they stay unmarried so as to be strong for God's work. But how can a man be strong without sons? This father here says that the Chambri people are his children. But we know who our fathers are. The priests must have many sons back home in their villages, waiting at home in the places they come from. This must be true because they are very powerful, bringing in trade stores, cargo, and many other things. They would not be powerful if they did not have sons. Their wives must be back home, like the wives of patrol officers. Although they could be like the bush-people—with few sons. But if this were true, then how did they become so powerful?

My informant's difficulties in defining the meaning of the social category, "priest" resulted from his incapacity to find the highest inclusive category within which to place the information he had acquired about those who held this position. He had no difficulties with nuns, defining them, simply, as married women. But priests seemed to be neither women nor men, patrol officers or bush-people. If he could have found a definition for them, then perhaps he could have explained inconsistencies in their behavior as either idiosyncracies or as alternative, lower-level components of their nature. But this was not possible because priests do seem to possess the essential characteristics and powers of men, women, bush-people, and patrol officers.

Another Chambri man expressed his anxiety over the identifications and divisions ambiguously united in the social category of priests by asking me: "How is it that the same people have the power to bring *makau* and the power to bring this no good grass?" When I requested clarification, he said: "Among us, one man has the power to bring fish, and another the power to bring fruits to the trees; one man has the power to bring mosquitoes, and another has the power to bring the dry water; but no one man has the power over all of these things."

This informant was referring to the egalitarian structure of Chambri patriclans, which depends upon the ownership by each of different totemic names and powers within a common social system. For a clan to be the equal of other clans depends upon certain divisions and identifications: Clan members claim descent from the same ancestor who, by definition, is not the apical ancestor of the members of other clans. Clan members own land and water rights in common which, by definition, are inaccessible to the members of other clans, who possess their own rights to different significant resources. Clan members have inherited totemic names and powers which, by definition, are theirs alone, in contrast to the totems of other cognate groups. Among the Chambri, to be equal is not to be the same, nor to own the same things, and conflict occurs—on both the ideological and socio-logical levels—when differences between groups become blurred, when two groups remove the boundaries between them while still insisting that they are distinct and equal. It becomes increasingly unclear which particular clans control which names, powers, and so on, and which clans are sym-metrically or asymmetrically related. And it seems that the Chambri per-ceive priests as embodying this ambivalent, conflict-ridden condition.

But how is this perception of theirs related to the introduction of *Salvinia molesta*? And why have they responded to the fern through a self-destruc-tive penchant toward weed warfare? The answer to the first question is re-latively straightforward. The presence of *Salvinia molesta* has been most destructive within the subsistence domain. Women have been unable to provide their families with food. They have been unable to fish and to travel to sago markets. And without the productive activities of women, men cannot survive. But no Chambri man believes that his difficulties are part of a general condition, as we learned from the sorcery trial I described earlier, when the Chambri father attempted to disenfranchise his sister whose clan status gave her the right to use certain sago palms to feed her family. Rather than blaming the fern for destroying their economy, Chambri men blame their women for supplying the wrong people with food. Most Cham-bri men believe that they and their agnates would have enough to eat if only their wives and sisters would maintain clear-cut allegiances. They be-lieve that if it were not for the ambivalence of female allegiances, the fern would affect only their neighbors.

Why, then, haven't the Chambri accused a woman of bringing *Salvinia molesta* to the region? First of all, Chambri men could not conceive of a woman with sufficient power. Second, although each Chambri man un-doubtedly has a particular woman in mind to accuse of divided allegiances, no one such accusation could adequately express the generally held belief that female ambivalence is responsible for the food shortage. In other words, although particular women may be blamed in specific situations, Chambri men would never assign a woman to head the class of such situations.[9] The priest, therefore, has become a symbol of the generality of their particular concerns.

That weed warfare is an attempt to resolve the problem of ambivalent clan allegiances becomes clear when we consider similar situations. For example, when Chambri groups are in conflict—when clan boundaries become blurred over time—their members generally express their grievances during elaborate public debates (see Gewertz, 1977b). All of the concerned individuals will arrive at one or another of their men's houses to argue their case. At every debate that I witnessed a Chambri, regardless of the irritant which brought the participants together, the issues concerned correct membership in kin groups or correct ownership of names, land, water, ceremonial accoutrements, or powers. Such debates occur when the internal cohesiveness of clans is disturbed. As Burke points out:

> In pure identification there would be no strife. Likewise, there would be no strife in absolute separateness, since opponents can join battle only through a mediatory ground that makes their communication possible, thus providing the first condition necessary for their interchange of blows. But put identification and division ambiguously together, so that you cannot know for certain just where one ends and the other begins, and you have the characteristic invitation to rhetoric. [1969: 25]

Clan boundaries become blurred over time, primarily through the establishment of patron–client relationships within the affinal exchange system. Public debates and semipublic discussions provide opportunities for dependent clients, whether individuals or clans, to assert personal power through displays of oratory and esoteric knowledge. By demonstrating such power, these individuals and clans hope to reinforce their identities, thereby preventing wholesale takeovers by large, powerful clans. They attempt to reestablish their autonomy and maintain the continuity of inheritance by publicly declaring their distinctiveness.

The same ambiguity of division and identification which results in verbal interchanges between debaters is also provoking Sepik River villagers to adopt weed warfare as a remedy to their environmental crisis. Warfare, like debating, provides an opportunity for individuals and clans to assert their identities and define their statuses. During warfare the internal cohesiveness of warring groups is counterpointed by the internal segregation of individuals and groups arising from their successes or failures during confrontations. In the past and under different circumstances these confrontations would have involved headhunting raids, where coincidence of luck, courage, and skill during the battle provided an unparalleled opportunity for dependent individuals to reaffirm their distinctiveness and worth.[10]

Today, Chambri villagers have translated the substance of these raids from a head for a head to the more relevant fern for a fern. By planting the *Salvinia* in their enemies' fishing grounds, they are attempting to validate the autonomy and integrity of their clans and villages by asserting their power to affect the destiny of others. The fact that the destiny of their victims presages their own is irrelevant to them because of the way in which they understand what is at stake. They do not perceive the "priest's fern" as destructive to ecosystemic relationships within their riverine environment, but rather as a threat to their totemic powers and sociopolitical statuses. This is why the people living in the Black Water, up the Karawari River where the fern has just begun to gain a foothold, told me that they were not worried about the situation. When I suggested that they build booms to prevent the *Salvinia* from penetrating their lagoons, they argued: "We've nothing to worry about from this no-good grass. Chambri ancestors were weak, and that's why Chambri Lake is now choked with grass. Our ancestors are strong, strong enough to keep our waters full of fish and free from ferns."

Cognitive Dissonance or Social Disintegration?

In what has become a classic article on social change, Lauriston Sharp has argued that the introduction of steel tools among the Yir Yoront, a population of stone-age Australians, led to the destruction of their society through the establishment of extreme cognitive dissonance (1952: 17–22). The Yir Yoront could not find a suitable totemic category within which to place steel tools, a situation that caused them to lose faith in the adequacy of their cognitive system.

> The most disturbing effects of the steel axe, operating in conjunction with other elements also being introduced from the white man's several sub-cultures, developed in the realm of traditional ideas, sentiments, and values. These were undermined at a rapidly mounting rate, with no new conceptions being defined to replace them. The result was the erection of a mental and moral void which foreshadowed the collapse and destruction of all Yir Yoront culture, if not, indeed, the extinction of the biological group itself. [1952: 21]

The situation I have described among the Chambri might be similarly analyzed: incapable of placing either priests or *Salvinia molesta* in one or another familiar category, these Middle Sepik fisherfolk lost faith in their world-view and are now suffering from extreme anomie.

A major problem with this analysis and, I believe, with Sharp's prototype, is that it overlooks the independence that Geertz has drawn our attention to between logico-meaningful and causal-functional domains of integration (1972: 142–69). By the former Geertz means "a unity of style, of logical implication, of meaning and value." By the latter he means "the kind of integration one finds in an organism, where all the parts are united in a single causal web; each part is an element in a reverberating causal ring which 'keeps the system going'" (ibid.: 145). The notion that each integrative domain determines the other, constraining and delimiting sociocultural reality upon pain of disfunction, or even extinction, is basic to most ahistorical anthropologists. It assumes that non-Western man has lived in static equilibrium within an unchanging ecosystem until the introduction of extraneous ideas, items, and behaviors have proven his equilibrations inaccurate and have led either to his cultural homogenization or to his social extinction.

I have searched for this static "dream-time" through more than 150 years of Middle Sepik history and have been unable to find it. Instead, I have found people, holding multifarious ideas about how their world works, sometimes changing their ideas in relation to shifts in their sociopolitical situations, and sometimes acting as the cause of these shifts through the adoption of new ideas, either autonomously and spontaneously devised or learned from other peoples with whom they have had the chance to interact. Never can the Middle Sepik be described as being in static equilibrium. Never have the logico-meaningful and causal-functional domains reflected each other perfectly, for the Iatmul, Chambri, and their neighbors have been too busy fitting one another into their interrelated although analytically separate systems of social reproduction to have had the time to establish such a perfect fit.

Nor, I would argue, have the Yir Yoront ever had time to integrate these domains, for they, too, have interacted with their neighbors, acquiring goods, services, behaviors, and ideas throughout their active history, and changing to accommodate these introductions while developing their own sociocultural system. And yet, I have no doubt that the situation described by Sharp is a real one, that the Yir Yoront have found it as difficult to accommodate the introduction of steel tools as the Chambri and the Iatmul have found it to live in a world overrun by *Salvinia molesta*. Since we can not assume that unclassifiable objects cum ideas will necessarily result in sociocultural breakdown, we must inquire about the historical context that resulted in the difficulties Sharp describes and I observed.

I should say, at this point, that the two situations are really more comparable than they initially appear to be. The environmental crisis being experienced by Middle Sepik peoples seems, at first, to place them in a class by themselves because of its serious effects upon their subsistence.

However, as I have shown, they do not perceive the crisis as we do, but in a way closer to that of the Yir Yoront in Sharp's description. In both cases, what seems to be at stake from the native points of view is autonomy, integrity, and power.

But who are the natives? I have reported that nearly 50 percent of the Chambri people have moved, more or less permanently, to the towns of Wewak, Madang, and Port Moresby; that a considerable number of those who have moved are young men and women who have begun to marry non-Chambri and have failed to engage in the appropriate affinal transactions; and that most of those who have remained at home are older men and women committed to the behaviors and values to which they are accustomed. Compare these facts to those reported by Sharp in the following paragraph:

> From what has been said it should be clear how changes in overt behavior, in technology and conduct, weakened the values inherent in a reliance on nature, in the prestige of masculinity and of age, and in the various kinship relations. A scene was set in which a wife, or a young son whose initiation may not yet have been completed, need no longer defer to the husband or father who, in turn, became confused and insecure as he was forced to borrow a steel axe from them. For the woman and boy the steel axe helped establish a new degree of freedom which they accepted readily as an escape from the unconscious stress of the old patterns—but they, too, were left confused and insecure. [1952: 21]

Certainly the insecurity and confusion of Yir Yoront men, whose power base had been eroded through the introduction of steel tools, was of a different nature from that of Yir Yoront women and boys, who had gained access to a social status previously denied them. Otherwise how can we explain the ready acceptance by women and boys of the new steel valuables?

It is also difficult to understand why the formerly powerful Yir Yoront men could not wrest control of the steel axes from these women and boys, much as Chambri men did with the shell valuables earned by their women through the sale of mosquito bags. Their incapacity to do so suggests that they lost the ability to affect the behavior of others early on in the process of modernization. A hint of what must have occurred can be found in Sharp's brief discussion of the method by which these men acquired the stone they formerly fashioned into tools. He reports that it "came from quarries 400 miles to the south, reaching the Yir Yoront through long lines of male trading partners" (ibid.: 19).

> Almost every older man had one or more regular trading partners, some to the north and some to the south. He provided his partner

or partners in the south with surplus spears, particularly fighting spears tipped with the barbed spines of sting ray. . . . For a dozen such spears, some of which he may have obtained from a partner to the north, he would receive one stone axe head. Studies have shown that the sting ray barb spears increased in value as they moved south and farther from the sea. . . . Apparently people who acted as links in the middle of the chain who made neither spears nor axe heads would receive a certain number of each as a middleman's profit. [ibid.: 19]

Thus it appears that the formerly powerful Yir Yoront men had not only lost control over their intragroup sociopolitical lives, but had also experienced the erosion of their intervillage socioeconomic relationships. They would no longer be interested in stone axheads, now that white men offered them steel, and their trading partners would probably be equally uninterested in obtaining the sting-ray-barb spears. Unless their relationships could be sustained through trade in other items, the intensity of the interaction between the partners must have steadily declined. In other words, Yir Yoront men, like their Chambri counterparts, were deprived of extragroup contacts and relationships once white men began to introduce European-produced commodities. Both groups were turned in upon themselves at the same time they were being encouraged by missionaries and labor recruiters to modernize.

Could it have been that Yir Yoront men, like many men from egalitarian societies, derived status and power through their maintenance of extragroup trading relationships, and that the stone tools they acquired from their partners were not only symbols of male virility but also reminders of the number of allies a man could count on? By eroding these alliances, had steel tools made Yir Yoront men aware of their vulnerability as individuals? Was this the reason they could not wrest the new commodities from their wives and sons—because without their status-defining intergroup relationships they simply didn't see the point? It was not simply that steel tools became "unthinkable," but rather that they made intergroup relationships untenable. No wonder Yir Yoront men could not adequately classify them; they had corroded the socioeconomic relationships that made totemic categories viable descriptions of a social reality regulated through egalitarian interaction. Yir Yoront society did not collapse when the ownership of steel tools became a matter of debate; the collapse began when the ownership of steel tools became a matter of indifference.

Earlier I discussed how the Chambri were able to negotiate the transition from stone to steel through the incorporation of currency into their affinal exchange system. In this sense, they were saved from a Yir Yoront fate by defining status and power in terms of intravillage exchange relationships.

When the Iatmul refused them shells in exchange for their stone tools and mosquito bags, the Chambri maintained their system by selling their labor for the new status-defining valuables. Now that both young Chambri men and women are marrying outside their villages, there is little of the system left to maintain, and it is this, rather than *Salvinia molesta*, that is destructive of the correct order of things, from the male point of view. They perceive the fern as a consequence rather than the cause of systemic breakdown—as an indication that their power has slipped. And they are correct, in this sense: *Salvinia molesta* is encouraging even more young Chambri to stay away from their homes. It is the straw that is breaking the camel's back.

Salvinia *and Starvation: Of Women, Men, and the Politics of Subsistence*

So far, I have described the *Salvinia molesta* problem from the male point of view. The Chambri women with whom I have spoken have a completely different perspective, primarily because it is they who return from the lake without enough fish to feed their families. They, like their husbands, are under stress, but the nature of the discomfort they are experiencing is profoundly different from that felt by Chambri men.

At first I did not understand the profundity of these differences. When I postulated that the increased earning and spending capacities of Chambri women would heighten their sense of self and make them aware of their potential political power, I believed, with Sharp, that Chambri women wished to "escape from the unconscious stress of the old patterns" (1952: 21), and that they were bringing these stresses to consciousness and learning to avoid them. I was wrong, and about more than my hypothesis, for Chambri women do not experience stress over the situations that we might expect.

They do not find it stressful to be betwixt and between two patriclans, uniting their fathers and brothers in complementary opposition. They expect to be in this position. Nor do Chambri women find it stressful to be coerced by their husbands and brothers for allegiance and valuables—be these valuables earned through the production of mosquito bags or through the sale of fish and artifacts. They expect to be so coerced. It is Chambri men who experience stress over the fact that Chambri women asymmetrically unite their clans; they expect to be able to win their equality but find that to do so means dependence upon women for production and reproduction.

Consider, as an example of the ease with which Chambri women accept their "liminal" positions, the following songs, collected at one of the many all-female dances held to celebrate various social events—births, initiations, homecomings, and so on. These particular songs were performed during the fifth birthday party of the grandson of an aging Chambri man. At the dance were women who described themselves as "the wives of the clan": the boy's mother, his paternal grandmother, her sister, the boy's father's brother's wife, her two sisters, and the boy's paternal grandfather's brothers' three wives. Also present were women who said that they were "sisters of the clan": the boy's father's three sisters and his paternal grandfather's two sisters. They sang nine songs in all, each repeated many times. Like all women's songs, they consisted of a short phrase followed by semantically meaningless chants. An annotated translation of the nine songs is as follows:

1. "We're happy with Woliwogwi," a totemic name belonging to the boy's clan. This song was sung by the wives of the clan.
2. "Our husbands don't bring us tobacco from the Nyaula. Our men are no good." This song was sung by both the wives and the sisters of the clan.
3. "Mandoi (a totemic rat owned by the men of the clan) wears beautiful decorations on his head and on his tail." This song was sung by the sisters of the clan, and refers to the elegance of their brothers.
4. "I'm worried about you. Come home." This was sung by both the wives and the sisters of the clan. It is about husbands and brothers away on plantations.
5. "Kapiakkupwan," a totemic fly owned by the clan of the boy's father's brother's wife, "sits down by the fire and eats with Mandoi." This was sung by the wives of the clan and refers to the relationship between their clans and those of their husbands.
6. "Kill a man; cut off his head; put it on top of our men's house." This was sung by the sisters of the clan, who describe the pride they feel when their brothers distinguish themselves in warfare.
7. "Your brother walks crookedly; he's not strong, Woliwogwi is strong." This was sung by the clan's sisters. It compares the club-footed brother of the birthday boy's paternal grandmother to the physically able men of the boy's own clan.
8. "When fathers go away, children cry: 'Take me with you in the canoe.'" This was sung by the wives of the clan.
9. "Take your bastards and go to jail." This angry song was sung by the sisters of the clan. It accuses their brothers of being cuckolds.

What strikes me about these songs is that both the wives and the sisters of the clan use them to express the same sentiments about the same men. Both groups of women sing about their anger at, their pleasure with, their commitment to, and their disappointment in their brothers and husbands. If wives and sisters found their structural positions within Chambri society to be stressful, I would expect their "talk play," as they put it, to express polarity between them. Instead, they seem to identify with one another—to share the same viewpoint toward the men.

What Chambri women find stressful is their incapacity to feed and care for their families, for this is not what they are socialized to expect, and it is why the *Salvinia molesta* problem is so upsetting to them. They can no longer adequately fish, expect to sell their fish in the towns, or anticipate sago markets with Hills women. Most of the rivulets in which they formerly placed their nets and traps are blocked by the fern. Those few that are still penetrable are insufficient to support the entire Chambri population. And many of their Sepik Hills sago-suppliers have decided to wait out the disaster in their original hamlets, where they hope that wild game will prove an adequate substitute for fish.

It is Chambri women who have been gathering the coconuts and wild greens from which to prepare soups for their families. And, as table 10.1 indicates, it is Chambri women who are spending the money they have saved to supplement their families' diets with trade-store foods. This should not surprise us, because Chambri women have been the procurers and preparers of food ever since the European intrusion allowed Chambri men to separate politics from subsistence.

What did surprise me was the degree to which Chambri men have been unable to recognize that the *Salvinia* crisis is a very serious threat to their biological survival. I was surprised at their lack of appreciation of their women's efforts to find food, at their unwillingness to contribute to a "relief

Table 10.1: The Monetary Transactions of Indingai Adults[a]
between June 25 and July 15, 1979

	Men		Women		Total
	Amount	Range	Amount	Range	
Earned[b] ($)	260.80	.20–42.50	106.60	.10–7.00	367.40
Spent[c] ($)	208.40	.10–10.00	181.43	.10–7.50	398.93
Donated[d] ($)	121.60	.10–20.00	93.10	.10–20.00	214.70
Gifts to men (%)	35		26		
Gifts to women (%)	23		16		
Received ($)	92.71	.10–20.00	88.29	.10–20.00	181.00
Gifts from men (%)	23		23		
Gifts from women (%)	36		18		

[a]The figures were collected from all 67 adult Indingai living at home during the study period, 37 women and 30 men.
[b]Monies were earned through the sale of fish, artifacts, betel nuts, and other native produce, the sale of motorboat taxi services, and the sale of labor by natives to natives at house buildings, canoe constructions, and shamanistic diagnostic sessions.
[c]Monies were spent on trade-store items such as rice, tinned fish, kerosene and petrol, on native produce such as sago and tobacco, and on native labor.
[d]By donations and receipts I mean gifts of money made between natives.

fund" designed to purchase food, and at their attempt to use the crisis for their own political ends.

Rather than appreciating their women's efforts, the men tend to blame them for the crisis. They believe, on some level, that if women aren't bringing home enough fish and sago, it's because they aren't working hard enough. Moreover, they argue that if sisters weren't pulling resources away from their brothers and fathers toward their husbands and children—and if wives weren't doing the opposite—then life would return to normal, or at least they themselves would flourish through the lean years. These arguments and accusations are, of course, a reflection of the association Chambri men make between changes in their affinal exchange system and their economic system. Women are practicing exogamy and people are hungry for fish and sago. That men associate these two stresses is understandable, given the structural and functional positions of women within Chambri society. Women not only link patriclans and produce children, but they also provide their husbands with food. If they are failing to function satisfactorily in the first role, it is no wonder that they are also failing to fulfill the second.

And perhaps Chambri men think that if they can regain control of their affinal exchange system, then their women will once again be able to catch enough fish within Chambri Lake. This is why, I was told, they do not wish to contribute their savings to the purchase of trade-store food. They have to hold on to what they have saved in order to be ready to engage in the politics of affinal exchange. If they are unprepared—if they have no money left—then there is no chance of ever emerging from the *Salvinia molesta* crisis.

Anton Bascam expressed this male perspective best when he arrived at my house to explain the *Salvinia* crisis as he saw it, to "story" with me about the events I had missed, and to request my help in solving the problem. Below, I include the sections of my field notes in which I describe our conversation.

> Bascam came to present me with a bill today—a bill I was to give to "the government" so that it would reimburse him for the money he spent while helping the Chambri people. Actually, he hadn't written the bill out, but came to give me the information I would need to do so. This is what he told me:
> On May 14, 1979, nine Chambri men died of starvation. Six hundred ninety-one Chambri hadn't any food. Five canoes and two outboard motor boats went out to search for fish. They came back with only forty-six fish.
> On May 15, 1979, Father Padlo gave Bascam two gallons of petrol to fill his motor tank so that he and his wife could search for fish. Bascam purchased another gallon, and also bought $K2.80

worth of batteries for the torches they would use to shoot fish at night. They found eighty-three fish.

On May 16, 1979, he and his wife went out again, after purchasing another gallon of petrol. They didn't find any fish.

On May 17, 1979, the pattern of the night before was repeated.

According to Bascam's calculations (which are incorrect), the government owes him $K9.60 for petrol, batteries, and motor-boat rent, as well as for the basket of fish he gave to the Chambri people "to help them eat strong food and stay alive."

When I asked him why he thought the government owes him anything at all, he said: "They must give me back the money if they want to get rid of the no-good grass, and they say that they want this on Radio Wewak."

Needless to say, I found his words incomprehensible, and so asked for an elaboration. He continued: "If Chambri men don't have money, they cannot pay their affines. If they don't pay their affines, then their children get sick. If their children get sick, then Chambri isn't strong. And if Chambri isn't strong, then the wind will never blow the no-good grass away. The government must give me the money to pay my affines to bring a strong wind to Chambri. But it's up to you because you can give it to me as well."

Compare Bascam's remarks to a similar request made by a Chambri woman named Ason, the mother of my daughter's best Chambri friend, Lucy. Again, I transcribe the sections of my field notes that describe the incident.

> I saw Akapina Ason this evening. She had come to the Windjammer Motel with Adam Manjantimi and with Andrew Kinjinkamboi to sell Lucas Yangim's carvings for him. When I asked her about her daughter, Lucy, she said: "Why hasn't your daughter sent Lucy a little present? They were sisters at Chambri, and she should have sent a little present, maybe $K20.00 or $K10.00. It's hard to find food at Chambri, and mama Margarita never sends us fish anymore. So why don't you give me some money for Lucy, and maybe some for Mariana and for Julie Kubusa and for me? We're all dying for want of food."

Although it appears that Bascam was devious while Ason was direct, this is neither true nor the point. Both had "exaggerated" somewhat in order to move me to act in their behalf. Nine Chambri men had not died of starvation; Bascam would probably have purchased the batteries and the petrol with or without the *Salvinia* crisis; and he and his wife had not collected the basket of fish by themselves, but had been assisted by numerous men and women of Kilimbit. Nor were Ason and her friends truly starving at the Kreer camp for migrants. Indeed, there was probably more money available to them then than they ever had access to before.

It is nevertheless interesting to compare the two requests because they summarize all of the differences that I have suggested exist between Chambri men and women. Bascam's argument can be expressed in the following way: the Chambri people can only be saved from the no-good fern if you give me money to engage in affinal exchange. On the other hand, here is Ason's argument: four women, to whom you are supposed to be committed, want your money to buy food.

If I were asked to describe the "kulturgeist" of the Chambri men and women, I would choose the requests of Anton Bascam and Akapina Ason as ideal representations. Indeed, I would argue that their two sexually differentiated concerns, for affinal transactions and for food, have informed most of the behaviors and activities that I have described in this book. At first I thought the male concern to be the more profound and hoped to find that Chambri women had adopted it as their own. Today, given the gravity of the environmental crisis faced by all of the Sepik peoples, I would give my money to Ason.

CONCLUSION:
THE IMPORTANCE OF
A HISTORICAL PERSPECTIVE

Early during my first field trip to Papua New Guinea I was asked by a man from Wombun Village to accompany him to his house on top of Chambri Mountain to see his secret book. As I climbed the mountain, my mind raced over the possibilities. Could it be that the Chambri had developed an indigenous writing system and that I was about to make a major historical discovery? How could Mead and Fortune have missed this, I wondered?

Sitting in the man's house, I watched him open two rusty locks on a metal patrol box he had acquired during the late 1930s. The contents lay beneath a covering of plastic tarpaulin, muddied and scratched by long use. He removed layer after layer of plastic until the book was revealed, nestled in a bed of cotton towels. He blocked it from my view as he removed it from its resting place, held it to his breast for a few seconds, and then handed it to me with a look of reverent expectation.

The book, a notification that a Melbourne homeowners association had amalgamated with a Brisbane insurance company, had been with him for a long time and had distinguished him from all of his fellow Chambri. He had been sending whatever money he managed to earn to an address he found in the book, having enlisted his mission-educated son as amanuensis. He was sure that I had come to his island to reward his efforts, and telling him what I knew about the book was the hardest thing I ever had to do.

He believed that the power of white men resided in their books, and that he had internalized some of their power through his ownership of one. Although familiar with Bibles, with local newspapers, and with patrol reports left in the village by government administrators,[1] my Wombun friend was convinced that written matter directed at natives was essentially different from that which the white men wrote for themselves—that writing was more powerful before it had become tamed by indigenous minds.

It has long been an assumption of anthropologists that the cognitive processes of preliterate peoples are so different from our own that it is impossible to translate their remembrances of things past into satisfactory historical narrative—that history is an artifact of "domestication."

On the other hand, consider Jack Goody's work on the evolutionary significance of literacy in *The Domestication of the Savage Mind* (1977). Goody is interested in documenting the very real transition between preliterate and literate societies, arguing that the written word adds a crucial dimension to social action—particularly in the politicolegal domain. He writes that:

> the growth of bureaucracy . . . depends to a considerable degree upon the ability to control 'secondary group' relationships by means of written communications. . . . The relation with both ruler and ruled becomes more impersonal, involving greater appeal to abstract 'rules' listed in a written code and leading to a clear-cut separation between official duties and personal concerns. [1977: 15–16]

To grant that literacy changed the way people thought and acted does not imply that they did neither before the invention of writing. That their thoughts and actions held consequences for them is nowhere more clearly demonstrated than in the fact that writing was adopted and bureaucracies grew. Goody, after all, in writing about preliterates, does so in historical terms. And my Wombun informant, intuiting that the power in his totemic names was surpassed by the power in our written words, and deciding to invest a portion of his resources in an Australian homeowners association rather than in affinal prestations, affected his own well-being. Although his decision was motivated more by a magical than by a historical consciousness, his actions presage the trajectory of the Chambri people.

What I am suggesting is this: preliterate peoples have a past. It is a past that they may not be aware of because it has not been explicitly recorded as history, but it is a past nonetheless. Because it has not been written down, objective observers find it difficult to describe this history, but sometimes the data we collect demand that we make the effort and take the risks to uncover it. In this concluding chapter I review these demands and these risks, particularly as they have affected my analysis in preceding chapters, but also as a basis for comparison with other New Guinea ethnographies.

To this end, consider table C.1, a summary of the book's argument in the form of a chronology listing events, dates, and the types of data I used in determining and evaluating the process of change through time. This table suggests that I am aware of very few historical events prior to the European intrusion, for nearly three-quarters of its entries occurred after the turn of the century. In fact, the table is somewhat misleading. I have chosen to eliminate certain of the events that I described as occurring before World War I (such as the attack of the Sawos village of Yamuk upon the

Table C.1: Chronological Summary

Event	Date	Type of Evidence*
Coming of Ndu	?	L, S
Trading partnerships (Iatmul–Sawos; Iatmul–Chambri; Chambri–Hills)	1700s–1800s	E, S, A
Barter markets (Iatmul–Sawos)	1800s	E, S
Growth of Iatmul villages	1800s	S, E
Manabi wars	1890	E
European intrusion	1890; 1900	D, E
Parambei-Chambri wars	1900s	D, E, S
Chambri exile	1905	D, E, S
World War I	1914	D, E
Incipient Chambri-Hills markets	1915	S, A, E
Restructuring of territories; missionization	1920s	D, E, S
Return from exile	1930	S, D, E
Labor migration	1930s	D, S, E
Margaret Mead, Reo Fortune, Gregory Bateson	1928; 1933	D, E
Kandingai-Yentchamangua war	1942	D, E
World War II	1942	D, E
Renegades on Sambungundei	1942	D, E
Iatmul intrusion into Chambri Lake	1943	D, E, S
Southern barter markets	1950	E, S
Growth of towns	1950s, 60s, 70s	D, E, S
Gaui Local Government Council	1964	D, E, S
Descent from Hills	1950, 1964	D, E, S
Money markets	1950s, 60s, 70s	D, E, S
Tribal exogamy	1977	D, S, E
Salvinia molesta	1973	D, S, E

*Types of evidence: A = educated assumption; D = documents; E = ethnohistorical accounts; L = linguistic data; S = socioeconomic data

Iatmul village of Suapmeri, the Kwolawoli involvement with Mindimbit and Timbunke, and the migrations of the proto-Gaikerobi), because my interest in them has more to do with the processes they reveal than with their actual occurrence. Given the data limitations of historical reconstruction among preliterate peoples, it is impossible to devise a complete chronology of dates and events. Without this chronology, the isolated case of Yamuk attacking Suapmeri is only interesting because it reveals the organizational potential of certain Sawos villages.

In other words, the early events I have gleaned through the conjunction of social structural and environmental data, linguistic analyses, and ethnohistorical narratives serve as barometers of the range of human activities and social processes characteristic of the region. Without reading these barometers, it is all too easy to view the Middle Sepik from Alexander Pope's viewpoint:

> All nature is but art, unknown to thee;
> All chance, direction, which thou can'st not see;
> All discord, harmony, not understood;
> All partial evil, universal good:
> And, spite of pride, in erring reason's spite,
> One truth is clear, WHATEVER IS, IS RIGHT. [1871: 370–71]

Although both theoretically and empirically unacceptable as an epigraph for ethnography, Pope's poem does express the perspective of many anthropologists working in the New Guinea Highlands since World War II. These anthropologists had been trained, by and large, by British structural-functionalists who had concentrated, in their African work, on the problem of group cohesion in societies without explicit political structures. They resolved this problem with reference to descent systems, arguing that lower-level biologically based relationships "nest" within higher-level biologically based relationships, whereby individuals related on each level coalesce on particular occasions.[2]

These students of functionalism discovered that the models they had inherited could not be made to fit the New Guinea situation. The descent paradigm in which political and economic activities were imbedded within templates of familial obligations could not explain social interaction in New Guinea, because Melanesian descent systems appeared to be no more than metaphors used to justify relationships established through other means.[3]

What followed were numerous ethnographic accounts of particular Highland societies using the principle of cumulative patrifiliation as a rubric designating processes of unknown origin. Watson, for example (1970), suggested that the Tairora social system organized a "flow" of personnel in space and time, while Langness (1964) described Bena-Bena warfare as a mechanism stimulating "flexible" alignments between weak and strong groups. Since these same anthropologists believed that the credibility of social science rested on a regularity in explanation and the ability to predict events, they found that "flux" could not replace "nesting" as an explanation of action, and called for a new method of investigation that would isolate the "structure" from the "flexibility" and identify the "organization" within the "flow."

Systems analysis was applied to the Highlands' data in the hope of identifying clusters of units that are dependent upon one another in a regular manner. The structure provided by systems analysis allowed ethnographers to organize their material economically. Whereas descent models had been a comprehensive shorthand for the interpretation of human behavior, systems analysis extended structural-functionalism into the realms of quantification and mechanical control.[4] The goal became to describe the homeostats that kept human populations within limits tolerable to the broader ecosystem, given the assumption that humans act in accordance with the laws of natural selection, that they strive to remain viable within their environments.

The most brilliant of the systems analyses produced from New Guinea data, for example, Roy Rappaport's *Pigs for the Ancestors* (1968), focused on ritual among the Tsembaga of the Western Highlands. Rappaport argued that a ritual complex called the *kaiko*, which includes the periodic slaughter of domesticated pigs, operates as both transducer and homeostat, "translating changes in the state of one subsystem into information which can effect changes in a second subsystem, and . . . maintaining a number of variables which in sum comprise the total system within ranges of viability" (1979: 41). In particular, by staging a *kaiko*, a local group of Tsembaga informs its potential opponents of its readiness to fight for its territory, while it reduces its pig population to a manageable size. Thus, the ritual "helps to maintain an undegraded environment, limits fighting to frequencies which do not endanger the existence of the regional population, adjusts man-land ratios, facilitates trade, distributes local surpluses of pig throughout the regional population in the form of pork, and assures people of high quality protein when they are most in the need of it" (ibid.).

Rappaport's analysis of ritual among the Tsembaga contrasts importantly with the earliest application of systems theory to New Guinea data by Gregory Bateson in 1933.[5] The theoretical importance of Bateson's work went unrecognized by anthropologists until the Highlands were opened to investigation after the Second World War.

While working among the Iatmul, Bateson recognized the necessity of explaining ritualized interactional patterns in the behavior of men and women. Analyzing these patterns in *Naven*, he introduces the concepts of symmetrical and complementary schizmogenesis—processes through which an individual internalizes his culture's preferred tendencies. Schizmogenesis is "a process of differentiation in the norms of individual behaviour resulting from the cumulative interaction between individuals" (Bateson, 1958: 175). Bateson believes that the predictability of response to culturally preferred behavioral acts is a positive reinforcement for behavior of the same sort. In symmetrical schizmogenesis the response is an augmentation of the stimulus, and in complementary schizmogenesis the response is the opposite of the stimulus. Thus, the sexually differentiated behavior of the Iatmul is indicative of complementary schizmogenesis, with women admiring the spectacular performances of the men who "are more exhibitionistic because the women admire their performances" (ibid.: 177). The spectacular performances themselves, on the other hand, reflect symmetrical schizmogenesis, with each man trying to outdo all others. "We have thus a potentially progressive state of affairs . . . unless other factors are present to restrain the excesses of assertive and submissive behaviour" (ibid.: 176).

Schizmogenesis is thus a process of character formation which culturally selects responses but is without a system of checks and balances to prevent their development ad infinitum. Having painted a "picture of schizmogenesis . . . [as] a process inevitably advancing towards such differentiation that some outside factor is bound to precipitate the final collapse" (ibid.: 190), Bateson's task is to delimit the controls which prevent the collapse from occurring—a task he does not accomplish to his satisfaction until 1958 when, in a new epilogue to *Naven*, he subsumes complementary and symmetrical patterns within the metalevel of cybernetic control.

By 1958 Bateson's interest in schizmogenesis had shifted from its role in character formation to its function as an internal generator of behavioral variability. The logic behind the shift is obvious: a culture is composed of individuals who become what they are through cumulative interaction with others; this cumulative interaction standardizes behavior but sets no limits on its augmentation; hence, schizmogenesis, as the standardizing process, must also be the source of progressive change.

Given the inevitability of progressive development, Bateson requires an operative homeostat to regulate the behavioral variables and thereby prevent systemic breakdown; parametric change can only be prevented through the regulation of schizmogenesis.

> Substituting the notion of self-correction for the idea of purpose or adaptation defined a new approach to the problems of Iatmul culture. Schizmogenesis appeared to promote progressive change, and the problem was why this progressive change did not lead to the destruction of the culture as such. . . . It was now necessary to ask, is there any communicational pathway such that an increase in symmetrical schizmogenesis will bring about an increase in the corrective complementary phenomena? Could the system be circular and self-corrective? [ibid.: 289]

Bateson pinpoints the selfcorrective circuits he seeks with the *naven* ceremonies. He believes that the "exaggerated caricature of a complementary sexual relationship between *wau* [mother's brother] and *laua* [sister's son], is in fact set off by overweening symmetrical behavior . . . [on the part of the *laua* whose] achievements in headhunting, fishing, etc., as particular examples of achieved ambition of vertical mobility . . . , place him in some sort of symmetrical relationship with the *wau*" (ibid.: 289–90). Furthermore, Bateson sees the transvestism of Iatmul women as a statement of "symmetrical rivalry *vis-à-vis* the men, compensating for their normally complementary role" (ibid.: 291).

However, the presence of corrective circuits is not enough to regulate oscillating variables. Communicational pathways simply transmit the regulatory signal from the homeostat to its goal. The model demands the presence of a "director" who recognizes the need for systemic regulation and sends the corrective impulse through the communicational pathways to the sources of variability.

Having found no isolable homeostat within Iatmul culture, Bateson designates schizmogenesis as both the source of variability and the director of its regulation. He believes that the Iatmul "learn, besides the symmetrical and complementary patterns, to expect and exhibit certain sequential relations between the symmetrical and complementary" (ibid.: 291). Each individual, therefore, is a self-regulator, having learned through the schizmogenetic process to introduce change in his dealings with others.

Bateson's analysis of the *naven* ceremonies is illuminating because, although concerned with maintenance and control, its presuppositions avoid the "functionalism of adaptation" that is expressed so well by Pope's *Essay on Man*, and has trapped many of the recent proponents of systems theory. Rappaport's thesis, for example, can be simplified thus: what exists is adaptive and must be maintained. Bateson's data, quite to the contrary, cause him to inquire why what exists appears to be maladaptive and yet is maintained. It is in the possibility of maladaptation, or rather of contradiction between elements within a system, that the alternative to the functionalism of adaptation lies.

Societies are not homogeneous wholes whose purpose is to maintain the larger ecosystem of which they are components. Nor, I believe, do social institutions function to maintain the societies within which they operate. The *post hoc ergo propter hoc* fallacy of functionalist thinking can only be avoided by assuming the autonomy of systems within their environments. Such an assumption demands a historical explanation of social formations in terms of the temporary compatibility—or incompatibility—of their subsystems, each ordered by its own laws of development.

Bateson, as we have seen, while recognizing the incompatibility between complementary and symmetrical schizmogenesis, limited his analysis of the Iatmul to their *naven* ceremonies and therefore never identified the more basic contradiction of which both male/female behavioral distinctions and the role-reversing *naven* ceremonies are expressions.

Forge, in "The Golden Fleece," comes closer to the real issue when he identifies Bateson's concepts of complementary and symmetrical interactions as basic to political and economic organization.

> Bateson's dualities and their expression in either equality searching symmetrical behaviour or in inequality emphasizing comple-

mentary behaviour, point directly at the two principles of exchange that form the majority of New Guinea social structures
and dominate their workings. [Forge, 1972: 539]

Forge believes that the exchange of classes of identical objects between
equals is a basic mechanism in the political and economic organization of
New Guinea societies. In an earlier article he elaborates on the importance
of symmetrical and complementary behavior and suggests a possible explanation of *iai* marriage in terms of "cosmology, and concepts of the fundamental nature of men and women, together with the interrelationship between equal and unequal exchange" (1971: 143). Specifically, Forge sees
the trigenerational renewal of *iai* marriage as consistent with the Iatmul
belief that women are the source of creativity while being simultaneously
inferior to men. The highly charged relationship between mother's brother
and sister's son, as celebrated in the *naven* ceremonies, is the supreme
expression of the relationships of inequality transmitted through women.
By the third generation, the intensity of the inequality diminishes, only to
be renewed through the ideology of *iai* marriage. Forge contrasts the Iatmul
with the neighboring Abelam, who prohibit affinal renewal while extending
the kin-term for wife to the prohibited women, and he suggests that in both
cultures attention is focused on marriage as the source of the ambiguous
category of competitive blood relations who are "equal unequals."

Iai marriage is therefore the Iatmul attempt to keep clear categorical distinctions between the symmetrical and the asymmetrical, the inferior and
the superior, the equal and the unequal. And, while agreeing with Forge
that the relationship between these dualities is important for an understanding of the Iatmul, I am disappointed that he finds mere metaphorical con-
sistency to be potentially explanatory, with a male/female cosmological distinction explaining an equally suprastructural marital preference. If there
are ambiguities in the concepts of man and woman, and if equal and unequal exchange are in need of reconciling, then the incompatibility of their
functions must be more than just the result of their definitions as opposed
modes of interaction. For Bateson their incompatibility is real, and therefore maladaptive. For Forge their incompatibility appears to be little more
than an ideological inconsistency, a problem capable of several structural
solutions.

The nature of this incompatibility can only be properly understood through
a historical analysis of the development of Middle Sepik societies in interaction with one another over time. Such an analysis demonstrates one undeniable fact: that the relationships linking groups together in mutual interdependence conflict with the goals, values, and social mechanisms that
necessitate this interdependence. Among the Iatmul, political autonomy—

control of the river and its resources— became contingent upon group size. Group size, however, demanded a loss of autonomy, for the integrative mechanisms that allowed large Iatmul villages to remain solidary required both a regular supply of Sawos sago and access to the shell valuables that only the Sawos could provide. Iatmul men resolved these conflicting demands by separating the domestic from the public domains. Their women acquired sago at barter markets using an essentially unequal exchange rate, while they maintained the reciprocal trading partnerships through which they acquired the shell valuables they needed to compensate their affines. The same incompatibility between autonomy and dependence was simultaneously being played out on the intravillage level, as prescribed marriage arrangements became an alternative to sister exchange, allowing for larger and better-integrated villages but demanding protracted interdependencies between affines, and between Iatmul men and their Sawos shell-suppliers.

South of the Sepik River, the incompatibility was the same, although its development reflected the particular position of the Chambri within the regional socioeconomic system. Autonomy, for these swamp dwellers, had become dependent upon Iatmul patronage. In return for their stone tools and mosquito bags, the Chambri lived in peace and acquired the shell valuables they needed to play at the politics of affinal exchange. Once the Iatmul withdrew their support—when Europeans introduced superior Western commodities—the Chambri had no choice but to shift their clientage to the dominant polity—namely, the Australian administrators who offered their protection in return for the sale of Chambri labor. This shift, from an autonomy-winning dependency upon the Iatmul to an autonomy-winning dependency upon the colonial government, allowed Chambri women to achieve control of subsistence transactions as Chambri men defaulted on trading partnerships. The women, gaining a new responsibility, also achieved the freedom of choice observed by Margaret Mead. Unfortunately, they lost it again when the Iatmul, fleeing from the river during World War II, intruded upon the lake and allowed Sepik Hills sago-suppliers to separate personal obligations from fish-for-sago exchanges.

What was at stake in both the Chambri and the Iatmul cases was much more than an ideological inconsistency. Both peoples were threatened with an actual loss of autonomy and independence. The Iatmul could easily have experienced the fate of their Sawos cousins, wrested from their advantageous positions along the Sepik River; the Chambri were threatened by Iatmul anxieties and were actually exiled among their sago-suppliers once the Europeans destroyed their commodity market; and neither people could hope to maintain their villages, nor their positions within their villages, without indebting themselves to their shell-providers and to their suppliers of women.

But doesn't the contradiction between autonomy and dependence operate within all human societies? Doesn't a Highland Big Man, for example, indebt himself to his constituents and to his allies so as to prevent encroachment by his land-hungry neighbors? Certainly the ethnographers of Highland societies have suggested as much. Consider Meggitt's description of group expansion and decline among the Mae Enga.

> To put the matter briefly, . . . groups grow and decline in a fairly regular manner that might be termed "spiralling." That is to say, a clan-parish whose membership . . . comes to be obviously larger than average . . . can not only more readily defend its territory from incursions, but it also becomes in the eyes of other people a group with which self-interested association is highly desirable. . . . The clan attracts more wives, who bear more sons to become workers and warriors and more daughters to bring in brideprice; affinal and exchange ties ramify; more wealth circulates and more credit is generated; the Big Men become more influential and are able to bring in immigrant protégés. . . .
>
> In time the increase in numbers builds up pressure on the land resources of the successful group, and, when a critical point is reached, it has no choice but to encroach on an adjacent clan (or clans) to secure more arable land. . . .
>
> . . . Before long its population again outruns its land resources. . . . If no weak groups are accessible, this clan comes into conflict with one of equal or greater strength. Rational appreciation of the situation may for some time dictate a military standoff; but sooner or later the continuing strains within the two groups force them to engage in intermittent and then, finally, internecine warfare that renders them vulnerable to invasion by other expanding clans. . . .
>
> Clans that are manifestly smaller than average . . . tend to be caught in a downwards spiral. They are less able to defend their land and pigs; they are not valued allies or exchange partners; they contract fewer marriages and produce fewer children; and consequently, they continue to stagnate or to decline until more-powerful neighbours seize the opportunity to destroy or disperse them and to expand into their territories. [1974: 198–200]

The loss of autonomy may be inevitable, as an expanding clan brings about its own decline through its very success at attracting the population it needs to maintain its territory, but a Big Man nevertheless achieves independence for himself and for his constituents by maintaining networks of exchange between himself and his allies. In other words, autonomy, for any Mae Enga clan, means dependence upon the good will and military support of other groups.

In another publication Meggitt suggests that the process of spiralling was, ultimately, directed by the Mae Enga perception that land was a "scarce and valued good, . . . [with] each local group assert[ing] its right to control as much land as it deemed necessary for its survival in a fashion befitting true Enga" (Meggitt, 1977: 183). The Enga, in other words, engaged in warfare, in exchange relationships, in alliances, and in marriages to insure control of their land. While they also valued their wars, their exchanges, their allies, and their affines, they viewed land as the sine qua non of all of these relationships. And they were correct in their perceptions, for without land a man could not raise the pigs he needed to engage in exchanges, grow the crops he needed to support his children, nor attract the affines he needed to supply his sons with wives. It might be said that, among the Enga, while there was land there was hope.

This Highland contradiction between autonomy and dependence—between land ownership and the relationships necessary to insure its ownership—is of a different kind than the one I have described among the Chambri and the Iatmul. To illuminate this difference, consider Bateson's discussion of the factors impelling changes in the size of Iatmul villages, a passage he wrote to demonstrate the integrating effects of the *naven* ceremonies.

> The reality of the integrating effect of *naven* might still be doubtful if the Iatmul communities were limited in size by some factor other than the weakness of their internal integration. It is conceivable, for example, that a community whose size was limited by its physical environment would never reach the size at which every contributory integrating factor becomes relevant. But actually, in Iatmul culture, it is clear that the factor which limits the size of the villages is the weakness of their internal cohesion. The larger villages are continually on the point of fission, and the fissions which have taken place in the past are always ascribed to quarrels which have split the parent community. [1958: 96–97]

Although the Chambri and the Iatmul needed certain essential resources—namely, sago and shell valuables—in order to maintain their societies, the crucial difference between their situation and that of the Mae Enga is this: these fish-suppliers never wished to gain direct control of the resources they needed, for to do so would mean to give up their identity and become the sago-suppliers upon whom they depended. Rather than wishing to control the territories inhabited by those who supplied them with sago and shells, the Chambri and the Iatmul have acted to maintain control of the relationships through which they were supplied with these items. Whereas the regional system within which the Enga and other Highland peoples operated was directed by their desire for land, Sepik peoples needed their exchange relationships per se.

Thus, Bateson is correct to suggest that village size is limited by its internal cohesion, for all fish-supplying groups were rivals and each other's principal competitors, competing inter alia for control of the exchange relationships upon which they each depended. Among the Iatmul, there were never periods of peace (as during the time before the *kaiko* ceremony among the Tsembaga), for hostilities were not affected by population pressure and land shortage, but by the continual possibility of alienating another group's exchange relationships or having one's own exchange relationships undermined. When villages grew larger, and the demand for both life-sustaining sago and group-sustaining shell valuables increased, the rivalry and competition that was generally directed against other villages began to erode intragroup relationships. Thus, as among the Mae Enga, the larger the group, the closer it was to disintegration. But, unlike the Highland situation, disintegration had nothing to do with real or perceived land shortage.

Bateson is correct in another sense as well, when he implies that there is no "director" in Iatmul or Chambri society comparable to those that have been discovered in the Highlands. Rappaport, for example, argues that the regional system within which the Tsembaga participate is directed by the wives of the owners of large numbers of pigs. These women find caring for their herds extremely burdensome when the energy they must expend in growing food to feed their animals becomes inordinate, and when the pigs start serious disturbances by invading neighboring gardens. Meggitt, likewise, suggests that the regional system of the Mae Enga is directed by men who perceive that they will not have sufficient land available to distribute to their sons unless they encroach upon the territory of a weaker neighbor. In both of these cases, there is a nonhuman referent against which to measure human capabilities and aspirations. Women can no longer manage to feed and care for their husbands' pigs; men perceive that their land will soon become scarce; and no Tsembaga nor Enga can conceive of circumventing the regulatory demands of their pigs and their land. Given their lack of technological capacities, they will have to slaughter their pigs and procure more territory.

In the Middle Sepik, however, the relationships established between men and women are not limited by their physical environments but, rather, are constrained by their mutual interdependence at any one point in time. The significance of these relational constraints is nowhere more clearly demonstrated than in the fact that Chambri quarry-owners could never establish hierarchical control over their less fortunate neighbors. Their inherited access to a significant resource allowed them to achieve the level of wealth acceptable to their Iatmul trading partners, and no more. They were not limited by their environment, but rather by their relationships, which is, perhaps, why the Chambri today attribute the ecological disaster wrought by *Salvinia molesta* to confounded affiliations.

Although Bateson was correct in locating the "director" of Sepik societies within the relationships established between groups of people, his mistake lay in suggesting that each individual Iatmul must learn to regulate himself—to introduce change into his dealings with others. In other words, Bateson identified the "rationality of the element while ignoring the rationality of the system" (Friedman, 1974: 459). Achievements of sisters' sons in headhunting or fishing, for example, are unlikely to be threats in any real sense to mothers' brothers, who have had a generation to achieve status within their villages. It is, rather, that during affinal exchange ceremonies celebrated for "achieved ambition" (Bateson, 1958: 289) on the part of sisters' sons, the *naven* ceremonies objectify the asymmetrical exchanges and unequal relationships between wife-givers and wife-takers.

Frequently, and generally during the largest affinal exchange ceremonies, representatives of more than two clans participate. The wife-givers and the wife-takers exchange foodstuffs and valuables on behalf of the mother's brother and his sister's son, but their patrons have donated many of the items exchanged. Thus, a large affinal prestation involves unequal and equal exchange relationships simultaneously. The wife-giving and wife-taking clans are involved in unequal, complementary relationships with each other and with their patron clans. These latter are in competition for control of their less adept neighbors but interact during the exchanges as unequals through their separate patronage of the wife-givers and wife-takers. The situation is inherently an ambiguous one, with conflicting relationships and allegiances prevailing. Although the stability of affinal inequality provides the perfect nonrepercussive context for competitive interaction, this interaction begins to undermine its context by obscuring the distinctions between wife-givers and wife-takers. In other words, the interdependency between affinally linked groups is based on social and symbolic differences that become confused as patrons make clients out of affines.

It is likely that the Iatmul *naven* ceremonies, which "are not very often performed . . . limited by the expense which they involve" (Bateson, 1958: 10), figure in those affinal exchange ceremonies involving numerous, ambiguously related clans.[6] Certainly this was true of the *naven* ceremonies I witnessed among the Chambri, which occur primarily when wife-givers and their supporters are beholden to the patrons of wife-takers—when they are in the difficult position of being in debt to individuals who are culturally defined as their inferiors.[7] This fact suggests that the ceremonies have a dual function. On the one hand, they delimit the sphere of interaction appropriate to unequals so as to distinguish it from the interaction of the equals who compete for dominance through control over the affinal prestations of smaller, weaker clans. In this sense, the *naven* ceremonies reaffirm the de jure stability of affinal inequality as a class of interactions distinct from de facto changes in the fortunes of corporate groups. On the other hand, the ceremonies indicate that competitive patrons have found the fiction of their de jure inequality an intolerable representation of the de facto situation. In this sense, the ceremonies mark the limits of patronization within the affinal exchange system—a time when symmetrically related groups can no longer compete without destroying the basis of their competitive interaction.

Thus Bateson was only partially correct when he described the processes of symmetrical and complementary schizmogenesis as inevitably leading to the destruction of Iatmul society, unless the *naven* ceremonies reversed the direction of positive feedback. The ceremonies do indicate the existence of a progressively destructive state of affairs, but they do nothing to reverse its direction. Instead, they reflect its ultimate development, the time when the society can no longer maintain symmetrical competitive interactions within the context of complementary affinal relationships—when the former threaten the existence of the latter.

Iatmul and Chambri society is not regulated by the *naven* ceremony but by the inability of "more than equal" patrons to find the wives they need to reproduce themselves—an inability that predictably follows upon their arrangement of the *naven* ceremonies.

It is this homeostat—the fact that each Iatmul and Chambri clan was destined to disintegrate for want of wives as soon as it became significantly more than the equal of the others—which has given Middle Sepik history its special thrust. Consider, for example, the history of the relationships between the Sawos and the Iatmul. To regulate their supply of sago, the Iatmul trapped their neighbors between political autonomy and economic dependence, which is to say that the Sawos accepted the fiction that the former followed from the latter. Thus, Sawos women agreed to an unfair exchange rate, while the dominant Iatmul maintained their reciprocal and interpersonal relationships with Sawos men. But to encourage political autonomy among the Sawos would only insure the Iatmul of a regulated economy for as long as the autonomy remained illusory—in other words, for as long as the autonomous sago-suppliers posed no real threat to Iatmul hegemony. The Iatmul could never achieve permanent control over their sago-suppliers, because these "princes of the Sepik" could never unite the region under a king. Their dependence upon the politics of affinal exchange to integrate their villages guaranteed that each Iatmul patron would remain symmetrically related to his counterparts, competing inter alia for control over his clients and his extratribal exchange relationships. And thus the Sawos were able to pose real threats to Iatmul hegemony quite regularly, and with varying degrees of success. Indeed, if more information were available, it might be possible to describe the Iatmul and Sawos as one people, composed of the "ins" and the "outs," who exchanged positions over time, as an Iatmul village or clan was pushed into the northern plains, vacating its river site to a successfully intrusive Sawos group.

The Chambri, too, seem to have been converging on the river, but by a more circuitous route. As commodity suppliers to the Iatmul, they were not only allowed the fiction of political autonomy, but were also encouraged in a false idea of themselves as a water-people equal to the Iatmul. How much more of a shock, therefore, when Iatmul warriors dispatched them to the hills so easily after the Europeans undermined the trade in stone tools and mosquito bags. If the Europeans had not intruded, the Chambri might well have tried to become peacefully incorporated into the villages of their Iatmul trading partners, leaving their island to the Hills people, who would assume the position of commodity-suppliers to the river villages.

In other words, the history of the region can be described as a confluence of peoples at the strategically important site of the Sepik River, a confluence perpetuated by the inability of any one group to gain permanent control but restricted by their general incapacity to support themselves alone.

The European administrators who entered the Middle Sepik during the 1920s did their best to reduce this confluence of peoples by organizing the region into permanent and inalienable village sites. And World War II partially reversed this direction by prompting many of the dominant Iatmul to seek safety in the southern backswamps. Simultaneously, European entrepreneurs reduced the significance of the regional socioeconomic system by allowing the natives to believe that wage labor promised liberation from the contradiction between autonomy and dependence—that to sell their time and purchase their food meant freedom from their trading relationships rather than just another form of subordination.

That the Chambri entered into this new form of subordination more readily than the Iatmul, who still acquire most of their sago through barter markets, has more to do with their precolonial past than it does with their present, a fact that I find very difficult to admit because it implies that "my people" made many serious errors in judgment. It occurs to me that anthropologists may often eliminate history from their analyses of social process to protect themselves from having to make similar admissions. If any group can be said to be living in an ahistorical "dream time," it is those of us who cannot risk acknowledging that times have changed, and that not all changes are directly attributable to the colonial intrusion. This is not to relieve colonial administrators and European capitalists of their responsibility for altering the balance of power within Papua New Guinea, but merely to suggest that all people, everywhere, must live with the consequences of their actions.

When anthropologists argue that they haven't the data to come to terms with the past, I think what they mean is that they haven't the heart to interpret facts they have collected about the past. After all, is my historical interpretation of the Yambukay-Samanday story (see chapter 4) any more or less accurate than my analysis of the Chambri kinship system would be? Both must be based on reflections about incomplete information, imperfectly understood. And how many of us, in the name of a fictitious tense we call the "ethnographic present," have selected ethnohistorical accounts for use in our ostensibly synchronic analyses—selected them because they seemed to cohere with our notions of what our people's society should be like.

My Wombun friend with the insurance pamphlet was convinced that our books bring us power, but he never conceived of the power that our synchronically structured monographs bring us. Our use of the ethnographic present allows us to create Papua New Guineans in our own idealized images of self-regulating primitives—to deprive our subjects of the human propensity to make mistakes, and of the human resilience to cope with these mistakes, for better or for worse.

Toward the end of my first field trip to New Guinea, I journeyed down the Sepik River and up one of its easternmost tributaries, the Keram River. My destination was the village of Kambot, where the son of an informant of mine was living. He had married a Kambot woman while stationed at Angoram and, after his only child had died of malaria during a trip to Madang, had moved in with his wife's parents. I had promised my informant to try to persuade her son to come home to Chambri, but was motivated to make the long trip out of self-interest. I wished to purchase a Kambot "story board," a flat wooden carving depicting a mythological scene or significant event in Kambot ethnohistory. The story board I bought portrays a large canoe, filled with warriors who are surrounded, above and below, by their ancestors, depicted both as humans and as totemic animals. When I returned home to Chambri (with my informant's son), my Papua New Guinea father, Tambwi Kwolikumbwi, visited me in my house to see the carving he had heard about. He came late at night and with his flashlight turned to its highest power, examined the artifact. He stood in front of it, totally engrossed, and said, as he moved the torch beam over the carved figures: "That's good. That's how it should be. No, that's not right. He's got it wrong. Good, that part's right. He knows his business. No, now he's wrong. I'm afraid of how many mistakes he has made." When I asked Tambwi why he was frightened by the Kambot carver's "mistakes," he said: "He's ruined me. I'm not the way he has carved me. And who knows, maybe he has the power to make me the way he says. He almost pulled Wundi's [my informant's] son away from here. If it hadn't been for your white power, he would have succeeded. I'm afraid of this carving."

Tambwi's fears resulted from the conflation of several significant social facts. First of all, he was expressing the common Middle Sepik belief that the ownership of totemic names defines group membership, and that the business of a clan is to maintain control of its totems. The Kambot carver had conjoined several totems belonging to Tambwi with those of two other Chambri clans, and Tambwi feared that the carving presaged the ultimate union of these clans—that he was destined to lose his autonomy as the head of a rapidly declining but still independent social group. This fear was related in his mind to another, more general anxiety about the loss of young Chambri men—and women—through their marriages to foreigners. Wundi's son had married a Kambot woman, and Tambwi knew that the Chambri people could not remain distinct and intact while marrying outside of their villages.

Tambwi's fears, it seems to me, were based on an accurate perception of his own social situation and on a broader understanding of the position of the Chambri people within a modernizing world. His own clan, which comprised only himself, his migrant brother, and his two disaffected sons, had already accepted patronage from a distantly related Kilimbit clan, and his people were becoming increasingly aware of how many of their sons and daughters were opting out of the affinal exchange system. But, his fears went deeper than this, and expressed an essential aspect of life within the Middle Sepik, where identity is transformed—or lost—through the establishment or disintegration of relationships with others.

The relationships Tambwi and his people established with European administrators and entrepreneurs seemed an excellent alternative to their trade in specialized commodities and were, indeed, their only viable option. But now, finding themselves trapped between modernization and development, with *Salvinia molesta* encouraging even greater numbers of their people to live and work in the towns, Tambwi and older Chambri have begun to doubt the wisdom of their choice.

NOTES

Introduction

1. Laycock writes: "The shape of the area occupied by the Ndu family suggests a northward migration; in the Maprik area, for example, will be noticed a large 'bulge', in which the Abelam speakers are surrounded by Arapesh speakers—a probable indication of penetration by the Abelam northwards into country already occupied by the Arapesh. It should be noted in this connection that the Ndu family is almost entirely surrounded by multiple-classifying languages (Arapesh, Urimo, Murik, Chambri); . . . it is possible that they may prove to be a related group which were split by intrusion on the part of Ndu-family languages" (1965: 193).
2. Newton (1967) agrees with Laycock (1965) that the present-day Ndu speakers originated south of the Sepik River in the foothills of the Korosameri and Karawari tributaries. He bases his judgment upon the occurrence of certain artistic traits throughout the East Sepik Province—namely, upon "a . . . kind of stylized face, suited to two-dimensional works such as barkpainting and relief sculpture, but also used for sacred masks; [upon] short-nosed masks; [upon] the serrated head ornament; [upon] the loop-nosed slit gongs; [and upon] cere-monial life centered on extremely large long-houses" (ibid.: 214). He estimates that the original Ndu populated the river over a span of about 250 years.
3. Dye et al. write: "Languages of the Ndu and Sepik Hill Families tend to share 10% to 15% cognates, with higher and lower cognate percentages in some cases. This suggests a genetic relationship, although borrowing between the parent languages of both families cannot be excluded" (1969: 153).

Chapter One

1. Margaret Mead began the long tradition of ethnographic comparison between Middle Sepik cultures in volume 2 of her comprehensive *Mountain Arapesh* (1970 and 1971), and in *Sex and Temperament* (1963). More recently, Forge (1966 and 1971) has compared cultural themes among the Iatmul and Abe-lam, while Tuzin (1977) has done the same for the Arapesh, Iatmul, and Banaro. Finally, Rosman and Rubel (1978) have attempted to isolate the evo-lution of certain structural patterns by comparing thirteen New Guinea cul-tures, three of which are found in the Middle Sepik region.

235

2. See Wurm et al., 1975, for a speculative reconstruction of the linguistic pre-history and the language migrations of Middle Sepik peoples.

3. Bateson compared complementary patterns to symmetrical ones, defining the latter as "a relationship between two individuals (or two groups) . . . [in which] each responds to the other with the same kind of behaviour, e.g. if each meets the other with assertiveness" (1958: 311). I find the following poem the best illustration of the concept: "Tit for Tat, Butter for Fat,/If You Kick My Dog, I'll Kick Your Cat."

4. The Iatmul-speaking villages of the Middle Sepik are divided into two dialect groups, Nyaula and Parambei. Nyaula is spoken from Japandai through Korogo; Parambei from Suapmeri through Tegowi. With few exceptions this dialect division is sustained by proximity and allegiance.

5. These figures were derived from the 1959 census data reported by Laycock, 1961.

6. The only detailed study we have of a Sawos village is Schindlbeck, 1980. His work took place primarily in Gaikerobi, a village whose members had adopted many of the social and ceremonial customs of the Iatmul. In fact, Schindlbeck's description of Gaikerobi could be applied to many Iatmul settlements, both in terms of village layout and social organization.

7. Schindlbeck's data were, of course, collected among the Gaikerobi living in a large and sedentary village during 1973 and can only partly inform us about the subsistence requirements of those original Sawos who began bartering for Iatmul fish. While it is likely that these early Sawos barterers were self-sufficient, their descendants are definitely not. Today's Gaikerobi need Iatmul fish, but their needs transcend the subsistence requirements of any one family—no matter what its size—and are determined by the requirements of their large and sedentary population.

8. I know little about the Minow market, having confined my marketing expeditions to those used by the Iatmul and Chambri of the Middle Sepik proper. Those Japandai living at Brugnowi and Tugwan were beyond my field of reference. Most Japandai living at Japandai Village trade at Wereman Market.

9. "Japanday" is spelled "Japandai" on official government maps.

10. In earlier publications I described four barter markets operating between the Iatmul and the Sawos (Gewertz, 1977a and 1978a). I now realize that these four markets are conglomerates of numerous other impersonal but patrilineally inherited markets, like the ones I have described here. It is fair to say, therefore, that trading partnerships evolved into barter markets which, under government and mission influence, have grown larger and lost their membership prerequisites.

11. I do not mean to suggest causality between a particular kinship or marriage system and a particular form of social organization. My point is simply that a transformation from one marriage pattern to another produces concomitant changes in the pattern of alliances between kin groups, and that a preference for one or another system indicates a great deal about the cultural possibilities within any social formation. The frequency with which the Iatmul practice *iai* marriage is irrelevant. What is important is that it could not have been culturally possible prior to the existence of large and sedentary villages.

12. Rosman and Rubel interpret this third marriage rule to refer "to a delay of one generation in the return of a woman and [to be] linked, as Bateson notes, to the formulation that women should be exchanged" (1978: 37).

13. Tuzin refers here to "the evolution of Ilahita's dual organization [which] has involved a condensation of function to structurally more confined groups: village functions have been transferred to the moiety sphere; moiety functions have devolved upon what are now sub-moieties. And yet, because the village was simultaneously growing in population, these shifts did not entail a transference of function to smaller-sized groups" (1977: 262).

14. Of the six former settlements Schindlbeck investigated, only the most recent exhibited the remains of more than one men's house. Moreover, the ethnohistories he collected suggest that today's Gaikerobi clans were once independent political units, living separately in a multitude of small hamlets. These hamlets seem to have been located near rivulets or brooks and were abandoned when the waterways dried up. Based upon genealogies, Schindlbeck was able to construct a shallow time sequence for the peopling of Gaikerobi. Its founders had inhabited the settlement called Ngətəpm for approximately eighty-eight years, and moved to Gaikerobi in about 1810. They were joined by six "clans" in two waves, one in 1860 and the other in 1885.

15. During my first field trip I assumed that the Iatmul, like the Chambri, rarely attacked their sago-suppliers. My second field trip clarified matters for me.

16. I wish to thank Mrs. Renata Jacques for her excellent translation of German texts.

17. Schindlbeck tells us that this carbohydrate was made from the palm tree called *yo* (1980: 216). I cannot identify it further.

18. Lami is the name of a former settlement of the Gaikerobi people.

19. The posture of the Gaikerobi women who presented themselves to Ngumoekumban seems to capture metaphorically the obsequiousness of the Sawos women who offer sago to the Iatmul.

20. Ngusai, Ngumoekumban's home, is located near the Iatmul village of Kararau.

21. See, for example, Bateson, 1958: 123–41.

22. Schindlbeck provides several versions of this myth. Some have the Sawos able to kill the seducer in the end, but all portray his death as extremely difficult to accomplish.

23. His concern is to demonstrate that the Iatmul do not necessarily follow their own marriage rules. This fact does not undermine my argument about the transformation from sister exchange to generalized marriage practices, for the significant developments involved asymmetrical exchange and the use of valuables, not marriage to the actual *iai*.

24. Rhoda Metraux tells me that the Iatmul villagers of the Lower Sepik guarded their rights to the bush tribes not only because they wanted sago but also because they wanted heads. It was almost as if the Iatmul cultivated the bush tribes as "head farms" (personal communication).

25. Bateson recognizes the difference between the marketing practices of the Middle and Lower Sepik Iatmul and writes: "This three-day week is characteristic of Palambai and Kankanamun, but is not adhered to by the Eastern [i.e., Lower Sepik] Iatmul whose villages are farther from those of their bush neighbours. The Eastern Iatmul hold their markets irregularly, on specially arranged days, the two parties meeting in the grass country which separates their villages" (1958: 143). I suspect that trading partnerships continued for a longer time on the Lower Sepik because the distances between the river and the bush allowed the Eastern Iatmul less control over their sago-suppliers.

26. Schindlbeck suggests that the Gaikerobi were as bothered by attacks from the north as they were by attacks from the south (1980: 3 and 63). Indeed, they viewed their northern neighbors as the more troublesome, probably because the bellicosity of these peoples was not mediated by their need of Sawos sago.

Chapter Two

1. Mead describes mosquito bags as "the most important manufacture . . . two of which will purchase an ordinary canoe" (1963: 253–54). Neither she nor Reo Fortune provide statistics that would help check my informants' recollections of past sales. Given these recollections, she was probably right about the commodities, if she meant the adjective *important* to mean that they were "worth the most."
2. Mead refers to green snail shells as "*talibun*." I prefer to spell them thus: "*talimbun*."
3. The Chambri valued three kinds of shell. These were *talimbun*, a green snail shell (*Turbo marmoratus*); *lin*, a bracelet or necklace that can consist of a variety of different shells, including cowrie and conus, which are pierced in the middle and strung together with hemp; and *kina*, the gold-lip pearl shell (*Pinctata margaritifera*). *Talimbun* were the most prized of the shell valuables.
4. Rights to quarries were inherited patrilineally.
5. Dr. Patrick Brock of the geology department of Queens College, C.U.N.Y., described the stone adze I asked him to analyze as "a fine-grained metamorphosed mafic volcanic rock, probably of basaltic composition."
6. Unfortunately, I have no samples of this harder variety of stone.
7. Neither Mead nor Fortune mention stone adzes in their field notes. My informants, recollecting past sales, set exchange rates at:

Size of Adze	Exchange Rate
Largest	6 *kina*, 6 *talimbun* and 3 *lin*, or 2 *kina* and 10 *talimbun*
Second largest	2 *kina*, 5 *talimbun* and 3 *lin*
Third largest	2 *kina*, 3 *talimbun* and 1 *lin*
Smallest	1 *kina*, 1 *talimbun* and 1 *lin*

8. These ceremonies involved the sacrifice of a chicken by the stone-adze salesman to his ancestors, who would, in turn, assure the supernatural *uncheban* of their descendant's good will. See chapter 4 for a fuller discussion of these ceremonies.
9. Kwaremanki's worry refers to an attack on his people made by the Chambri living on Timbunmeri Island shortly after the Chambri were forced to flee their own island by the Parambei Iatmul. See chapter 5 for a fuller description of the incident.
10. As ancestors who transubstantiate into sago palm, Maiyum and Abundimi are particularly averse to bloodshed. This could be because they—like the mothers to whom they are frequently compared—"cry" over the spilling of their descendant's blood. I do not know why the Chambri fear asphyxiation.
11. In order to earn the right to wear black paint at ceremonials, a young Chambri man had to take a head in warfare. If this was not possible, his mother's brother would purchase an infant so that he could slaughter it ceremonially. Between one and three *kina* were paid per child. Of the twenty Indingai men alive in

January 1976 who had infants bought for them, eight killed children from Mali, four killed Milae children, two killed Garamambu children, and six killed children from neither Sepik Hills nor Garamambu hamlets. Mead distinguishes the Iatmul from the Chambri by asserting that "the Tchambuli were not enthusiastic about warfare or head-hunting; it is true that a ceremonial house must have heads, but they preferred to buy the bastards and orphans and criminals of the bush people and kill them ceremonially in the village, rather than run the risks of battle" (1963: 242–43). My Iatmul informants assured me, however, that they also frequently bought bush infants to be ceremonially slaughtered.

12. Unfortunately, although I was shown this white earth, I never had it analyzed, and do not know its components.
13. Mensuat is a hamlet composed of speakers of the Bisis language, a member of the Sepik Hills language family.
14. I do not know the Latin name of *pliplimank*.
15. Chambriman is now called Changriman. It is a Bisis-speaking Sepik Hills hamlet.
16. The Heve speak a Sepik Hills language.
17. Milae is a hamlet composed of speakers of the Mali language, a member of the Sepik Hills language family.

Chapter Three

1. Hauser-Schaublin estimates that each adult Iatmul woman brings home an average of nine fish per day after approximately four hours of work (1977: 28).
2. Margaret Mead describes the productive lives of Chambri women thus: "There is no need for daily labour; sago is stored, fish is smoked, the market does not come every day, and it is always possible to stop all work for several days and attend whole-heartedly to a ritual or a feast. This is the normal course of life, but occasionally, when there has been much war among the sago-producing bush people, or particularly bad fishing for the Tchambuli, and it is the season when the supplementary taro gardens are all under water, there is hunger" (1963: 242). My informants remembered few occasions when they suffered from hunger, and none due to environmental rather than socioeconomic causes. In other words, even before the introduction of *makau*, Chambri Lake was full of fish, although occasionally the people found them inaccessible during times of warfare or exile.
3. Bateson sets this myth within the following context: "As a further documentation of the respect which is paid to women of strong and courageous personality, we may cite here a traditional myth which was told to me in Mindimbit in explanation of the head-hunting alliance between that village and Palimbai. Both of these villages have a traditional feud with the village of Kararau which lies between them" (1958: 145).
4. Bateson tells us in a footnote that Iatmul men frequently confuse sisters with wives in their myths (1958: 145–46, n. 1). This is so, I believe, because they blame all women for establishing relationships of inequality between otherwise equal groups of men. I think it clear, however, that Au-vitkai-mangka was acting, in this story, as a wife would. If she had been the dead man's sister, then she would not have felt free to offer herself in marriage to the men of

Parambei. As his wife, her self-evaluation was not tied to the successes of her husband's corporate group.

5. Government maps spell the name of this Iatmul village thus: Parambei.

6. Each Iatmul and Chambri clan possesses its own ceremonial mound or ceremonial stone, near to which members would bury the bodies of enemies taken in warfare.

7. Bateson elaborates upon this sentence in a footnote. He writes: "The nakedness of the women in this context seemed so natural to me when I was told the myth, that I did not enquire into the reasons for it. I have no doubt, however, that this nakedness is the mark of the suppliant and that it is, in some degree, analogous to the nakedness of the women in *naven* when they lie down before the hero" (1958: 146).

8. Bateson admits that he has condensed the conversation in the following four paragraphs.

9. Bateson explains in a footnote that: "This phrase is substituted for a list of technical terms which do not concern us here" (1958: 147).

10. In an early descriptive article, Bateson describes the totemic system of the Iatmul. He writes: "Comparing the lists of totems belonging to different clans, we find that there are certain general differences. Thus the clans of the Sun moiety tend to have suns and stars and clouds for their ancestors and to place their ancestral pigs, canoes, etc., in the sky. The clans of the Mother moiety, on the other hand, connect their ancestors with the earth. Some clans say that they have totems connected with the bush, while others are especially connected with the Sepik River. Others again are connected with certain geographical areas—the South-East River or the Sawos plain. But, broadly, the most important sorts of totemic ancestors are to be found common to the list of each clan. Every clan numbers among its ancestors a certain number of each of the following: shamanic spirits, fires, waters, dwelling houses, ceremonial houses, crocodiles, gingers, masks, eagles, and many other important categories" (1932: 403). Bateson's description could be equally as well applied to the Chambri totemic system. Among both peoples, their totemic names are translated as, for example, "Leg-fishhook-man" or "North-bank-earth-tree" (Bateson, 1932: 410), and refer to the ancestors who once held them, to the ancestral spirits and magical powers invoked by their recitation, and to the natural objects, territories, and resources owned and lived in by the ancestral spirits. Although group members claim descent from their groups' founders, it is the inheritance of totemic names and not the transmission of blood that links them together.

11. Wobunprendu and Kabunprendu, the myth's wooden women, are living examples of the danger inherent in females. The myth describes them as *chambɔn*, carved wooden hooks that normally represent particularly significant patrilineal ancestors. The Chambri recognize two types of *chambɔn* by their respective functions. The first is hung by every married or initiated man from the ceiling of his wife's or mother's house. These *chambɔn* are carved by their owners to represent personally significant patrilineal ancestors, perhaps the ancestor for whom the man is named or one who is thought to dwell in the house. A man's wife or mother is responsible for keeping the woven reed bag which hangs from her husband's or son's *chambɔn* filled with sago and fish, so that he can eat whenever he returns from his spirit-house. Women do not own *chambɔn*, for, I was told, "they prepare their own food whenever they like."

The second type of *chambɔn* resembles the first in construction, but is suspended from the ceiling of a man's spirit-house. These *chambən* are passed down from generation to generation and represent apical ancestors. Their baskets are filled with ceremonial accoutrements—human bones, shell valuables, or feather decorations. These objects are used during the various ceremonies in which the particular ancestor plays a significant part. Thus, when it is time for the ancestor Saungai to make the "white water" of the Sepik River return to Chambri Lake after the dry season, the leader of the Saungai clan places his Saungai *chambən* and ceremonial basket close to the area where the ceremony is performed.

Chambən, therefore, are repositories of patrilineal power. They are extremely important in both the secular and sacred lives of Chambri males, and they are never used by women nor carved to represent female ancestors. Wobunprendu and Kabunprendu are female *chambən*, a dangerous contradiction in terms. Women are safe, or at least controllable, when relegated to the position of mediators between patrilines. Through marriage they move from one male group to another, to reproduce their husbands' patrilines. Wobunprendu and Kabunprendu, however, represent to Chambri males their greatest fears about the reproduction and continuity of patrilines. Not only do they take the forbidden form of *chambən*, thus invading the cultural realm, but they also try to steal Wundan and Pumbun's hawks by hiding them underneath their sago baskets. Hawks figure prominently in Chambri mythology as representatives of the male ancestors or of living men, who magically assume the likeness of birds. Sago, on the other hand, is symbolic of female sexuality (see Ruddle et al., 1978, who discuss the widespread association between women and sago palms throughout Papua New Guinea). Wobunprendu and Kabunprendu, by hiding the hawks underneath their sago baskets, were attempting to steal away the essence of patrilineality. This is precisely what Chambri males fear will happen during sexual intercourse. Wundan and Pumbun were not, however, deceived by the girls' ploy, but instead coerced them into marriage, the Chambri means of controlling female sexuality. But, as we have seen, marriage is only the lesser of two evils, for although it allows for the control of females, it necessitates unpleasant social relations.

12. When a boy is initiated into his father's patriclan, the scarification ceremony is explicitly intended to rid the initiate of the weakening influence of his mother's blood.

13. I determined the number of persons related through the exchange of this *kina* by analyzing Mead's data. She does not explicate these data herself but simply records them under the heading: "History of a Kina during four months with further notes on the Tchuikumban-Yebiwali incident."

14. Seven of the fifteen affinal transactions to which I refer occurred at initiation ceremonies, two took place during marriage transactions, two during sorcery trials, one after a young man had his hair cut for the first time, one at a mortuary ceremony, one at a birthday celebration, and one at a house-opening party. For a fuller discussion of several of these ceremonies, see Gewertz, 1977b and 1977c.

Chapter Four

1. Wombun Village, also called Walintimiingai, or "belonging to Walintimi," is said to have been founded when Walintimi left Indingai after fighting with

Yambukay over the ownership of a banana tree. Kilimbit Village, or Saungai, was ostensibly founded when Saun, the youngest of the three "brothers," argued with Yambukay over a woman. Each of these brothers is the leader of one of the three Chambri phratries, the highest order genealogically based divisions that the people recognize. The territory of the phratries coincides with that of the villages. They are not, however, landowning groups.

2. The stories that are told to explain these emigrations to Chambri generally involve sociological or supernatural troubles at each ancestor's place of origin. Those who came from the small Chambri Lake islands, for example, had been plagued by a huge supernatural hawk; while the Milae-born ancestor sought refuge from his older brother, with whom he had had a serious argument.

3. All Nor Pondo speakers are multiple-classifiers who use full concord. To the best of my knowledge, there has been no comparative analysis of the Nor Pondo languages.

4. There is considerable bi- and trilingualism throughout the Middle Sepik, although with the widespread use of Melanesian Pidgin, there is less than there used to be.

5. Yenimp, located approximately 400 feet up Chambri Mountain, is the site of a major stone quarry.

6. The events described in this myth are said to have happened after Walintimi founded Wombun Village.

7. Nowhere in the field notebooks of Margaret Mead and Reo Fortune is there mention of a woman donating shell valuables to a man other than her brother, husband, or close relative, all of whom use the valuables on their own behalf.

8. The baskets referred to by Kosemp were not produced before tourists became interested in purchasing native artifacts. They are generally made of reeds, colored with European-produced dyes, and woven into geometric patterns. Sometimes Chambri women will weave a common European name into their baskets, hoping the tourists will be encouraged to spend $K2.00 on the baskets "marked for them."

Chapter Five

1. The Nyaula- and Parambei-speaking Iatmul were always antagonistic, attacking one another's villages more frequently than they attacked villages within their own dialect groups. Although the Chambri were never directly involved in these hostilities, they perceived themselves as allied to the Nyaula.

2. The grasses that grow up in Chambri Lake during the dry season lose their anchorage during the rainy season and drift throughout the lake like small floating islands. These floating islands figure in many Chambri myths and stories.

3. Sunmali is the name of a land-boundary between Chambri and Kandingai territories.

4. Nearest the largest men's house of Indingai Village stands a conical hole filled with muddy water, about twenty feet in diameter and fifteen feet deep. This hole is where the Chambri believe Emosuie Apankay and Kwolimbank anchored Chambri Island. They occasionally remove the water from the hole in order to prove their contention by showing doubters the stone and palm anchors located at the bottom of the hole.

5. The conical hole in which Emosuie and Kwolimbank are said to have anchored Chambri Island can be interpreted as a microcosm. The Chambri say that in it are mingled the waters from the north, south, east, and west, from the River, Hills, White Man's Land, and the Lake itself. It is thus a representation of the Chambri world, which they explicitly use to predict the future and explain the past. When the water in the hole was last removed, Kwolimbank's anchor had moved closer to the center of the hole, a fact that upset the Chambri considerably. They said that the arrangement of the anchors indicated that the Kandingai Iatmul had intruded into Chambri Lake, where they do not belong and whence it will be hard to extract them.

6. The Iatmul referred to the Chambri as *numanki*, literally, "incompetents."

7. It would, perhaps, be more accurate to suggest that both the Chambri and Iatmul lacked access to the same resource zones, thereby necessitating that each engage in exchange with bush-people who could help them support their populations.

8. Among both the Chambri and the Iatmul, large-scale ceremonial transactions between relatively egalitarian groups do not occur. Exchange takes place primarily between affinally linked groups which, by definition, are involved in an unequal relationship of dominance and subordination. Status division, therefore, cannot be established and maintained by overcoming an equal through a large ceremonial transaction but only by controlling the affinal prestations of unequals. Both systems create and maintain status divisions, but their structures are inverse. Whereas Highland's Big Men are the foci of all interaction involving large, ceremonial transactions, Sepik leaders are points of connection and dispersal for their subordinate clients who are involved in unequal exchange with their respective affines. And where Highlands ceremonial exchange networks have "indefinite potential outer limits . . . [extending] in point-to-point chains" (Schwartz, 1964: 90), Sepik ceremonial exchange networks rarely extend beyond a village or ethnic group where the participants are united by a "theoretical all-to-all linkage" (ibid.).

9. I do not know why many Wombun chose to flee to Kabriman. The "trade-ties" that Mead says existed between Wombun and this Korosameri River village (1963: 243) were actually between Wombun and emigrants to Kabriman from the Sepik Hills hamlet of Yambi Yambi. Presumably, the Wombun felt safer living on a river than in the hills.

10. See Gewertz, 1978b, for a sociosymbolic analysis of this war with the Manabi.

11. Kurapio is a site located on the southeastern side of Timbunmeri Island. Today, many Mali people live there, but formerly it was used by Chambri and Garamambu trading partners to exchange their produce.

12. This is an estimation based upon genealogies. My guess would be that approximately 150 Wombun fled to Kabriman.

13. The Annual Report to the League of Nations does not credit Kassa Townsend with writing the Sepik section, but since he was District Officer at the time, I have assumed that he authored it.

14. B. P. stands for Burns Philp, an Australian-based chain of stores found throughout the Pacific.

15. Malmansi and Yangandimi were two Chambri leaders, the former from Kilimbit and the latter from Indingai.

16. Buka is an island located off the northeast coast of mainland New Guinea.

17. Lakindimi refers here to certain renegade police who were captured by Austra-

lian administrators on Sambungundei Island in Chambri Lake just before the Japanese invasion into the region. I discuss this incident in chapter 7.

18. Margaret Mead and Reo Fortune report that shell valuables were still being used for affinal transactions while they worked among the Chambri in 1933. They also mention that European-produced commodities were exchanged. My informants told me that European goods had completely replaced indigenous valuables by the beginning of World War II, circa 1942.

19. Consider, for example, the following passage from Sidney Shurcliff's record of the Crane Pacific Expedition. Arriving at Wogamush on May 20, 1928, Father Kirschbaum, the Catholic priest accompanying the explorers up the Sepik River, "became very excited."

He rushed down to the laboratory and soon returned with his arms full of steel knives, hatchets, and adze blades.

"Look," he said, pointing out something we had not noticed before, "these are Stone-Age men! Those sticks they are waving at us are stone axes. We must be in territory where the white man is little known, if at all."

He went down the gang-plank to the bottom step and waved one of the hatchets toward the natives. At first they did not notice it. Then one of the most elaborately decorated men gave a gutteral shout, pointing at the same time toward the hatchet. . . . Apparently they had *heard* of steel before, at any rate.

By this time seventy or eighty of the wild men in nearly as many canoes had closed in on the ship. . . .

[Father Kirschbaum said:] "We may have to get out of here in a hurry. For the present they will not bother us as long as I pass out steel implements at frequent intervals. . . ."

He distributed among us a few dozen of the steel articles so that we could each trade for ourselves. Then the fun began! We had only to lean over the rail and point at whatever article in the canoes or in the natives' hands had caught our fancy. Immediately the natives nearer the ship would snatch it from the owner and thrust it into our hands, at the same time grabbing from us the piece of steel which we had offered. Within fifteen minutes there came over the rail enough spears, arrows, axes, bone knives, paddles, stone adzes, lime boxes, shell ornaments, head plumes, and nose-plugs to outfit an exhibition room in a museum" (1930: 252–53).

20. Several informants told me that after their Kamanbo exile they would only visit their trading partners when they wished to get away from their villages. Although they had always found trips to the bush to be somewhat diversionary, they now viewed them as primarily so, having become uninterested in acquiring what their bush friends had to offer.

21. When Mead worked among the Chambri they were busy rebuilding their villages. In her field notes she refers to three of Indingai's five men's houses being opened or constructed during the four months she lived there. During the Parambei war, all of these houses, and most of the ceremonial accoutrements they contained, had been gutted by fire. See chapter 6 for a fuller discussion of these facts.

22. Fifty-two percent of all Chambri adult men between the ages of 15 and 45 were absent from their villages during 1933. See chapter 6 for a fuller discussion of this fact.

Chapter Six

1. I am not sure why Namowi chose a door to turn into a crocodile, or why the door moved up and down before it turned. I can only say that the episode reminds me of the ceremony held by the Chambri after the death of an adult member of their tribe as a means of diagnosing the individual or ancestor responsible for the death. Members of the deceased's clan place a long, thick piece of bamboo near his grave. After a day or two, sufficient time for the deceased's spirit to have entered it, the bamboo is removed. It is kept near the dead person's house until night falls. Then the men who retrieved it place one end in the door or window of the house and rest the other on a small wooden gong. Between three and five men grasp the bamboo, underhand, and ask questions of the deceased's spirit. Occasionally they are his affines, but frequently they have no traceable genealogical relationships to him. Invariably, however, they prove to be either members of, or affines to, the clan or clans which are later found to be responsible for his death. Their questions concern the causes of his death and are always asked in a yes/no form. "Was the 'cross' between you and the Mangemeri over the woman, Tupikumban?" is a typical example. If the deceased's spirit answers affirmatively, the bamboo moves vertically to pound the split gong. If not, the bamboo slides horizontally along the drum. As the questions touch on events approaching the present, the bamboo's movements become increasingly violent and frequently the frame of the window or door is torn from the house. The association I sense between the *mambu* ceremony and the mythic transubstantiation of the door as a crocodile may be based on the fact that during both events inanimate objects are imbued with spirits of deceased individuals. Could the door of the myth stand for the boundary between life and death?
2. Klinjambang is a Sepik River village located upriver from Angoram. On maps it is referred to as Krinjambi.
3. Men's houses are supported by elaborately carved posts, each of which is incised with the totemic markings of those whose house it is.
4. I do not know how to interpret Wobowi's statement, primarily because I have been unable to locate Andena on a map of the Lower Sepik. If, as I suspect, Andena is a sago-supplying bush-village, then Wobowi's message is clearly: "I am subservient to you."
5. Being most impressed with stories of British kings and queens, the Chambri reject the notion that the Australians could be without such notables.
6. Indingai Village supports three traditional Big Men and one entrepreneur who has achieved prominence within an Australian-imposed political organization. Two of the three traditional leaders are older brothers, while the third is a younger brother whose two older male siblings could not achieve leadership. The first of these older siblings died while still a young man, while the second lost the desire to lead after his children died in infancy. The entrepreneur is a younger brother, whose older male sibling is a deaf-mute.
7. Chambri fathers assume that their educated older sons will obtain lucrative work and then pay the school fees for any additional children in their families. Since not many young men have finished their educations or obtained well-paying jobs, it is difficult to say whether their fathers' assumptions are well-founded.

8. In most myths that I collected from Chambri and Iatmul, conversations between characters always escalate as they engage in either symmetrical or complementary interaction. Men either challenge each other to prove their equality or demure from such challenges.

9. The Iatmul recognized no permanent social position called "fight leader." Ma-
mandai must have been a man who was unusually and consistently successful
in warfare.

10. Consider, for example, Ion Idriess's description of the different peoples who
worked carrying cargo to the goldmines in the Markham Valley: "Here individ-
uality came in, for the carriers were from numerous localities; many came
from distant rivers and from islands across the sea. Some were truculent or
sullen, others were fightable or full of fun; some were steady boys, others plain
dodgers; some were 'wooden-headed,' others were cunning" (1949: 131).

11. Obviously I have no population statistics from before the time of the European
intrusion. My statement that Sawos villages expanded over time is based on
the assumption that sedentary populations will be larger than migratory ones.

12. The most controversial of Mead's claims about the Chambri—that women
dominated their men—must be understood in terms of the historical circumstances that prevailed during 1933. When Mead's household surveys are compared with my genealogies, it appears that nearly 52 percent of Indingai men
between the ages of fifteen and forty-five were absent from their villages, probably for the purpose of labor migration. Mead's household surveys are organized according to men's house affiliation. She lists all the initiated men who
reside in the same spirit-house and then records their wives, their children,
and their other dependents, such as widowed mothers. My genealogies are
relatively complete for the generation of Indingai men among whom Mead
lived. According to my records, 18 young men between the ages of fifteen and
twenty-five, and 22 older men between the ages of twenty-six and forty-five are
unaccounted for by Mead. I think it likely that these men were living away
from Indingai, probably on plantations, because otherwise Mead would have
recorded their names and families. Since her surveys are organized according
to male household heads, it is not surprising that the wives and children of
these migrants appear nowhere in her records.

In other words, there may be a straightforward demographic explanation for
the female dominance Mead describes. Mead's surveys indicate that there were
three adult women for every two adult men living in Indingai during 1933. If
I am right about the number of women who resided there without being recorded by Mead, then females must have appeared to be even more numerous
than the figures indicate. Chambri women may have appeared dominant to
her because they had temporarily become the most numerous of the adult
social groups living on the island. I do not mean to give the impression of an
island exclusively inhabited by women. There were men living there too, but
they were preoccupied with rebuilding the villages the Parambei had razed to
the ground. Thus, when Mead writes that: "Beneath the Pax Britannica
Tchambuli culture is undergoing a renaissance, and the lake-shore rings to the
sound of axes hollowing canoes. Every man's hand is occupied etching a pattern on a lime-gourd, plaiting a bird or a piece of mask, brocading a house-
blind, or fashioning a cassowary-bone into the semblance of a parrot or a horn-
bill" (1963: 244), she was indeed describing the most immediate concern of

Chambri men. All of their men's houses, containing most of their ceremonial accoutrements, had been gutted by fire, and it is likely, therefore, that "every [male was] an artist and most men [were] skilled not in one art alone, but in many" (ibid.: 245) because there was so much restoration to be done. In fact, her field notes refer to the construction or opening of an extraordinary number of men's houses—three altogether—during the four months she lived at Chambri. During the time I spent among the Chambri, no men's houses were opened, constructed, or redecorated. There had been one built the year before I arrived in New Guinea, and another was built in 1977.

13. These were primarily Mensuat and Changriman women, although Mali women would also occasionally attend.
14. Mead and Fortune lived among the Chambri between January 1933 and April 1933.
15. The incident I refer to is most completely described in Reo Fortune's notebooks under the heading "The Tanum Affair." Since I discuss this incident in detail in chapter 9, I will not do so here. Let it be said, however, that Tanum's clan co-members were surprised to learn that he had gone off to market, suggesting that his decision to journey to the Hills was made on an impromptu and individual basis.
16. I can find no confirmation of this encouragement in any official documents. This does not surprise me, however, because most of the more descriptive patrol reports were lost during the war.

Chapter Seven

1. This market had been servicing both the Yentchamangua and the Kandingai, along with some Korogo and Suapmeri.
2. See chapter 5, pp. 100–02, for a fuller discussion of the events to which the Chambri attribute their "brotherhood" with the Kandingai.
3. These hostilities are too numerous to discuss here, but generally involve Sepik Hills peoples attempting to intrude into the lake region.
4. Unfortunately I have not been able to obtain the proceedings of these hearings.

Chapter Eight

1. Kurapio and Mepen are the names of settlements on Timbunmeri Island. They were inhabited by the Manabi and were then used by Chambri and Garamambu trading partners before the Garamambu moved in. Now they are inhabited by the Mali and Kandingai, respectively.
2. Nyeminimba and Nauinimba are totemic patrimoieties that are said to regulate Chambri marriages. If a man belongs to Nauinimba (sun people), his wife should come from Nyeminimba (moon or mother people), and nearly 60 percent of the people do marry into the opposite moiety. When my informant suggested that mothers must hold shields to protect their children, he was referring to the ideal relationships between these moieties. Under normal circumstances, Nauinimba do not act toward Nyeminimba as children act toward their mothers.
3. Date notation has been changed to conform to the American system of listing the month before the day.

4. K. Dowrie's store is still located in Pagwi.
5. The Sepik Hills people were not the first to think of selling sago. The idea was first instituted by Catholic Fathers at Chambri, whose motto is Industry through Example. During the late 1950s and early 1960s they taught industry by selling sago and other Sepik Hills produce to the Chambri and to the Kandingai of Timbunmeri at a mission-run trade store at Indingai.
6. I do not believe a plane has landed at Kilimbit since 1964. The Kilimbit airstrip is short and narrow, and the people, having received little encouragement and guidance from the local Catholic Father, have allowed it to become overgrown.
7. I was told by several informants that maintenance of the bartering system was discussed as a precondition to allowing the Mensuat to move to Peliagwi Island. A small barter market still exists at Peliagwi, attended only by very old women.
8. Schindlbeck suggests that increasing numbers of Iatmul and Sawos women have become interested in selling their produce for money, but not to one another. In other words, though they journey to government and mission stations to earn currency, they still barter their fish and sago when back home (1980: 154–56).
9. In all seven cases where men sold fish to the government, their wives had caught and smoked the produce.
10. This figure was derived by multiplying the three-month arithmetic mean by twelve.

Chapter Nine

1. Fortune fills twenty-two pages of his field notes with a detailed description of this incident. He does not analyze it, however.
2. Recently I learned of another major initiation of Chambri women (see the *Post Courier*, February 13, 1981). During December 1980, Matias Yambumpe arranged for the initiation of an Australian man, Brian Taylor, who had applied for Papua New Guinean citizenship. Taylor wanted to establish kin ties within a native village and thought this a good way to go about it. He, together with eight men and six women, were initiated at the cost of $K10,000. Taylor is said to have contributed generously to the expense. After the ceremony, he was adopted into Yambumpe's clan and was given the name Yanklpang Intekaiwan, which means "small talk." Yambumpe undoubtedly believed that Taylor, as personnel manager of the Burns Philp Company, could assist him in instituting his socioeconomic schemes. Although many of the newly initiated women may also have been able to contribute their earnings to their patriclans, or to those of their husbands, I doubt that this is why they were initiated. Chambri men never had difficulty acquiring their women's earnings before, when female initiation was only occasionally practiced. Rather, I suspect that many Chambri men were beginning to feel considerable discomfort at the developing predilection of their young women to marry non-Chambri. By elevating these young women in status to full-fledged members of their clans, the initiators may have hoped to obligate the women—both jurally and supernaturally—to remain in their villages and marry their Chambri kinsmen and neighbors. See chapter 10 for a fuller description of the practice of extratribal exogamy by Chambri women.

3. By the time I worked among the Chambri, they had become thoroughly used to the European custom of paying rent. Although this may not have been the case when Mead and Fortune lived with them, I do know that they were paying fees to their informants, in valuables and commodities.
4. The Chambri point to Kubusa as living their equivalent of a Horatio Alger life. He used the money sent to him by his army corporal son to buy the outboard motor used by his second son. Now he has two sources of money to support his network of affinal debts. This network consists of nineteen individuals from ten different patriclans, all of whom are unrelated to Kubusa. He pays all the debts owed by these individuals to their respective matrilateral kinsmen and receives whatever recompense is due to them.
5. Yarapat's network of affinal debts consists of five different individuals from five different patriclans. Like Kubusa's clients, these individuals are unrelated to their patron.
6. Wapiyeri died in 1980. When I last talked with him during 1979, he asked me to contact his migrant sons and ask them to come home. As far as I know, they never did.
7. In 1976, the independent country of Papua New Guinea began to use its own currency. Today, one *kina* is worth $US1.40.
8. By inviting three Timbunmeri men to cure her children, Scolastica was flaunting the will of many of her covillagers, who view the Iatmul living on Timbunmeri as their major enemies.
9. Yambumpe's trade store is very successful. It is the only store opened by the Chambri in the past ten years that seriously competes with the Catholic Mission's store. This is primarily so because Yambumpe acquired a liquor license and supplies his covillagers with beer.
10. Blaming an illness on a ghost is usually the first step in a series of transactions between the living representatives of the ghost's clan and those who represent the invalid.

Chapter Ten

1. I do not know Mangi Pingang. He mentions in his Letter to the Editor that he hasn't "lived through the years of suffering in [his] village, [but has] been told and [has] experienced some . . . hard times which have come about since the salvinia weed was first introduced" (*Post Courier*, 1979: 4). This suggests to me that he is an educated man who has been living in a town, visiting his village only during holidays.
2. This is the Pinang Lagoon near Angoram, just northeast of the village of Moim.
3. In 1974 the population of Indingai Village was 365 persons, including migrant laborers. One hundred and forty-eight of these poeple, or 40.5 percent of the population, lived more or less permanently away from their village. In 1979 the population of Indingai had grown to 414 persons, 195 of whom, or 47 percent, were living away from home. Although these figures indicate a growth in the number of migrants that exceeds the rate of population increase, what is more significant is that today's migrants do not perceive themselves as Indingai who happen to be away from home, but rather as townspeople who happen to have been born at Indingai.
4. I would characterize the great majority of Chambri I spoke to in 1979 as suf-

fering from an acute case of anomie. Life seemed to hold little promise for them. My Papua New Guinea father, for example, after I had refused to buy his clan's sacred totemic bones for $K10,000, insisted that I take them anyway, saying: "Deborah, you're the only young man who cares about them."

5. Bulolo and Wau are towns located in the Morobe Province of Papua New Guinea.

6. I do not wish to impute blame to the priest or to anyone who may have unwittingly introduced the fern into the Sepik River.

7. Tambwi Kwolikumbwi, for example, while discussing marriage prohibitions with me early in 1974, asked if I knew the story of Adam and Eve. When I told him that I did, he said: "Well, since Adam and Eve shared one bone, they must have had the same father. They were brother and sister, and if Adam was allowed to marry Eve, then we can marry anyone we like." Tambwi was referring to the common Middle Sepik belief that agnates acquire their bones from their fathers but was concerned to justify his own slightly irregular marriage in any way he could.

8. See Gewertz, 1977b, for a detailed description of the procedures used to overcome a case of environmentally destructive ancestral displeasure.

9. The same is true of patriclan leadership, where particular women may become de facto clan heads due to the death or absence of their brothers and sons but are never accorded de jure recognition.

10. Stalemate is impossible during warfare, where a head is either taken or not.

Conclusion

1. These last were called Village Books. They were left by administrators with the village's *luluai* to encourage native responsibility and to insure compliance with their content.

2. See, for example, E. E. Evans-Pritchard's classic analysis of segmentary opposition, or nesting, among the Nuer (1969).

3. This fact was first implied by Barnes in his "African Models in the New Guinea Highlands" (1962). His point was to distinguish Africa from New Guinea with respect to descent or filiation as mechanisms of recruitment to social groups.

4. Consider, for example, Andres Vayda's famous foreword to Rappaport's *Pigs for the Ancestors*. He writes: "Part of the interest of Rappaport's study is that it constitutes a sustained attempt to isolate such systems and to validate hypotheses about their operation through the use of extensive quantitative data on the systemic variables. A way is being shown here for using empirical procedures in functional analysis" (1968: xi).

5. Bateson himself did not recognize this aspect of his work until he was a member of the Macy Conference shortly after World War II, where cybernetics, or systems theory, was formulated.

6. Bateson witnessed four *naven* ceremonies but never explains why they were performed when they were, a question which interests me because it seems that the Iatmul could have as acceptably chosen not to perform them.

7. I refer here to *naven*-like behavior as Bateson describes it (1958: 6–22). Many Chambri affinal exchange ceremonies involve some of this behavior.

REFERENCES CITED

Allen, B. J. 1976. *The 1974–75 Rural Survey: A Study of Out-Migration from Fourteen Villages in the East Sepik Province.* Port Moresby: I.A.S.E.R.

Bateson, Gregory. 1933. "Social Structure of the Iatmul People." *Oceania* 1: 245–91, 401–53.

————. 1958. *Naven.* Stanford: Stanford University Press.

————. 1972. *Steps to an Ecology of Mind.* New York: Ballantine.

Bragge, L. W. 1973. "Ambunti Patrol Report for 1972–73." Unpublished manuscript. The District Commission, Papua New Guinea.

————. 1974. "Ambunti Patrol Report for 1973–74." Unpublished manuscript. The District Commission, Papua New Guinea.

Brown, Paula. 1978. *Highland Peoples of New Guinea.* Cambridge: Cambridge University Press.

Burke, Kenneth. 1969. *A Rhetoric of Motives.* Berkeley: University of California Press.

Cohn, Bernard. 1980. "History and Anthropology." *Comparative Studies in Society and History* 22: 198–221.

Curtain, Richard. 1976. *A Study of Outmigration from Fourteen Villages in the East Sepik Province.* Port Moresby: Institute of Applied Social and Economic Research.

————. 1978. "Labor Migration from the Sepik." *Oral History* 6: 1–114

Durkheim, Emile. 1933. *The Division of Labor in Society.* New York: Free Press.

Dye, W. et al. 1969. "The Sepik Hills Languages: A Preliminary Report." *Oceania* 39: 46–56.

Epstein, A. L. 1963. "The Economy of Modern Matupit." *Oceania* 33: 182–215.

Evans-Pritchard, E. E. 1969. *The Nuer.* Oxford: Oxford University Press.

Forge, Anthony. 1966. "Art and Environment in the Sepik." *Proceedings of the Royal Anthropological Institute for 1965*, pp. 23–32.

————. 1971. "Marriage and Exchange in the Sepik." In *Rethinking Kinship and Marriage*, ed. Rodney Needham, pp. 133–44. London: Tavistock.

————. 1972. "The Golden Fleece." *Man* 7: 527–40.

Fortune, Reo. 1933. "A Note on Some Forms of Kinship Structures." *Oceania* 2: 1–9.

————. n.d. "Field Notes." Unpublished manuscript, University of Auckland.

Friedman, Jonathan. 1974. "Marxism, Structuralism, and Vulgar Materialism." *Man* 9: 444–69.

Gardi, René. 1960. *Tambaran*. London: Constable.

Geertz, Clifford. 1973. "Ritual and Social Change: A Javanese Example." In Geertz, *The Interpretation of Cultures*, pp. 142–69. New York: Basic Books.

Gewertz, Deborah. 1977a. "From Sago-Suppliers to Entrepreneurs: Marketing and Migration in the Middle Sepik." *Oceania* 48: 126–40.

————. 1977b. "On Whom Depends the Action of the Elements: Debating among the Chambri." *Journal of Polynesian Society* 86: 339–53.

————. 1977c. "The Politics of Affinal Exchange: Chambri as a Client Market." *Ethnology* 16: 285–98.

————. 1978a. "Tit for Tat: Barter Markets in the Middle Sepik." *Anthropological Quarterly* 51: 36–44.

————. 1978b. "The Myth of the Blood-Men: An Explanation of Chambri Warfare." *Journal of Anthropological Research* 34: 577–88.

————. 1979. "The Consequences of Constancy among the Chambri of Papua New Guinea." *Oceania* 49: 295–310.

————. 1981. "An Historical Reconsideration of Female Dominance among the Chambri of Papua New Guinea. *American Ethnologist* 8: 94–106.

————. 1982. "The Father Who Bore Me: The Role of the Tsambunwuro during Chambri Initiation Ceremonies." In *Male Initiation in New Guinea: New Findings*, ed. Gilbert Herdt. Berkeley: University of California Press.

Goody, Jack. 1977. *The Domestication of the Savage Mind*. Cambridge, Cambridge University Press.

Haantjens, H.A. et al. 1972. "Detailed Description of the Aitape-Ambunti Area and Its Resources." In *Lands of the Aitape-Ambunti Area*, ed. H. A. Haantjens, pp. 15–35. Australia, C.S.I.R.O.

Harris, Marvin. 1975. *Cows, Pigs, Wars, and Witches*. New York: Vintage.

Hauser-Schaublin, Brigitta. 1977. *Frauen Von Kararau*. Basel: Museum für Volkerkunde.

Idriess, Ion. 1949. *Gold-Dust and Ashes*. Sydney: Angus and Robertson.

Langness, L. L. 1964. "Some Problems in the Conceptualization of Highlands Social Structures." *American Anthropologist* 66: 162–82.

Laycock, D. C. 1961. "The Sepik and Its Languages." *Australian Territories* 1: 35–41.

————. 1965. *The Ndu Language Family*. Canberra: Australian National University.

Laycock, D. C., and Z'graggen, J. 1965. "The Sepik-Ramu Phylum." In *Papuan Languages and the New Guinea Linguistic Scene*, ed. S. A. Wurm. Canberra: Australian National University.

League of Nations. 1921–38. *Report to the League of Nations on the Administration of the Territory of New Guinea*. Geneva: League of Nations.

Lévi-Strauss, Claude. 1960. "The Problem of Invariance in Anthropology." *Diogenes* 31: 19–28.

McCarthy, J. K. 1972. *Patrol into Yesterday: My New Guinea Years*. Melbourne: Cheshire.

Mead, Margaret. 1963. *Sex and Temperament*. New York: Morrow.

————. 1970. *The Mountain Arapesh: Arts and Supernaturalism*. Garden City, N.Y.: Natural History Press.

————. 1971. *The Mountain Arapesh: Stream of Events in Alitoa* Garden City, N.Y.: Natural History Press.

————. 1972. *Blackberry Winter*. New York: William Morrow Company.

————., n.d. "Field Notes." Unpublished manuscript. Library of Congress.

Meggitt, M. J. 1974. "Pigs Are Our Hearts." *Oceania* 44: 165–203.

————. 1977. *Blood Is Their Argument*. Palo Alto, Calif.: Mayfield.

Mitchell, D. S. 1979. *The Incidence and Management of Salvinia Molesta in Papua New Guinea*. Port Moresby: Office of Environment and Conservation.

Newton, Douglas. 1967. "Oral Tradition and Art History in the Sepik District, New Guinea." In *Essays on the Verbal and Visual Arts*, ed. June Helm. Seattle: American Ethnological Society.

Philpott, Malcolm. 1972. *Economic Development in the Sepik River Basin*. Port Moresby: Department of Transport.

————. 1974. *East Sepik District Growth Centre Study*. Port Moresby: Central Planning Office.

Pinang, Mangi. 1979. "Salvinia Weed: The Sepik Villagers Can't Fish, Can't Gather Food—Some Will Starve." Letter to the Editor, *Post Courier* (Port Moresby), September 18.

Pope, Alexander. 1871. "Essay on Man." In *The Works of Alexander Pope*, vol. 2, ed. John Wilson Crocker and Whitwell Elwin, pp. 341–524. London: John Murray.

Post Courier. 1979. "Weed Warfare Erupts in the Sepik," August 14. Port Moresby.

————. 1981. "Ordeal in the Haus Tambaran," February 13. Port Moresby.

Rappaport, Roy. 1968. *Pigs for the Ancestors*. New Haven and London: Yale University Press.

————. 1979. *Ecology, Meaning, and Religion*. Richmond, Calif.: North Atlantic Books.

Reed, S. W. 1943. *The Making of Modern New Guinea*. Philadelphia: American Philosophical Library.

Romer, A. S. 1933. *The Vertebrate Story*. Chicago: University of Chicago Press.

Rosaldo, Renato. 1980. *Ilongot Headhunting, 1883–1974*. Stanford: Stanford University Press.

Rubel, Paula, and Rosman, Abraham. 1979. *Your Own Pigs You May Not Eat*. Chicago: University of Chicago Press.

Ruddle, Kenneth et al. 1978. *Palm Sago*. Honolulu: University of Hawaii Press.

Sahlins, Marshall. 1972. *Stone Age Economics*. Chicago: Aldine-Atherton.

————. 1976. *Culture and Practical Reason*. Chicago: University of Chicago Press.

Schindlbeck, Markus. 1980. *Sago Bei Den Sawos*. Basel: Museum fur Volkerkunde.

Schwartz, Theodore. 1964. "Systems of Areal Integration." *Anthropological Forum* 2: 56–97.

Schuster, Meinhard. 1965. "Mythen aus dem Sepik-Gebiet." In *Festschrift Alfred Buhler*, ed. Carl Schmitz and Robert Wildkaber, pp. 369–84. Basel: Pharos-Verlag Hansrudolph Schwabe.

————. 1969. "Die Topfergottgeit Von Aibom." *Paideuma* 15: 140–59.

Seiler, Donald. 1974. *Aspects of Movement and Socio-Economic Development in the Maprik Area of Papua New Guinea*. Port Moresby: Department of Transport.

Service, Elman. 1962. *Primitive Social Organization*. New York: Random House.

Sharp, Lauristan. 1952. "Steel Tools for Stone Age Australians." *Human Organization* 11: 17–22.

Shurcliff, Sidney. 1930. *Jungle Islands*. New York: G. P. Putnam's Sons.

Staalsen, Philip. 1965. "Brugnowi Origins: The Founding of a Village." *Man* 65: 184–88.

Strathern, Andrew. 1971. *The Rope of Moka*. Cambridge: Cambridge University Press.

Tourraine, Alain. 1977. *The Self-Production of Society*. Chicago: University of Chicago Press.

Townsend, Patricia. 1969. "Subsistence and Social Organization in a New Guinea Society." Ph.D. dissertation, University of Michigan.

Tuzin, Donald. 1977. *The Ilahita Arapesh*. Berkeley: University of California Press.

Uberoi, J. P. Singh. 1971. *Politics of the Kula Ring*. Manchester: Manchester University Press.

Vansina, Jan. 1961. *Oral Tradition*. Chicago: Aldine.

Vayda, Andrew. 1971. "Phases of the Process of War and Peace among the Marings of New Guinea." *Oceania* 41: 1–24.

Watson, James. 1970. "Society as Organized Flow." *Southwestern Journal of Anthropology* 26: 107–24.

Wiener, Annette. 1976. *Women of Value, Men of Reknown*. Austin: University of Texas Press.

Wurm, S. A. 1971. "The Papuan Linguistic Situation." *Current Trends in Linguistics* 8: 541–657.

INDEX

Adoption: in myth, 78; and labor recruitment, 121–22. *See also* Kinship
Affinal bond. *See* Marriage
Affinal exchange. *See* Marriage
Affines. *See* Marriage
Age grades: and moiety subdivisions, 24. *See also* Kinship
Age dominance: in myth, 117–20. *See also* Inequality
Aggression. *See* Conflict
Agnates: in myth, 117–20; advantages of birth order, 120; Chambri views on, 138–39; rivalry of, 178–80. *See also* Kinship
Aibom: commodity production of, 80, 81 (*see also* Commodities); history of, 80–81; and Iatmul trade, 81. *See also* Exchange—relations
Alliances: political, 5, 78; maintenance of, 28, 63; between bush–water people, 34–35, 237n25; Chambri and Iatmul, 139; military, 151; to social group, 181
Ambunti, 110. *See also* Boundaries; Colonial Administrators
Ancestors: uncheban, 39, 87–88 (*see also* Quarries); sago, 41; bush spirits, 80; and revenge, 192–93
—apical, 85, 101, 206; in myth, 101; Emosuie Apankay, 101
Anopheles faranti. See Mosquitoes
Artifacts: sales of, to Europeans, 164–65. *See also* Markets
Autonomy: loss of, 13; and group size, 226; and patron–client relationships, 226; and dependence, 226, 227–28
Avatip, 137
Axes, steel: male control of exchange of, 210–11. *See also* Exchange

Balus. See Birds
Bananas: leaves of, in exchange, 48; fruit of, in exchange, 49

Barter. *See* Exchange; Markets
Barter markets. *See* Exchange; Markets
Barter-partners. *See* Exchange
Baskets, 92, 164, 242n8. *See also* Artifacts; Income, Chambri
Bat bones: in myth, 119
Bates, Charles, 133–34
Bateson, Gregory: see his *Naven* passim; on schizmogenesis, 19, 223–24; on male mortuary ceremonies, 71; on the Mindimbit, 130–31; on Mindimbit–Kwolawoli marriages, 130–31; on Iatmul male ethos, 136; on systems analysis of Iatmul, 222–23; on symmetrical relations, 236n3
Behavior: barter, 19, 40–41 (*see also* Exchange; Markets); of Iatmul men, 19; of Iatmul women, 19; assertive, 20
—complementary, 19; of Iatmul men, 19; A. Forge on, 224–25
—subservient, 20; in myth, 30, 237n19
—symmetrical: A. Forge on, 224–25
Behavior maximization. *See* Markets
Betel nuts: in exchange, 19, 40; access to, 109. *See also* Exchange
Big Men, 48, 176, 180; roles in exchange, 4; in myth, 82; description of, 104; as Chambri clan leaders, 120; power of, 175, 190; networks of, 189. *See also* Exchange; Leadership; Power
Birds: *balus*, 41; in myth, 67, 24n11. *See also* Exchange; Valuables
Bisis, 11. *See also* Environment, physical; Settlement pattern
Bisnis. See Alliances
Black-birders, 111
Books: and white man's power, 218. *See also* Power
Boundaries:
—indigenous: European restructuring of, 122–23; flexibility of, 123
—physical: arbitrary nature of, 2–3; cre-